Baedeker

Venice

www.baedeker.com

Verlag Karl Baedeker

SIGHTSEEING HIGHLIGHTS ✷ ✷

The list of attractions in Venice is long; from the Piazza San Marco with St Mark's Basilica and the Doge's Palace, Gallerie dell'Accademia, Santa Maria Gloriosa dei Frari, or the lagoon island of Murano – we have compiled what you really shouldn't miss.

✷✷ Basilica di San Marco
Church of the doges, state church of the republic, monumental shrine for the state saints, and a cathedral since 1807
▸ **page 160**

✷✷ Burano
Most picturesque island in the lagoon, famous for its point ▸ **page 171**

✷✷ Canal Grande
Main traffic artery of Venice and the »most beautiful street in the world« ▸ **page 173**

✷✷ Ca' d'Oro
The »golden house«, the most famous private building in Venice ▸ **page 185**

✷✷ Ca' Rezzonico
The interior of this palace is still the same as it was 300 years ago. ▸ **page 188**

✷✷ Collezione Peggy Guggenheim
Palace and collection of modern art from the American patron of the arts ▸ **page 190**

✷✷ Gallerie dell'Accademia
The picture gallery has the most important collection of Venetian paintings in the world, from the gothic to rococo. ▸ **page 193**

✷✷ Murano
With its main canal and the many small side canals, the »Island of the Gaffers« is reminiscent of Venice. ▸ **page 220**

The floor in St Marcus Basilica is worthy of your attention

✶✶ Santi Giovanni e Paolo
27 doges are buried in the largest church in Venice, also known as San Zanipolo. Their tombs are a museum for sculpture connoisseurs.
► **page 264**

✶✶ Scuola Grande di San Rocco
The brotherhood building contains one of the most comprehensive cycles of Italian paintings by Tintoretto.
► **page 271**

Goldsmiths from Constantinople and Venice used over 3000 precious stones in the Pala d'Oro.

✶✶ Palazzo Ducale
The centre of power of the Republic of Venice, residence of the doge, and state prison for over 1000 years ► **page 224**

✶✶ Piazza San Marco
Centre of Venetian life and, according to Napoleon, »most beautiful salon in Europe« with the most famous buildings in the city ► **page 238**

✶✶ Santa Maria Gloriosa dei Frari
With its gorgeous interior decorations, it is almost a Pantheon of Venetian history.
► **page 257**

✶✶ Santa Maria della Salute
The domed church at the mouth of the Canal Grande to the lagoon was erected to give thanks for the end of the plague.
► **page 262**

Mosaics cover all walls and domes of St Marcus Basilica.

BAEDEKER'S BEST TIPS

Of all the Baedeker tips in this book, we have assembled the most interesting ones for you here. Experience and enjoy Venice from its best side.

Secret Paths
A tour of the »Itinerari segreti« offers insight into the dark side of the Serenissima. ► **page 39**

Waiting Times
Waiting times when arriving or leaving by train can be spent here. ► **page 75**

Where can you meet Venetians?
You want to meet young locals? This is where you need to go... ► **page 82**

Nice Discounts
Booking a hotel via the internet can be worthwhile, since many of them offer special »internet rates« ► **page 70**

Venice Card
So that the vaporetti trips don't affect the budget so much – and because it's so much more convenient ► **page 133**

Off Piazza San Marco
Venice is more than just St Mark's Place. ► **page 150**

Excursions into the Lagoon
The lagoon and its islands are introduced on trips with the RiViviNatura. ► **page 154**

In the Arsenale
The arsenal is only accessible during the biennial. A trip on the Rio dell' Arsenale offers a bit of insight. ► **page 159**

A Boat Trip
You can see any attraction in Venice on foot, except for the Canal Grande. ► **page 173**

Alla Vedova
»To the Widow« is the name of an original Osteria where Venetians like to enjoy a few Cicheti and a glass of wine at the counter. ► **page 186**

❗ Hire a bike

Lido is best explored by bicycle.
► **page 215**

❗ Fortuny

The plisse fabrics by the all-round genius Mariano Fortuny are a very special souvenir. ► **page 237**

❗ For gourmets

Hobby chefs can make discoveries in the Drogheria Mascari. And after the shopping excursion, there are cosy and inviting wine taverns in the vicinity ► **page 244**

❗ Dalla Marisa

The small trattoria cooks using traditional (mainland) recipes. ► **page 246**

❗ For Nautical Fans

The Mare di Carta bookstore carries (almost) everything regarding marine navigation. ► **page 249**

❗ Ice cream dream

The Gelateria Millevoglie between the Frari Church and the Scuola Grande di San Rocco has especially good ice cream.
► **page 261**

❗ Nightlife alla Veneziana

Venetian nightlife concentrates here on the Campo. ► **page 270**

❗ Pearls

Select handcrafts and real Venetian pearls are available in the Croccio di Marina.
► **page 276**

❗ Al Ponte del Diavolo

The Osteria on Torcello is a good location, and not just because of its shady terrace.
► **page 277**

BACKGROUND

12 Queen of the Lagoon
16 Facts
17 Population • Politics •
Economy
18 Transport
21 The Lagoon of Venice
24 *Special: Is Venice Sinking?*
31 Legendary Beginnings
32 *3 D: How Venice Was Built*
34 Queen of the Adriatic
36 The Government of Venice
40 From the Fall of Venice to
the Present
45 Romanesque and Byzantine Art
46 The Gothic Period
49 Renaissance
54 17th and 18th Centuries
56 *Special: Death in Venice*
58 19th and 20th Centuries
58 Early Printing

PRACTICAL INFORMATION FROM A TO Z

70 Accommodation
75 Arrival • Before the Journey
78 Beaches
79 Children in Venice
80 Electricity
80 Emergency
81 Entertainment
82 Etiquette and Customs
84 Festivals, Holidays and Events
86 *Special: Madcap Days*
91 Food and Drink
94 *Special: Liquid Shadwos*
105 Health
105 Information
108 Language
116 Literature
118 Media

*Lagoon island Torcello with
the Alps in the background*
▶ page 277

118 Money
119 Opening Hours
119 Post and Communications
120 Prices and Discounts
121 Shopping
129 Sports
130 Theatre • Concerts
131 Time
132 Tours and Guides
132 Transport
136 Travellers with Disabilities
137 When To Go

TOURS

142 Out and About in Venice
143 Tour 1: Sestiere di San Marco
146 Tour 2: Sestiere di San Polo e Santa
　　　Croce
148 Tour 3: Cannaregio
151 Tour 4: Dorsoduro – »hard back«
152 Tour 5: By ferry to the lagoon
154 Trips

*Children playing in the city on the
lagoon; one of the many fountains
serves as a meeting place*
▶ page 113

Scala dei Giganti, crowning stair-case in the doge's palace
▶ **page 233**

SIGHTS FROM
A to Z

158 Arsenale
160 Basilica di San Marco
164 *3 D: St Mark's Basilica*
171 Burano
172 *Special: All About Lace*
173 Canal Grande (Grand Canal)
178 *Special: Obscure Secrets*
185 Ca' d'Oro
186 Ca' Pesaro
188 Ca' Rezzonico (Museo del
　　　Settecento Veneziano)
188 Chioggia
190 Collezione
　　　Peggy Guggenheim

190 Fondaco dei Tedeschi
192 Fondaco dei Turchi Museo di Storia
　　　Naturale
192 Fondazione
　　　Querini-Stampalia
193 Gallerie dell'Accademia
199 I Gesuiti
200 Ghetto
202 *Special: Oldest Ghetto in the
　　　World*
206 Giardini Pubblici
207 *Special: Biennial*
208 La Giudecca
211 Islands in the Lagoon
214 Lido di Venezia
216 Littorale del Cavallino
217 Madonna dell'Orto •
　　　Santa Maria dell'Orto
218 Mercerie
220 Murano
222 *Special: Blown Jewel*
224 Palazzo Contarini del Bovolo
224 Palazzo Ducale
232 *3 D: Doge's Palace!*
237 Palazzo Pesaro degli Orfei Museo
　　　Fortuny
237 Piazza San Marco
243 Ponte di Rialto
245 San Francesco della Vigna
245 San Giacomo dell'Orio
246 San Giobbe
247 San Giorgio Maggiore
248 San Giovanni in Bragora
249 San Giovanni Crisostomo

Prominent centre of the city on the lagoon: Campanile
▶ page 235

249 San Nicolò da Tolentino
250 San Pietro di Castello
251 San Polo
252 San Sebastiano
252 San Trovaso •
Santi Gervasio e Protasio
254 *Special: Queen of the Canals*
256 San Zaccaria
257 Santa Maria Formosa
257 Santa Maria Gloriosa
dei Frari – Frari
262 Santa Maria dei Miracoli
262 Santa Maria della Salute
264 Santi Apostoli
264 Santi Giovanni e Paolo •
San Zanipolo
268 Santo Stefano
270 Scuola Grande dei Carmini
271 Scuola Grande di San Rocco
274 Scuola di San Giorgio
degli Schiavoni
276 Teatro La Fenice
277 Torcello

280 Index
284 List of Maps and Illustrations
285 Photo Credits
285 Publisher's Information

Background

VENICE, THE ENCHANTING CITY IN THE WATER, HOLDS MORE THAN 1,500 YEARS OF HISTORY: FROM ITS FOUNDATION VIA ITS RISE TO BE QUEEN OF THE SEAS, FROM ITS FALL TO THE PRESENT – ONE OF THE MOST BEAUTIFUL CITIES IN THE WORLD.

QUEEN OF THE LAGOON

Venice is a fragile work of art made up of bridges and canals, palazzi with crumbling plaster and churches in which golden mosaics shimmer next to precious Madonnas by Titian and Last Suppers by Tintoretto.

Venezia is far more than the obligatory trip on the Grand Canal and »the most beautiful open-air salon of the world«, where a cup of espresso in Caffè Florian is not overpriced for the unbeatable style of the surroundings. It is more than the Byzantine atmosphere of St Mark's Basilica and the pattern of St Mark's lions which guard the Doge's Palace, more too than an evening of opera in the Teatro La Fenice, a theatre steeped in tradition which was only recently restored to its full splendour after damage by fire. Venice is a labyrinth in which beauty is everywhere, in the nameplates beside doorbells, in secret gardens, wine bars, or simply in the waves of the lagoon, lapping against shell-encrusted colourful gondola poles. Those who wish to discover Venice must drift, and let themselves get lost.

Doge's Palace
Centre of power for Venice and the republic for over 1,000 years

Looking Back, Looking Forward

Venice is a unique city of fascinating clichés, an island, seemingly detached from time and space, in which modern standards lose their importance and the decaying glory of La Serenissima, the old republic of the doges, which once controlled the Levant and the oriental trade, still rules. It is a permanent photographic motif, and not just during carnival. The city which for centuries inspired the romantic dreams of tourists and artists is also under threat: a city inaccessible to cars and where apartments are expensive is unattractive to most young people. Are postmen, garbage collectors, gondolieri and souvenir salesmen destined to be the last Venetians?

Fortunately there have recently been signs that the tide has turned: young people from the surrounding mainland have discovered Venice as a place to go out in the evenings, and are no longer leaving the historic city centre to the tourists. For a city with an aging population, the fact that in the popular sestiere (city district) of Cannaregio

Ca' d'Oro

One of the most famous Venetian palaces.
Paintings, frescoes, and sculptures
from the collection of Baron Giorgio Franchetti
are on display here.
The view from the loggia
onto the Canal Grande is magnificent.

Piazza San Marco

Heart of the city on the lagoon,
it was the »most elegant salon in Europe«
for Napoleon with a view
of St Mark's Basilica
and the Palazzo Ducale.

Santa Maria della Salute

The baroque church of monumental dimensions
was built to give thanks for the end
of the plague epidemic of 1630.

Murano
*The »Island of Glass« is also home
to an architectural attraction,
the church of Santa Maria e Donato
from the 12th century.*

Carnival
*The carnival is a high point
in the holiday calendar of the city.
There are no limits on the imagination;
here a costume in the national colours.*

Burano
*Certainly the most picturesque island in the lagoon,
it is famous for lace and the
brightly painted facades of the houses.*

and around Piazza Santa Margherita, restaurants are finally open past midnight again, represents a return to normality. In Casanova's time, here in the city of courtesans, celebrations lasted all night long throughout the eight-month carnival! It is encouraging, too, that more and more of the persons responsible are trying to ensure that the city's attention is not directed solely towards tourism and the past, but also to the future.

From Fishermen's Settlement to Metropolis

The beginning of Venice was when fishermen set their nets at the Rialto. Later, merchants drew customers here with exotic wares.

From above, the city is shaped like a fish, and the Ponte della Libertà, the Bridge of Freedom which was built in 1846, has the appearance of a fishing line. In fact, Venice floats at the northern end of the Adriatic, barely 4km/2.5mi from the mainland and 2km/1.2mi from the open sea, in the lagoon of the same name. Venice rests on millions of straight tree trunks which, from ancient times, were driven down into an archipelago of 118 islands and bits of land to form foundations. There are 177 narrow canals and about 400 bridges.

But Venice consists of more than the centro storico, the old quarter. Since 1962, the city community – the Comune di Venezia – has also included Mestre, which lies on the mainland on the other side of the Ponte della Libertà, with a few other districts and the other islands of the lagoon, among them Lido, Burano, Murano, Torcello and Pellestrina. Overall, Venice is approximately 450 sq km/173 sq mi in size, which makes it the second largest city in Italy after Rome.

Twin Towers
Lighthouse of San Giorgio and the Campanile of Venice – signposts in the lagoon

Discover Venice

With more than 20 top-class museums, 90 churches (all richly decorated with paintings and sculptures) and approximately 10,000 palaces, the city itself is a work of art and holds a special place in Europe's cultural heritage. With its unique lagoon and lovely islands, partly famous, partly little-known, Venice is one of the most beautiful destinations in the world.

Facts

Read on for a compact description of what you need to know about Venice, its residents, what is special about the city and how to get around there. Learn how the lagoon – Italy's second-largest wet biotope – came into existence and about the threats to it.

Population · Politics · Economy

Population and City Districts

Venice has about 271,750 residents, of whom the old city, the centro storico, houses about 64,000 (in 1951, the figure was 174,800, and the exodus continues). The islands are home to about 31,600 people, and a further 176,150 live on the mainland. The old city is divided not into city quarters but, since the 12th century, into »city sixths« or **sestieri**. They are named San Marco, Castello, Cannaregio, Santa Croce, San Polo and Dorsoduro (which also includes the islands of Giudecca and San Giorgio). Every »sixth« has its own atmosphere. **San Marco** is the glamorous gateway to the city and its heart. The atmosphere is more down-to-earth in Castello and San Polo. **Castello**, even when Venice was known as the Serenissima, was the home of the arsenalotti, who were employed in the famous shipyards. **San Polo**, the smallest of the sestieri, and Rialto represented the old commercial centre of the city. Wide open spaces are found in **Cannaregio**, one of the largest sestieri. Until the construction of the railway embankment, it was the main entrance to Venice. Today, the majority of craft businesses and an everyday atmosphere are found here. Via Piazzale Roma, **Santa Croce** connects Venice to the mainland; this sestiere has probably experienced the most changes in the course of its history. **Dorsoduro**, the »hard back« (the name refers to the solid ground of this city district) is probably the liveliest sestiere. It was chiefly inhabited by fishermen and sailors; at the end of the 19th century, industrial workers came to live here as well, a development that also occurred on the island of Giudecca. The university in the western part of Dorsoduro ensures a young population, which likes to gather on Campo S. Margherita. Towards the Salute church, Dorsoduro has developed into one of the most up-market residential areas of Venice.

Politics and Administration

Venice was the first republic of the Middle Ages, a great constitutional achievement of the 11th and 12th centuries. It existed until its conquest by Napoleon in 1797. Today, Venice is the capital of the province by the same name which includes a total of 43 districts, as well as being the capital of the northern Italian region of Veneto. Like all major Italian cities, it is administered by a mayor (sindaco; currently Massimo Cacciari) and a magistracy (giunta municipale) who are newly elected every five years. The seat of local government is the Ca' Farsetti near the Rialto bridge.

← *Venice has around 400 bridges. The Ponte dei Sospiri, here the topmost of the many canal crossings, is certainly one of the most well-known.*

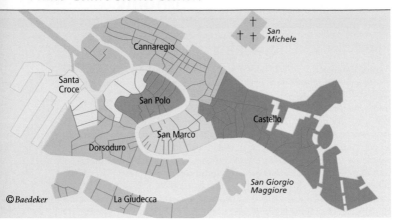

Venice Centro Storico Sestieri

San Michele

Cannaregio

Santa Croce

San Polo

Castello

San Marco

Dorsoduro

San Giorgio Maggiore

© Baedeker

La Giudecca

Economy

The main source of employment in the island city is **tourism**. After Rome, Venice is the most visited city in Italy: every year, approximately three million overnight guests and more than ten million day visitors come here. Most businesses in the inner city live from tourism. This also explains the high density of craft workshops and souvenir stores by comparison to the population, producing glass art, lace, textiles, handmade paper and especially masks. Many Venetians also work in the **public sector**.

Furthermore, Venice is Italy's third largest **port** (after Genoa and Trieste). The port is on the mainland in Marghera, the location of Petrolchimico, Italy's **chemical centre** with 45,000 workers. Aside from the giant chemical plants, the largest **heating power plant** in Italy and the largest **crude oil depots** on the Mediterranean are here and in Mestre. Every day, about 25,000 residents of the insular part of Venice travel to the mainland to work, while 20,000 commuters, 5,000 of them from the surrounding islands, come to the historic centre to work or study. The university Ca' Foscari and the architectural college (IUAV) have 20,000 registered students.

Transport

Venice's international airport Marco Polo lies on the mainland, at the north edge of the lagoon at Tessera. The Canale di San Marco diagonally opposite the Doge's Palace serves as a port for passenger ships. From here, there are connections to many Adriatic ports. Ven-

Facts and Figures Venice

Venice

©Baedeker

Venice
► capital of the province of Veneto as well as the region of the same name

Location
► at the north end of the Adriatic, 4km/2.5mi from the mainland and 2km/1.2mi from the open sea, latitude 41° 25' north and longitude 12° 02' east

Size
► historic centre (centro storico): 4.3km/2.7mi at the widest and 1.4km/0.9mi at the narrowest part; including the islands of San Giorgio and Giudecca, 7.06 sq km/2.7 sq mi; length: 11km/7mi

► Comune di Venezia: includes the centro storico, Mestre, Malcontenta, Marghera, Favaro, Zelarino and Cavallino (mainland, terraferma), and the lagoon islands (estuario) Lido, Burano, Murano, Torcello and Pellestrina: 450 sq km/173 sq mi (by comparison: London 1,579 sq km/609 sq mi), which makes the Comune di Venezia Italy's second largest urban area after Rome.

Population
► centro storico: 64,000, including about 7,500 foreigners from 122 nations
► Comune di Venezia: about 271,000, including about 32,000 on the lagoon islands.

Economy
► Most important employer: tourism (the 3 million annual overnight guests can choose from 400 hotels and bed-and-breakfasts with about 16,000 beds; in addition, there are about 10 million daytime visitors), government, industry and port

Local Government Headquarters
► Ca' Farsetti on the Grand Canal, near the Rialto bridge

? DID YOU KNOW ...?

■ More than 13 million people visit Venice every year. More than 80% of them spend less than eight hours and under 15 in the city. 90% of them visit only the Piazza San Marco. So it is not surprising that the authorities would like to limit the number of day trippers.

»High Street« Canal Grande

ice is also a popular starting point for cruises – preferred landing sites include Zattere and Riva degli Schiavoni. Since 1846, the island has been connected to the mainland by a railroad bridge. In 1933, the »freedom bridge«, Ponte della Libertà, was opened for motor traffic. Of course, cars have to be parked no further than at the Tronchetto parking site or in the car park at Piazzale Roma at the end of the road bridge. From here, progress is only possible on foot or by boat.

Water travel in Venice The approximately 118 islands which form Venice are very close together and built up to their very outer edges, but the waterways between the islands were kept clear. This resulted in a network of more than 170 canals. Boats are the most important mode of transport. In addition to the canals, Venice has about 3,000 »streets«. There is only one so-called **strada**, Strada Nova, which was built through the labyrinth of Cannaregio at the end of the 19th century, and two known as vie, Via 22 Marzo in the sestiere of San Marco and Via Garibaldi in Castello. All others are called either **calle** (plural calli) – the second name of many calli is a reminder of the guilds which once resided here, such as the Calle dei Lavadori (washers), dei Saoneri (soap makers), dei Spezieri (spice dealers) or dei Boteri (barrel makers) – or **ramo** (branch), **ruga** (groove), **salizzada** (from selciato meaning paved, the name for the first paved streets in the city), **rio terrà** (filled-in canal), **fondamenta** or **riva** (shore road); **sottoportego** is a narrow passage which even leads under houses in some cases.

There is also only one **piazza**, namely that of San Marco. The adjacent smaller squares are called Piazzetta (in front of the Doge's Palace) and Piazzetta dei Leoncini (next to St Mark's Basilica). All other squares in the city are called **campo** (meaning field, plural campi) or, if they are very small, campiello. Corte (plural corti) is a term for a closed inner courtyard.

400 bridges (**ponte**, plural ponti) hold the city together and lead the twisted alleys and streets over the canals, three of them across the Grand Canal: the wooden Ponte del'Accademia, the famous Rialto bridge and the Ponte dei Scalzi at the railway station. A fourth bridge is currently under construction outside Venice to designs by Santiago Calatrava. It is to cross the Grand Canal between the railway station and Piazzale Roma.

? DID YOU KNOW ...?

- The houses within a sestiere are continuously numbered (only the island of Giudecca has its own numbering).
  For instance, Castello ends with the record number 6828, while Cannaregio ends at 6426 – a system which goes back to Napoleon and is practically incomprehensible to non-Venetians.

The Lagoon of Venice

Flat land and water as far as the eye can see, many islands and islets of which twelve are inhabited today, innumerable small banks of sand or slick (barene) some of which are only visible at ebb (velme): this is the Laguna Veneta, **Italy's second-largest wet biotope** after the Po delta, in which Venice lies like a pearl. This land-locked lake in the shape of a half-moon is about 40km/25mi long and no more than 15km/9mi wide. The laguna viva, the »living« lagoon, reaches as far as salt water at high tide. Salt water rarely penetrates the laguna morta, which accounts for nearly half of the lagoon. The water in the canals near the port has a depth of 15–20m/50–65ft, but otherwise only 50cm/20in on average, and is more or less brackish, depending on the tides. The lagoon, in which fresh water and sea water mix, provides excellent living conditions for plants, water birds and

Lagoon of Venice Plan

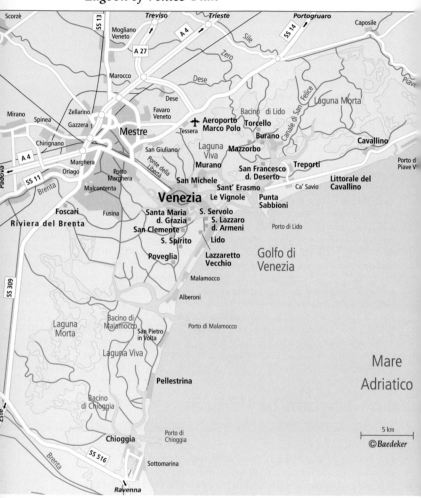

fish. The south is occupied particularly by valli da pesca, fish ponds, where fish, mussels (cozze) and hard-shell clams (vongole) are farmed (recognizable by the nets and ropes stretched between poles). By contrast the north has remained an almost unspoiled world of islands and is a protected nature reserve.

Origin This unique landscape was created in prehistoric times when the rivers that flow into the Mediterranean here – particularly the Brenta,

Sile and Piave – deposited the masses of sand and stone which they had carried down from the Alps. The changing watercourses, ebb and flow of the tide, storms and the constant sea surf formed this material into sand banks (litorali or barre) and coastal strips (lidi) about 20km/12mi in front of the actual coastline. The lagoons disappeared where humans did not intervene (e.g. at Ravenna). Since increasing silting damaged the shipping, commerce and also the defence of Venice, the lagoon residents began to redirect the large rivers as early as the 14th century.

Today, the lagoon has only three large through-flows (bocche): the 900m/2950ft-wide Bocca di Lido, the 470m/1540ft-wide Bocca di Malamocco and the nearly 500m/1640ft-wide Bocca di Chioggia. The Adriatic flows through these into the lagoon twice daily; seawater flushes the channels and flows back. In order to maintain shipping and this »natural« drainage system, the bocche are kept open with major technical efforts.

At the time of the maritime republic, the Magistrato alle Acque was set up in 1501 to protect the lagoon. It initiated the regular cleaning of the canals (which were used for sewage disposal). The canals were dredged to give them a minimum depth of 180cm/6ft. The rivers

Protection and hazards

In constant flux in tidal rythm: the lagoon

IS VENICE SINKING?

From an urban perspective, the ancient queen of the seas, now over a thousand years old, is up to her neck in water. More and more residents are turning their backs on their city, for it is sinking into the lagoon while sea levels rise.

Venice was created in the early Middle Ages and has remained almost unchanged. However, there have been dramatic changes in the **size of the population**. In 1951, approximately 174,000 people lived in the lagoon city. Today, there are only 64,000, and some sources even speak of 60,000. Of these, more than 33% are over the age of 65. And the exodus continues.

Population Decline

Every year, about 2,000 Venetians leave the city centre. Most remain within the Comune di Venezia, but move to the mainland, to Mestre (in 1926, Venice and Mestre merged), Marghera or another area of the city. Young people, in particular, move away. There are numerous reasons, among others the **high rents** in apartments that are often uncomfortable,

lacking heating and bathrooms, and the high investments needed to maintain apartments or houses. **Mass tourism** with more than 13 million visitors annually has enormous effects on the city infrastructure. Grocery stores, kindergartens and schools are displaced by souvenir stores, restaurants, hotels or recently bed & breakfasts. Prices in cafes, bars and restaurants are much higher than normal. The city also offers little to young people in general – there is limited **nightlife**, and trips to the mainland require a car, which costs a lot in parking fees. Venice is also inconvenient. All goods must be brought from the mainland, loaded onto boats and transported on foot and by hand cart. Due to the many bridges, shoppers and mothers pushing their children need to be fit. In the inner city, **employment oppor-**

tunities are **very limited**, and the exodus has caused the loss of many jobs. Today, about 25,000 commuters go to work in Mestre or the surrounding area.

The City Sinks

Venice's buildings stand on larch piles. Every year, these piles sink a little deeper under this weight **into the muddy lagoon bed**. This also happened in past centuries. Venetians reacted by building one floor on top of another, up to six layers. However, the situation worsened dramatically when, after 1930, ground water was taken in greater quantities, particularly for the emerging industry on the mainland in Mestre and Marghera, and the three entrances into the lagoon were enlarged to a depth of 12m/40ft so that the oil tankers could reach the refineries. In consequence the ground sank even more rapidly. Since 1908, it has dropped by 12cm/ 5in (more than in the two preceding centuries). Ground water removal was finally stopped at the end of the 1970s, and the situation became a little less critical.

Floods

In the same time period, sea levels rose by 12cm/5in. Acqua alta, flooding, is the name of the danger, which is mainly concentrated in the period between September and March. Conditions become critical at a level of 80cm/32in above normal sea level, when visitors to the atrium of St Mark's Basilica (from only 63cm/ 25in) and on St Mark's Square get wet feet. Between 1923 and 1932, flood waters higher than 110cm/44in occurred only every few years. From 1943 to 1952, flooding occurred once annually, and from 1993 to 2002, five times annually. Since the flood catastrophe of 1966, with levels of 194cm/ 6ft 4in, the acqua alta has exceeded the one-metre mark (3ft 4in) more than 220 times. If the forecast global warming and the associated rise in sea levels occurs, this would mean acqua alta on one day in three within 50 years! But extremely low tides are also damaging. Too little fresh sea water in the lagoon means **insufficient oxygen**, which acutely threatens the marine life, mussel farming and fishing. Very low water levels are also dangerous to

The constant movement of the water eats through any and all walls.

the city, since the thousands of larch piles on which Venice is built start to rot having contact with oxygen.

Environmental Pollution

The pier of San Marco is currently being raised, the edges of the Piazzetta lifted, and all foundations renewed. The magic formula against rising sea levels goes by the name of MOSE (▶ p.29). However, critics object that this is only fighting the symptoms. For the toxic industry of Marghera, which has been pouring thousands of tons of highly poisonous wastes such as chlorine or nitrogen solutions, cyanide and heavy metals directly into the lagoon, continues to operate. And even though a recycling system is meanwhile being built, the effluents of the hundreds of thousands of residents still flow unfiltered into the lagoon. This and the exhaust gases from the 1,500 factory chimneys of Marghera continue to eat away at the piles and the brickwork of the buildings. They are probably also responsible for the fact that the province of Venice has a 50% higher rate of cancer than the world average.

What's New in the Lagoon

For over a decade work has been proceeding intensively on city planning policies, not only for the historic centre, but also for the twin city of Venice-Mestre. Numerous projects have been planned or already completed, all with the goal of making Venice more attractive to the people who live here.

With **affordable apartments**, which are currently being built on the island of Giudecca among others, city subsidies and low-cost loans, young Venetians and small entrepreneurs are being encouraged to stay in or even return to the old city. **San Giuliano**, the island between Venice and Mestre, is currently undergoing major change. Where toxic wastes from the industrial zones were stored for decades, a nature park, a technology and science park as well as other research and government facilities are now being built. 70ha/170 acres of the Parco San Giuliano had been inaugurated by 2003. Currently, a bridge is being built outside Venice (architect: Santiago Calatrava). It will be the **fourth bridge across the Grand Canal.**

Since St Marcus Plaza is rather low, it is especially prone to flooding. Apparently, pigeons also do not like getting their feet wet …

Another bridge for motor traffic will span the port basin of Marghera (Alberto Navarin). In Dorsoduro, the new headquarters of the architectural institute IUAV (by Enric Miralles) was created in the Magazzini Frigoriferi. The neighbouring old freight port is purely a passenger terminal today (Ugo Camerino and others). New construction projects on both sides of the bridgehead on the mainland in Mestre and **an enlargement of the cemetery island of San Michele** are enlarging the northern profile of the lagoon (David Chipperfield). At Marco Polo Airport, a small boat docking basin is under construction (Frank Gehry). There is great, almost untapped potential for future development in the city centre, on the site of the arsenal.

Undersea Railway

Thus far, the Ponte della Libertà is the only connection between Venice and the mainland. At the end of 2003, the city government decided to build an 8km/5mi-long underground railway. The **Sublagunare** is planned to take 9 minutes from the airport via the island of Murano to the Arsenale, leaving the city core untouched, but making it easier for the 25,000 commuters, 30,000 tourists and 20,000 students per day to come in and go home. Work on the €150 million railway is to be completed in 2010. However, financing questions are still unsolved and environmentalists warn that the construction of the undersea tunnel will stress the unstable ground below the city.

Information about the **lagoon ecosystem** and the development of the flood protection program MOSE is available in English at www.salve.it and the office in Punto Laguna, Campo S. Stefano 949.

were redirected to prevent silting in the lagoon, and the shorelines were stabilized. The rivers that flow into the lagoon were monitored, and the drinking water supply and the well system were also very carefully monitored. Intentional contamination was strictly punished, by the death penalty in the worst case. The system of water management functioned until the unification of Italy. Then the Magistrato alle Acque was subordinated to Rome. In the early 20th century, large areas of land around Venice were then filled in, developed as an industrial site, and deep waterways dredged out for giant tankers. Since then, the aggressive **exhaust gases** and particularly the **effluents** produced by industry (especially nitrogen and phosphate compounds), but also from the households (Venice still has no sewage system) and last but not least, the excrement of the innumerable pigeons have threatened the lagoon and the city. Significant damage is also caused by motorboats in Venice and the boats of the mainland Venetians, which are often high-powered and cause **waves** and underwater eddies. This washes the cement out of the joints of the house walls and gradually destroys walls and shorelines. Buildings and foundations sustain serious damage much faster than in older times. This is why house façades and gondola mooring sites more and more frequently display protests: **stopp moto ondoso** – stop the waves from motorboats.

MOSE The most keenly felt of all threats are the frequent floods. Since the major storm flood in 1966, when the flood waters rose to 1.94m/6ft 5in above the normal sea level, numerous ideas have been presented about how the city could best be protected. In 2003, Prime Minister Silvio Berlusconi laid the foundation stone for the project **MOSE**, which was developed in the 1970s. MOSE, actually Modulo Sperimentale Elettromeccanico, is a plan to install 78 mobile protection dams at the three entries of the lagoon. These dams could then be raised or lowered depending on water levels. In normal conditions, the water-filled, 5m/17ft-thick and 20m/66ft-high bulwarks lie anchored to the ocean floor on hinges. If sea levels rise above 1.10m/3ft 7in, compressed air is forced into the gates until they stand almost upright in the water, holding back the floods. The lagoon could be closed off in this way within one hour.

MOSE is intended to function in this way up to a further increase in the water level of 60cm/2ft. This means it would provide safety from floods for the next 150 years. The Consorzio Venezia Nuova, a pool of companies which are mainly from the Veneto, has been mandated to carry out the work. Construction is to be completed by 2011. The cost of the work is estimated at €6 billion. Critics state that the climate-related increase in sea water levels will be much higher than calculated. They also warn of the consequences of the (even temporary) separation of the lagoon from the open sea, since it depends on the cleaning effect of the tides for survival. And the poisonous industry of Marghera continues to operate.

Venice Mose Flood Protection Programme

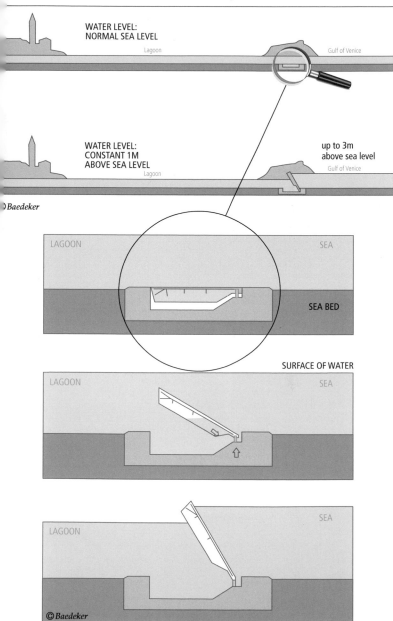

WATER LEVEL:
NORMAL SEA LEVEL

Lagoon

Gulf of Venice

WATER LEVEL:
CONSTANT 1M
ABOVE SEA LEVEL

Lagoon

up to 3m
above sea level

Gulf of Venice

© Baedeker

LAGOON

SEA

SEA BED

LAGOON

SEA

SURFACE OF WATER

LAGOON

SEA

© Baedeker

City History

It all started with a few merchants and fishermen who sought protection on the inaccessible islands in the lagoon. Through a brilliant combination of trade and diplomacy, the island state rose to power in the following centuries, then surrendered in 1797 to Napoleon Bonaparte, who did not even require weapons for the conquest.

Queen of the Adriatic

828	Translation of the bones of St Mark
1204	Conquest of Byzantium; Venice becomes stato da mar, the ruler of the Mediterranean
1381	Victory over Genoa, beginning of expansion on the mainland, Venice becomes stato da terra

Rise:
9th to 11th
century

In a contract between Charlemagne and Byzantium in 812, Venice (along with Dalmatia and the port cities of Istria) became a province of the Byzantine Empire. The political and intellectual centre of the city was on the Rialto archipelago. This was the site of the buildings that preceded today's Doge's Palace and cathedral. And when two merchants from Venice brought the remains of **St Mark** (Mark the Evangelist) from Alexandria in 828, the young lagoon state finally had »its« saint as well. The relics were kept in the newly constructed St Mark's Basilica, the house chapel of the doges. Its symbol, the winged lion, became the sign of the city. As talented ship builders, skilled ferrymen, courageous sailors (with a legendary tendency towards piracy) and clever merchants, the island Venetians gradually conquered the maritime and trade routes through the Adriatic to the east. Distant Byzantium generously opened all ports and trade routes to its ally. It was from here that the Venetians brought velvet and silk fabrics, ivory, gold and particularly pepper and other spices as well as rice, coffee and sugar to Venice. But domestic goods such as oil and wood from the hinterland as well as the salt which was harvested from the lagoon were also sold. Individual families became rich, and the city also developed into Europe's greatest financial centre.

? DID YOU KNOW ...?

■ The »thieves« of the body of St Mark concealed the bones in a barrel of bacon and easily passed through customs, since the Moslem guards were not allowed to touch pork for religious reasons.

The growing success of Venice as a commercial power and the inflow of people from near and far ensured its rapid development. Influential merchant families dominated the economic, political and social development of the city. A powerful war fleet ensured external safety in the battle against pirates, but also steadily acquired new territory in the Adriatic, Istria and Dalmatia (AD 1000). Dalmatia provided Venice with an inexhaustible source of slaves and wood. Since this year, every year on Ascension Day the »marriage of the doge and the sea«, **sposalizio del mar** has been celebrated in front of the church S. Nicolò.

Ca' Rezzonico: The festival hall decorated with gold chandeliers, carved furniture and ceiling frescoes on the first floor, the so-called Piano nobile.

In the past, the larch and oak posts required to build Venice were tied together and transported to Venice as rafts. A barge makes the job easier.

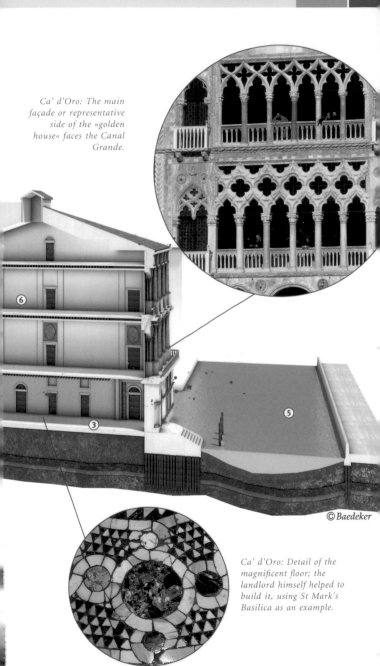

Ca' d'Oro: The main façade or representative side of the »golden house« faces the Canal Grande.

© Baedeker

Ca' d'Oro: Detail of the magnificent floor; the landlord himself helped to build it, using St Mark's Basilica as an example.

HOW VENICE WAS BUILT

Venice was built on 118 islands and islets located close together in a lagoon. The first island dwellers lived in huts reminiscent of the »nests of waterfowl« (Cassiodorus). Until the 13th century, all houses except for the churches were made from (lightweight) wood. For improved fire safety and in order to erect more representative stone structures, the Venetians developed a special construction technique for the swampy terrain.

① Venice floats on a submerged forest

Entire forests in the Venetian alps were cut down and transported to Venice on rafts (zattere). The 2 to 20m/7 to 66ft long oak or larch posts were driven into the mud and down to the solid bottom of the lagoon (caranto) close together. In salt water, where there is no oxygen and no bacteria to cause decay, the posts gradually became as hard as rock. The builders then nailed horizontal walnut or mahogany planks onto this carpet of wood, and sealed them with sand, tar and oil.

② Actual foundation

The actual foundation followed at the water level: brickwork and a thick base made from water-resistant rock or marble from Istria, which then supported the building itself. According to estimates, the Basilica della Salute rests on over one million posts and each side of the Rialto bridge is supported by approximately 6,000 posts.

Almost 20,000 buildings in Venice »float« on this upside-down submerged forest.

③ Floor

This floating base also explains the Venetian preference for mosaic and terrazzo floors. Unlike large-scale marble installations, they can follow the »floating movements« of the base. Stones with a certain hardness, structure and thickness such as porphyry, serpentine, chalcedony, lapis lazuli and malachite were used. Terrazzo was already known in ancient times: Marble pieces of various shapes, colours and granulation are interspersed into a limestone and cement mortar bed and are polished once it has hardened; the Palazzo Ducale has some very nice examples.

④ Wells

Until a water main from the mainland was built in 1884, the population obtained their water from cisterns within the city. Rainwater was guided into clay-lined cisterns through drains underneath the pavement. A layer of sand acted as a natural filter. The cleanliness of the water was strictly protected.

⑤ Canals

Sewage and all other wastes ended up in the canals. They were regularly cleaned out by the rise and fall of the tides and the occasional storm surge. Since this was insufficient, they were brought to a statutory minimum depth of 180cm/ 71in and cleaned regularly.

⑥ The Venetian house

The floor plans of the palaces (called Casa, house, or Ca' for short in Venice) were more or less the same and have changed little over the centuries. The Palazzo normally has two entrances; the representative entrance faces the canal, the simple one is at the rear. The ground floor was used for storage and commercial space. The reception or festival hall was located on the first floor, the Piano nobile. The actual living quarters for the family were located on the second floor.

Legendary Beginnings

5th century AD	Mainland Venetians fled into the lagoon from Germanic invaders
Late 7th century	Election of the first doges

According to legend Venice was founded on 25 March, AD 421. But there is no exact date. The city was born when a storm of migrations brought about the end of the Western Roman Empire, and Germanic peoples poured into northern Italy. At that time, mainland residents sought protection in the inaccessible island world of the lagoon (lacuna, the Latin word for puddle, pond). The first settlers moved onto Malamocco (now Lido), Torcello and Murano, cleared the partly swampy islands and drained them. They probably made a rather scanty living as fishermen, coastal sailors, salt workers and vegetable growers. The Huns under Attila (452) and later the Lombards (from 568) triggered further waves of flight and settlement. A lively description originates from the Roman scholar Cassiodorus, the chancellor of the Ostrogoth king, Theodoric, who resided in Ravenna. In 537, he wrote of the Venetians: they »seem to be equally at home on the ocean and on land«. »The land is alternately covered and laid bare by tide and ebb«. Their huts appear like »the nests of water birds, before which their boats are tied like horses«. Venice was not yet a city when the small lagoon population placed itself under the protective rule of the Byzantine Empire, which had grown out of the Eastern Roman Empire.

5th–6th century AD

In 697, the Byzantine exarch of Ravenna named the first in a long series of 120 doges (Latin: dux, leader), Paoluccio Anafesto. His first seat of government over the lagoon settlements was in Heraclea on the mainland. In 742, this was moved to Malamocco (Lido). The first century of rule by doges was marked by rivalries between the lagoon settlements and by pro- and anti-Byzantine conflicts. Few doges (there were nine up to the year 804) died natural deaths. Influential families who owned property on the mainland fought over the rights to the lucrative salt production. Unification came through an external threat: when the Emperor Charlemagne and his son Pepin besieged the lagoon in 809 and destroyed Malamocco, the islanders played to their strengths. Through a trick – by pulling out the poles which marked the numerous sand banks in the lagoon – they won a battle over the enemy forces and relocated their seat of government to Rivus Altus (Rivoalto, Rialto). This group of islands at the centre of the lagoon was the core of the rapidly growing city of Venice.

Unification of the city: 7th/8th century

← *A flag with a winged lion, the symbol for Mark the evangelist, flies in front of St Mark's basilica.*

Venice, which maintained lively trade connections to the Muslim world, played a relatively small role in the first crusades to the Holy Land. This was profitable to the trade competitors Pisa and Genoa, which successfully encroached on the Venetian sphere of interest. When Constantinople gave privileges to its rival Genoa, Venetian restraint came to an end with the Fourth Crusade (1202–1204). With skilful diplomacy, the 92-year-old and half-blind Doge Enrico Dandolo obtained support for the conquest of the Dalmatian coastal city of Zara and particularly Constantinople as a reward for providing ships and crew for the transport of the crusader army (1204). The richest city of Christendom and capital of the Byzantine Empire was thoroughly plundered. Valuable art treasures, among them the four famous bronze horses of San Marco, came to Venice. At the same time, Venice secured for itself nearly half of the former territory of the Eastern Roman Empire: the coast of Epirus to the Peloponnese, Euboea, Crete, Rhodes and other islands of the Aegean. Thus Venice had become a Mediterranean power. Brief thought was given to moving into the conquered city on the Bosporus. The plan was discarded in 1224 with a majority of only two votes.

Crusades 12th/13th century

The mosaic above the Porta di S. Alippio shows the transfer of the bones of St Mark's

Venetian sea power now had a monopoly on all major trade routes between the Levant and the west. Such a surplus of power brought an old rival, Genoa, to the table. The struggle for first rank in the Mediterranean trade lasted until 1381, when Venice defeated its old enemy. Venice was now a **stato da mar**, a maritime power. Venetian merchants reached far-away places on their commercial travels. Nicolò and Antonio Zeno sailed to Newfoundland, Greenland and Iceland in 1390, while Nicolò Conti crossed the Indian Ocean to the Persian Gulf and to Ceylon in the 15th century. Venetian settlements were found in the Crimea, Armenia, Syria and Egypt. In the late 15th century, Venice was the third-largest city in Europe after Paris and Naples with about 150,000 residents.

Proud maritime republic 13th–15th century

The Government of Venice

The constitution of Venice provided inner political peace for many centuries, even among the social groups that were excluded from power. The constitution's roots are in the 11th and 12th centuries, but continued to develop in accordance with demands. It owed its success to a well-developed system of mutually controlling forces, in which the checks and balances of modern democratic constitutions were already present. The difference was that this involved »democracy« for only one class of the people, the nobility.

Organization of the republic

Venice was an **oligarchy**. Power lay in the hands of a few families who had become rich through trade. They were members of the so-called Greater Council. After its numbers had risen to several hundred, it was closed to newcomers in 1297 and known as the **Serrata**. From then on, membership was open only to those who (or whose families) were recorded in the **Libro d'Oro**, the Golden Book of the republic (at the end of the republic, this book contained 1218 names). The Greater Council chose the members of the various committees which carried out state business, and elected the doge from among its own members. Every noble held an office in the state apparatus, usually as an unpaid servant of the state. He was not allowed to refuse a service with which he was mandated, nor a command. Persons who failed in office, whether through their own fault or otherwise, were subject to the strictest punishments. These measures promoted the development of a highly stable class of leaders which determined all the affairs of the city. Not all members of the population were satisfied with this regulation; coup attempts were inevitable.

The »bourgeois« families were entered in the **Silver Book**. They had no part in government decisions, but some offices in government were open to them. The families entered in the Golden and Silver Books did not account for even 15% of Venice's total population, but controlled nearly 90% of the republic's wealth.

Office of doge

In AD 697, the first doge (from Latin dux, meaning leader) had been named by the representative of the Byzantine emperor. From 726 onwards, the lagoon population exercised its voting rights. In 1797 Doge Manin, the last of the long line, returned the doge's hat with the words: »It is no longer needed.« In these eleven hundred years, 120 doges who were elected for life represented the republic of Venice. Their sign of office was the famous **corno**, the doge's hat, which was decorated with gold and jewels worth 194,000 ducats. The people confirmed the election of the doge by cheering the announcement »This is your doge if you accept him«. At first, the power of the doge was nearly unlimited. In the 10th century, when Doge Pietro Candiano IV (959–976) tried to make the office of doge inherit-

Venice from a birds-eye view, painting by Josef Heitz Junior from the 17th century

able, there was an uprising. The Doge's Palace and the basilica went up in flames; the doge and his son, who was still a minor, were murdered. Following this, the power of the doge was increasingly restricted. Finally, the people were also excluded from the election of the doge. Now the announcement was only »This is your doge« (mid-12th century). A highly complicated process was intended to prevent cheating in the election of the doge. 30 people were chosen by lot from the Greater Council. They elected nine from among themselves who then chose another 40 electors. These 49 were reduced to 12 by drawing lots, and they chose another 25. These were again reduced to nine, each of which chose another five. These 45 then selected eleven men from their group, which determined the 41 final electors. The election process could take months.

The doge represented the republic, had a seat on every committee (but only one vote in elections), presided over the Greater Council, and had the duty of bringing about decisions and controlling the holders of state office. However, his authority was strictly limited: the doge and his wife had to reside in the Doge's Palace. They had to pay for their furniture and other expenses out of their own pockets. The doge was not allowed to hold private or external offices. No members of the doge's family were allowed to participate in commercial undertakings, and his sons and daughters were not allowed to marry outside the city without the permission of the Greater Council. In the absence of the councillors, the doge was not allowed to open letters from outside powers, receive ambassadors or accept gifts (unless they were flowers, scented herbs or rose water). In the 14th century, Francesco Petrarch described the situation of the doge with the words: »Doges are not rulers, not even princes, but only the glorified slaves of the republic.«

Duties of the doge

Government

If there was anything similar to a state government, then it was the **Lesser Council** which consisted of six consiglieri, representatives of the six city districts. The consiglieri discussed all state matters, monitored and represented the doge, who also had only one vote within this circle, and chaired the various bodies together with him. The two most important ones included the Quarantia (named after its originally 40 members) and the senate. The **Quarantia** was already in existence in 1179. It was initially only a court of appeals, but from about 1230 developed into a financial and legal organization. From about 1230, the **senate** mainly dealt with matters of shipping and

Porta dell Carta: The doge Foscari kneels before the lion of St Mark's

trade. It later developed into the actually ruling parliament – responsible to the Greater Council, but entitled to make important decisions. In the first third of the 14th century, the senate gave rise to the **Collegio dei Savi**, which was mandated to prepare senate sessions and handle matters of commerce and marine duties, and in the 15th century to the **Collegio**, which, together with the doge, the Lesser Council and three representatives of the Quarantia, functioned as a sort of ministers' council. The last great constitutional organ to emerge was the **Council of Ten** (Dieci). The background was the coup attempt of Baiamonte Tiepolo in 1310. The task of the Dieci was to examine the background and the processes and punish the guilty parties. In 1335, the decision was made to maintain this type of special court. It was charged with investigating all occurrences which might endanger the security of the state. The principle of distrust which marked Venice's constitution was practically institutionalized in this body. Naturally, the names of the ten members, whom the senate elected every year, were kept secret.

Many institutions

In this way, many institutions were created which delegated and shared power and controlled each other. A network of usually unsalaried office-holders ensured that the enacted regulations were carried out precisely, and that individual groups did not become too powerful. The periods of service of the most important state offices were very short (except for the doge, who was elected for life and very closely monitored). State office terms usually lasted only a year. Furthermore, the office holders could only be elected into other offices after a waiting period. One of the most important offices was that of the cattaveri, the tax assessors. All Venetians, regardless of rank and person, had to disclose their entire financial situation to them and pay the taxes that were thus determined.

There are many hypotheses about why the Venetian population, the middle classes and craftsmen, but also the merchants and sailors, accepted their lack of power. In some periods many new citizens were ennobled. Truly outstanding wealth enabled citizens to become councillors at any period. Perhaps the so-called scuole, the typically Venetian guild brotherhoods, also played a special role.

Scuole

By the 13th and 14th centuries, the constitution of Venice had largely been completed. It changed little in later times, although 95% of the population did not partake in political power. An important role in the social structure and the stability of the republic of nobles was played by the so-called scuole, which formed from the 12th century onwards – lay brotherhoods which usually consisted of men of a particular trade. They elected their representatives, created association regulations, but also fulfilled a number of social tasks: they founded and maintained hospitals and shelters for the poor. The scuole developed into a very complex group of associations and unions and thereby offered a substitute for political activity to a large number of Venetian citizens. Longworth (»Rise and Fall of the Republic of Venice«, 1976) refers to them as the »most democratic systems of Venice«. There were numerous small scuole, comparable to guilds. The most significant ones included the Scuole di San Rocco, dei Carmine, San Giovanni Evangelista and San Giorgio degli Schiavoni. The members paid fees and supplied the men who marched in the most important processions. The large scuole had their own buildings, and it is testimony to their importance that the Scuola Grande di San Rocco has one of the most impressive cycles of paintings in the world: Tintoretto painted 56 large-format works for it. But even the interiors of the small scuole are surprising – for instance, Vittore Carpaccio created a fabulous set of paintings for the Scuola di San Giorgio degli Schiavoni. Marco Polo and many great artists were members of the scuole. The end of the republic was also their (temporary) end. Napoleon forbade the scuole as well as the monasteries. However, they were refounded (the Scuola Grande di San Rocco in 1797, others followed in the early 20th century).

Baedeker TIP

Secret paths

The Council of Ten usually met at night. The seat of office was the Palazzo Ducale, where the prison, torture and execution rooms were also located. However, they were very well camouflaged and not visible from the outside. A look at these rooms and the way in which this secret police worked is provided by the tour »Itinerari segreti« in the Palazzo Ducale (►page 228).

From the Fall of Venice to the Present

1453	Conquest of Constantinople by the Ottomans – the Turks become competitors in the Aegean
1508	Founding of the League of Cambrai, an alliance against Venice
15th–16th cent.	Venice conquers its hinterland
1797	Resignation of the last doge, Venice surrenders to Napoleon without a fight

Venice was the unchallenged ruler of the seas. The merchant fleet consisted of 3,900 ships with about 17,000 sailors. Domestically the republic was stable. Only its hinterland was not secured, and so the »stato da mar« began expansion to the west in the early 15th century – finally making Venice the greatest territorial power in northern Italy.

Conquests on land 15th century With paid troops, led by renowned condottieri (mercenary leaders), the queen of the Adriatic conquered large parts of the mainland (terraferma): Padua, Vicenza, Verona (1405). In 1489, when the island of Cyprus fell to Venice, the city state reached its greatest size: its rule extended from the Greek islands of the Aegean west via Dalmatia and Friuli to Bergamo, north to the Alps, including a large part of Triente, and south to Ravenna. A great variety of economic activity had developed within the city. At the end of the 15th century, Venice had more printers than Rome, Milan and Florence together. Silk and cotton weaving blossomed; the glass-blowing factories on Murano grew into large-scale operations. The differentiation in crafts was far advanced, still recognizable today from the repertoire of street names – rope makers, soapers, dyers, brewers, weavers, bakers, goldsmiths, spice dealers, tanners, candle makers. This period also produced many of the magnificent churches and lovely palaces which fascinate visitors to Venice to this day.

External threat In 1453, the Ottomans quickly conquered Constantinople, and then, one by one, the Venetian possessions of Cyprus, Crete and the Peloponnese. They even penetrated the waters of the Adriatic, and in 1499, temporarily occupied part of Friuli. At the same time (1504), France, Spain, Hungary and Austria formed the League of Cambrai with papal support. The maritime republic was able to withstand the league, which soon dissolved due to internal troubles. Calm had only just returned west of Venice when the Turks resumed their challenge in the east. In 1517, they conquered Egypt, and from then on, controlled Venice's trade routes to Asia Minor, Persia and the Far East.

The barbaric and destructive war for control of the eastern Mediterranean, which had now lasted for 300 years with interruptions, led to the destruction of the stato da mar. In 1492 the Genoan Christopher Columbus sailed to the New World, and in 1499 the Portuguese Vasco da Gama discovered the sea route across the Atlantic to India – events with far-reaching consequences, since the centre of world trade increasingly shifted to the Atlantic coast, Lisbon, London and Antwerp. The Mediterranean trade, and with it the commercial power of Venice, increasingly lost significance. In 1510, trade with Flanders had already stopped, and the spice trade had lessened by 60%. The despair of the Serenissima regarding these developments in the 16th century is shown by plans for the construction of a Suez canal, which, however, could not be technically realized at that time.

Venice faced great difficulties: in terms of external politics, the republic was isolated from the European royal houses. But the Turkish fleet threatened not only the remaining trade activities of Venice, but also the interests of the other

Proud Condottiere: Colleoni monument in front of Santi Giovanni e Paolo

Mediterranean countries. Under Pope Pius V, a »Holy League« was finally formed. A fleet was created with the aid of Naples, Austria, Sicily and Genoa – a total of 450 ships with 120,000 crewmen, and on 7 October 1571, the decisive battle took place in the Gulf of Corinth near the small port of Lepanto (today Naupaktos). Even though the Venetians won an outstanding victory for the last time in history, they were unable to free themselves from isolation in foreign affairs.

Battle of Lepanto 1571

There were signs of internal decay as well. Poverty became a much greater problem. Corruption and mismanagement caused the collapse of several renowned banks. Syphilis spread so severely that in 1522 the duty to report and treat it was introduced. In 1575 and 1630, Venice experienced two epidemics of the black death, from which nearly one third of the population died each time. The Turks returned, attacked Crete and drew Venice into another Mediterra-

Long twilight

nean war with large losses (1644 to 1669). When the new forces of the Habsburgs pushed back the Ottoman Empire and acquired the conquered regions for themselves, Venice gave up its last trade bases in the Aegean and concentrated its efforts on preserving its independence as a small state – in the protection of its home lagoon.

End of the republic 18th century

The republic of Venice had lost power, but culturally it rose to greater heights, recorded in the paintings of Tiepolo, Canaletto and Guardi as well as the writings of Casanova and Goldoni, as if carefree enjoyment could delay the imminent end of a glorious past. In the early 18th century, there were still 216 Venetian patrician families, who were just able to supply members of the Greater Council and the large apparatus of officials. After 1750, in order to clean up state finances, the senate began to confiscate the possessions of the churches. The funds were used, among other things, to build the 15km/9.3mi-long, 14km/8.7mi-wide and 4.5m/15 ft-high dyke system to protect the lagoon (murazzi), a final great achievement of the republic.

In 1796, **Napoleon** had declared war on Austria and marched his troops into northern Italy. In 1797, he finally stood before Venice. The Greater Council met on 17 May 1797. The last doge, Ludovico Manin, declared his resignation. With 512 yes votes and only 30 opposing votes, the end of the republic was decided. Disrespectfully, Napoleon burned the Libro d'Oro, the Golden Book of the city which contained the names of all great patrician families, and plundered the city. At that time, many works of art were taken away to Paris – among them the four bronze horses from St Mark's Basilica – buildings torn down, churches and monasteries destroyed or rededicated. In the same year, France ceded the entire Veneto, including Venice, to Austria.

19th century From Austria to Italy

After more than 1,000 years of independence, Venice was only a province of the distant capital Vienna. The new rulers had streets paved, gas lighting installed, sea defences strengthened, and in 1846, they built the railway bridge which connected Venice to the mainland. In the first half of the 19th century, the Serenissima bore the occupation without resistance. In the European revolution year of 1848, Venetian freedom fighters under Daniele Manin, were able to free the city from Austria for 15 months. In 1866, the Habsburgs ceded the region of Venice to the newly united kingdom of Italy. At this time, Venice was only a shadow of its former self. Marked by mismanagement and local political power struggles, the city was like a poorhouse – approximately one third of the 130,000 residents lived in poverty.

New prosperity 20th century

The desired economic and social upturn took a long time to come. In 1917, during the First World War, the construction of industrial facilities began in Marghera. The port was also moved here from

Regatta in honour of Napoleon in 1807; he is standing on the balcony of the Palazzo Balbi

Venice. In 1926, Venice, Mestre and Marghera merged. In 1933, a road traffic bridge was constructed between Mestre and Venice, parallel to the railway embankment. Despite its industrial facilities, Venice was left unscathed by Allied bomb attacks. In the 1950s, the mainland became home to the centre of the Italian **chemical industry**.

Insular Venice reached fame as a tourist destination in the second half of the 20th century. However, the city and its lagoon are facing great challenges, including environmental contamination, increased flooding, sinking foundations and rising numbers of visitors. The future of the city depends on the solutions to these problems ▶ Baedeker Special p.24.

Venice today

Art and Culture

The city is a work of art in itself; and it has almost immeasurable treasures in its museums, churches and palaces. A special feature of Venice is that many works of art are still found in the places for which they were originally created.

Romanesque and Byzantine Art

Close links to Constantinople marked the development of art in Venice. The state and court church of the doges, **San Marco**, was built with five domes in the image of the Church of the Apostles of Constantinople. After 1100 the vestibule, later the interior of the church too, was covered with Byzantine mosaics. Byzantine mosaic artists worked on them with Italian helpers. The iconography is strongly oriented to its eastern model, although the execution departs from the sense of form of Byzantine art through the lively design of the surface and the figures as well as the stylized folds. A further example is found in the Last Judgement mosaics of the west wall in **Santa Maria Assunta** on Torcello (12th century). This link between western elements of style and eastern models is an important attribute of Romanesque art in Venice.

Byzantine influence

The architecture of **Santa Maria Assunta** on Torcello shows important hallmarks of Romanesque architecture: a tall campanile towers above the column basilica, which has wooden ceilings and no transept; narrow blind arches are generously applied to structure the walls, and in the interior the wall surfaces above the narrow arcades are emphasized.

Architecture

On the basis of a Byzantine model, **Santa Fosca** was built on Torcello in the late 11th century. It has a central plan with a dome, in which the forms of the octagon, cross and circle interact to create a square interior space. The octagonal outer mantle is dominated by slender arcades on high columns.

Romanesque-Byzantine influences are evident in the cathedral of **SS Maria e Donato** on Murano: the column basilica, through the insertion of a large transept, gains the spatial effect of a centrally-planned structure, and the exterior of the eastern apse is built as a façade. A two-storey arcade on double columns stands out, enclosing niches on the lower level and standing free before a wide gallery on the upper level. This vertical structuring with galleries that are relatively far away from the wall is a characteristic of secular pre-Gothic architecture in Venice.

Sculpture of the 11th and 12th centuries also shows strong Byzantine influences. It is frequently difficult to decide whether the sculptures were made in Venice or imported. The screens in the cathedral of Torcello (11th century), on which a symmetrical pair of peacocks surrounded by vines picks grapes from a bowl, came from Byzantium. The symbolism refers to the renewal of life by partaking in the death of Christ. The relief with the ascension of Alexander on the

Sculpture

← *With their extravagant gold grounding the mosaics in St Mark's basilica cover an area of almost 4,000 sq m/43,060 sq ft.*

Richly decorated spolia pillar in front of the south side of St Mark's.

northern façade of San Marco is dated to the 11th century, due to its simple form and reduced corporeality. It might have come from the Christian east.

Aside from the numerous imports of reliefs and sculptures, Venice possesses numerous **spolia**, pieces from older buildings. Through commercial relations, trade bases and particularly through the conquest of Constantinople in 1204, many spoils of war reached Venice. Many of the polychrome marble columns and the fine ornamentation on the pilasters of St Mark's Basilica are such plundered pieces. The two free-standing columns on the Piazzetta today are among the best-known spolia. They were brought to Venice by sea at the end of the 12th century. The figures on the columns are also spolia from the orient. The bronze St Mark's lion was originally a chimera, whose meaning was changed by adding wings and the open book. The figure of St Theodore is a Roman work, reshaped to show Christian meaning.

The Gothic Period

Architecture A decorative system developed in Venice during the Gothic period, particularly through the redesign of the façade of the Doge's Palace. All forms show a certain grace and colour here. The arcade of the low ground floor consist of wide pointed arches, while that of the upper loggia is much narrower, with quatrefoils cut into the spandrels to produce a more transparent effect. The wall above it seems less massive due to the white-red-green bricks and the diamond patterns. Wide pointed-arch windows as well as oculi with quatrefoils pierce the wall, and the balconies have beautiful Gothic window frames. Even the »flame-shaped« crenellations are perforated to form a filigree top.

The exterior of **San Marco** was also fundamentally changed in the late 14th century, when the row of arches on the upper floor was

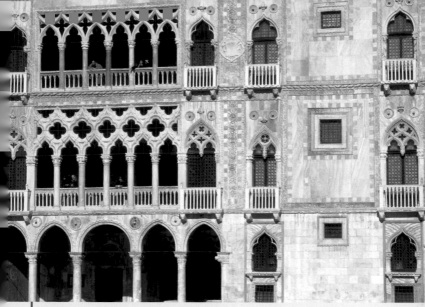

Ca' d'Oro, one of the most famous palaces in Venice

crowned in late Gothic style. Figure tabernacles, curving canopies and statues on the gables, typically Gothic decorations, were added. The most famous late Gothic palace façade is that of the **Ca' d'Oro** (1421 to 1440). The Gothic elements of the façade, which was formerly partially covered in gold, are slender arcades with various forms of tracery, balconies, friezes and finely applied decorations as well as the polychrome work.

The Dominican church **SS Giovanni e Paolo** and the Franciscan church **Santa Maria Gloriosa dei Frari** are the two largest late Gothic churches in Venice. Both were built according to the scheme of Gothic churches of the mendicant orders, as vaulted column basilicas with transepts and side chapels in the choir.

Sculpture

In the field of sculpture, styles from the most diverse sources met in Venice. Byzantine influences remained of decisive importance; elements from antiquity were taken up and combined with Gothic characteristics. The sculptural decoration on the main portal of San Marco dates from the mid-13th century and shows complete individuality in its lively narrative and the detail of its depictions.

The brothers Jacobello and Pierpaolo dalle Masegne participated in important projects in Venice: their sculptures on the rood screen of San Marco (1394) show that they attached great significance to the individual design of the figures, the precise rendition of body volumes and lively gestures. On some apostles, they even worked at contrapost.

View from the Palazzo Ducale across to the Island of S. Giorgio Maggiore

Nowhere in Venice can the development of tomb art be followed better than in SS Giovanni e Paolo, for this mendicant church was a popular burial church for the doges. The design of the tomb of Michele Morosini on the right wall in the presbytery is typical for the 14th century. A pointed arch with a gable, bordered by tabernacle towers on its sides, stands high over the tomb. The deceased lies on a bed here, with an inscription between the consoles for the coat of arms. The small sculptures, angels, apostles and the Annunciation show northern influences; the mosaic of the crucifixion with the donor figures are close to the art of Giotto.

Painting Oil painting was introduced by Antonello da Messina at the end of the 15th century. The works that he produced during his stay in Venice had great influence on Venetian painting. Antonio Vivarini shared a workshop with his brother Bartolomeo. Starting with a rather decorative late Gothic style in which the figures look rigid, he refined his painting from 1400 onwards. His work displays astounding nearness to reality and empathy in characterization. Bartolomeo developed a pictorial language with depth. His work excels through strong colours and hard contours. The son of Antonio, Alvise, produced large altar and devotional paintings and had close links to Giovanni Bellini.

Renaissance

In the 15th century, few new churches were built in Venice. How- **Architecture**
ever, the commission to sculptor and architect **Pietro Lombardo** in
1481 to rebuild Santa Maria dei Miracoli was of outstanding significance. Retaining its classical proportions, he had the entire exterior
covered in polychrome marble, the lower storey rhythmically structured with pilasters and the upper storey with arcades. Marble also
dominates the interior – a barrel-
vaulted hall with a raised presbytery. Special emphasis is placed on
the relief decorations of the pilasters, consisting of ornamental bands
enriched with animals, vases, heads
and masks. They have depth, and
are delicate and densely worked.
Aside from Lombardo, who was also responsible for the Scuola
Grande di San Marco with perspective design of the reliefs at the base
of the walls, important commissions had also been entrusted to
Mauro Coducci. Among other
work, he covered the façades of
San Zaccaria and San Michele in
Isola. Semicircular tops to façades
and segments of circles are charac-

> **? DID YOU KNOW ...?**
>
> ■ Items of special interest: Venetian floors,
> which were made from the 9th century, first
> by oriental masters, later by craftsmen from
> the region of Ravenna and from Venice itself.
> Many of the motifs have special significance;
> for instance, a circle symbolizes the sky, a
> square the earth (paradise on earth). The
> eagle is the king of the air, the lion king of the
> desert and the incarnation of majesty, courage
> and justice. Occasionally it represents Christ
> himself. The peacock stands for resurrection
> and immortality, while the deer embodies
> belief in God. Mythological monsters like the
> griffin or the basilisk symbolize evil.

teristic of his work. San Zaccaria shows his strict system of design,
consisting of pilasters, columns and round-arch windows or blind
arches as vertical elements, receiving a horizontal accent through
wide cornices which separate the storeys. Round oculi are a frequent
element in his façades. Both architects, Lombardo and Coducci,
played a significant role in the development of the Venetian palace
façade by piercing the previously closed walls with large windows.
Andrea Palladio, in his Venetian period, devoted himself solely to religious architecture. He planned three important church façades: San
Giorgio Maggiore, Il Redentore and San Francesco della Vigna,
which excel in terms of austere lines and clear proportions. Colossal
arrangements of columns, a columned vestibule crowned by a gable
and a balanced ratio of wall to column lend a special effect to the
church fronts.

In the development of tombs, that of Pietro Mocenigo in SS Giovan- **Sculpture**
ni e Paolo (1476–1481) was ground-breaking. **Pietro Lombardo** con-
ceived a design which built on the motif of the triumphal arch. Nine
warriors based on ancient models stand in the niches or support the
sarcophagus, on which the deceased doge is no longer shown lying,

but standing. The tomb of Andrea Vendramin by Tullio Lombardo (1493), the son of Pietro, is a further well-known monument in this church. Once more, a central arcade of columns is framed by restrained side sections. The iconographic programme combines Christian motifs with humanist ideas. An examination of the individual figures, particularly those of the warriors, suggests that the artist made a precise study of ancient sculpture. The artist lent similar vivacity to the double portrait in the Galleria Franchetti (Ca' d'Oro) by expressing emotions in the faces.

Antonio Rizzo, the second important Venetian sculptor of the Renaissance, created the figures of Adam and Eve, which originally stood at the Arco Foscari of the Doge's Palace, in the second half of the 15th century. In the proportions, Eve in particular, with her narrow shoulders and wide hips, is characteristic of the Gothic sense of form, but it is precisely her posture and gesture that make her seem sensual and withdrawn, while Adam is moved and outward-looking, as his open mouth and right hand held in front of his chest indicate. The figures were made from models – sculptures from antiquity were surely not used.

In the design of Piazza San Marco and the Piazzetta, the architect **Jacopo Sansovino**, who planned the Libreria di San Marco and the Zecca, played an important role. Even though he also worked as a sculptor, he did not himself carry out the rich sculptural decoration that he designed. Nonetheless, Venice contains significant examples of his work: the reliefs of the singers' galleries and the vestry doors of San Marco, the Madonna in the Arsenal, St John the Baptist on the font in the Frari church and the figures in the niches of the Loggetta (Pallas Athene, Mercury, Apollo, Pax) next to the Campanile, which embody the main principles of Venetian politics. In these haunting bronze sculptures, outstanding in their cohesion and the fine detail of the surface structure, the influence of ancient sculpture cannot be overlooked.

Painting

One identifying characteristic of Venetian painting is the variety of colours; it can be explained by the influence of Byzantine art, the location of Venice on the water, and the numerous narrow canals in the city which create extraordinary effects of light and shade. Contrary to Florentine painting of the time, which particularly focused on narrative and pathos, Venetian painters preferred to record lyrical subjects and moods. **Giorgione's** painting *The Tempest* in the Gallerie dell'Accademia is a well-known example. The painting, which cannot be clearly decoded iconographically and may represent an allegory of human life, shows a calm, peaceful scene, to which the restless, almost ominous mood of the stormy skies forms a strong contrast. Light and colour to convey mood in a sensual, poetic world are important characteristics for this painter.

Gentile Bellini, who worked in the highly influential family studio with his father Jacopo and his brother Giovanni, had the honourable

Giorgione's »Thunderstorm«, a famous painting in the Accademia

task of painting every newly elected doge. Today, few originals but many copies of these paintings survive. The portraits of the Bellini school reveal an intense concern with the individual.

The sketchbooks of **Jacopo Bellini** show that he took an interest in antiquity, though more in formal terms than in terms of content. Here Venice differs from other cities of the arts such as Florence and Mantua, where mythological representations became popular as early as the second half of the 15th century. In the early Renaissance, patrons in Venice preferred paintings with Christian content.

Vittore Carpaccio was frequently employed by brotherhoods to produce cycles of paintings for their meeting rooms. His paintings display a fascinating joy in narration and love of vivid details, while impressing formally through a strict composition, clear perspectives and precise modelling of figures.

Vittore Carpaccio: »Dream of St Ursula« (Accademia)

Titian painted the central altar image of the Assunta for the Frari church (1516–1518). Here, the ascension of the Virgin takes place in a space filled with light: below are the apostles, frightened, gazing after the departing Virgin with arms raised high, and in the highest zone, God receiving Mary. In this monumental work, Titian found a composition for this theme which set a standard for decades to come. While Titian worked for a variety of prominent European patrons, **Jacopo Tintoretto** concentrated on his home city of Venice. Aside from numerous commissions for secular buildings, he painted large altarpieces. His compositions emphasize the three-dimensionality of moving figures and place them in spaces with depth and a precise perspective structure. Particularly in his late period, light increasingly became a means of conveying atmosphere, drama or vision. This makes him one of the most important masters of Mannerism.

In the paintings of **Paolo Veronese,** the main scene unfolds in the foreground as if on a stage, while further scenes related to the main theme take place in the background. His joy in narrative and decorative style can be seen in the church San Sebastiano, where he did the ceiling and wall paintings.

Palazzi

Strictly speaking, Venice has only one palace, the Palazzo Ducale or Doge's Palace. All buildings commissioned by well-off families were referred to with deceptive modesty as a casa (house), ca' for short.

Palazzo Contarini del Bovolo, »Snail Staircase«

Unlike other north Italian cities, palace architecture in Venice remained unaffected by two important problems: the buildings were naturally protected by the water, and Venice was not affected by conflicts between rival families, which meant that the individual buildings could be created with a free and open design. And since Venice had numerous rich nobles and citizens, it became home to unusually large numbers of palaces. Less expensive housing was built for those with lesser financial means, as many townhouses with functional ground plans and numerous architectural refinements still show today.

Palaces were both residences and places of work. This meant that their layout had some special characteristics which remained into the 18th century. On the ground or water floor, a hall extends right through the building and provides access to the adjacent rooms. From the Renaissance, these somewhat uncomfortable rooms were used as commercial space, store-rooms and offices. Intermediate floors were frequently inserted next to the hall. A stairway led to the residential rooms on the first and second floors. On the first floor, the piano nobile, there was a large hall with a loggia. This was a space for celebrations, feasts or theatrical performances. The sala was correspondingly furnished and decorated with paintings, weapons and trophies. The actual living rooms are on the second floor.

The Venetian palazzo generally has two entrances: the fine entrance faces the water, while the simpler one is on the opposite side. From the Renaissance, the entrance area was improved and richly decorated with paintings or sculptural ornamentation. The outside stairs which were customary until that time, and of which the spiral staircase in the courtyard of Palazzo Contarini del Bovolo still provides a beautiful example today, were increasingly moved inside the house. Large inner courtyards were frequently omitted due to the high property prices.

Façade The main façade also always faces the water. The foundation of the façade design is a base of dressed stone which terminates in a clearly marked cornice. A portal of one or more arches leads to the palace interior via a stairway. An arcade may also be built in front of the water storey. On the upper floor, the window group of the sala is the determining element. The side rooms usually had two windows placed far apart, leaving broad surfaces of wall between them. Their form depends on the period: round arches, pointed arches, tracery decoration and rectangles with triangular gables are found. The structure may be embellished with pilasters, columns or other, sometimes very detailed, decorations. The palace, originally a two-storey structure, gained another floor in the Gothic period; however it was ensured that all palazzi were of the same height. Only in the 16th century did some structures begin to exceed the uniform height.

Wood remained the preferred building material until the 13th century, when the more durable stone came into favour. Brick walls became common. They were plastered and could then be painted or clad in marble or limestone. The varied colours and grains of the stone contributed to the effect of the façades.

17th and 18th Centuries

Painting In Venice, in contrast to other regions, painting continued to develop, continuing the independent tradition of the city and supported by a well-off citizenry. Sebastiano Ricci, Giovanni Battista Tiepolo and his son Domenico made a significant contribution to this development. **Ricci** sought to include many ideas from Bolognese art and expanded his repertoire through travels to Rome and Florence. He influenced **G. B. Tiepolo**, who developed a style of painting that was flooded by even light with fine and highly differentiated colours. He mastered the composition of spatial depth, in which figures move lightly and playfully, and received numerous commissions, both from the church and private patrons. The frescoes of Palazzo Labia are his work.

The paintings of **Pietro Longhi** depict Venetian everyday life, often in very small formats. Harmonious colouring characterizes Longhi's French-influenced art. A new genre came into being beside the description of contemporary festivities and everyday life: the vedute of Calevarijs, **Francesco Guardi** and **Canaletto**. Canaletto initially painted views of the city in strong colour contrasts, but then altered his style. His topographically meticulous pictures had become routine and rigidly formulaic by the end of his creative life.

Architecture **Baldassare Longhena** is regarded as the leading Venetian architect of the Baroque period and was the builder of the city's most significant

Pietro Longhi: »The Concert« (Accademia)

Baroque church, Santa Maria della Salute. For this site, which has a prominent place in the city, he created a central plan, a domed rotunda with an ambulatory and radiating chapels. Strong architectural decoration and rich sculptural ornamentation contribute to the imposing exterior.

The architects of the 18th century sought to take up the tradition of preceding centuries, the building methods of Sansovino or Palladio, thereby producing spacious buildings filled with light. **Giorgio Massari** designed Palazzo Grassi-Stucky (1749), a clear, simple building with a classical façade and an austere staircase. For the Chiesa dei Gesuati (1726–1743), he planned a façade of great sculptural effect with columns, gables, entablature and niche figures. A similarly classical columned façade was added to the church San Nicolò da Tolentino by **Andrea Tirali**.

DEATH(S) IN VENICE

Melancholy, mysterious, morbid – these attributes are frequently bestowed on Venice. Those who have experienced the city in fog or fine rain may be able to understand this. It is therefore no surprise that Venice's own particular charm has inspired writers and filmmakers: to dark stories which send a shiver down the spine of readers or audiences.

However, in other films Venice provides a joyous, romantic or exotic backdrop for pleasurable holidays, carnivals, colourful thrillers or spy films. Katherine Hepburn, in David Lean's *Summertime* (1955), plays an old maid who vacations in Venice and blossoms when she meets Rossano Brazzi, who fills the role of the Italian cavalier particularly well. In *The Venetian Affair* (1966), Elke Sommer stars in a spy story revolving around a suicide bombing. And in *The Venetian Woman* (1986), Sean Connery experiences the joys of love.

Black Comedy

However, the true Venice film is a different matter altogether. It not only presents the city's beautiful façade, but also tempts people to come and then diverts them from their course – not only in a geographical sense. Something of this atmosphere is found in *The Honey Pot* (1965), a black comedy by Joseph Mankiewicz in which Rex Harrison awaits three former lovers, plays the dying rich man to them and plans murder.

City of Errors

That the crumbling façades conceal an abyss, that the sinking city has a strange effect on visitors and residents and may become the place for obsessions, becomes clear in Luchino Visconti's *Senso* (1953). Alida Valli plays an Italian duchess who, against her convictions, falls in love with an officer of the Austrian occupying forces (played by Farley Granger) during the Italian wars of liberation. She wants to escape him and flees through the empty alleys at night.

*Scene from
Visconti's 1970 film
»Death in Venice«*

Finally, her lover catches up with her, and later she even turns traitor. 17 years after *Senso*, Visconti's film of Thomas Mann's novella **Death in Venice** was a declaration of love for the city. The composer Aschenbach comes for recuperation. But Venice, which is threatened by cholera, is the wrong place. He falls in love with a beautiful boy. The magnificent images of the film exude an elegiac atmosphere, culminating in the final scenes in which the dying musician lies in a deck chair on the beach, make-up running across his face.

City of Obsessions

Obsessions and death are also at the centre of Nicolas Roeg's thriller **Don't Look Now** (1973). After the accidental death of their child, an English artist couple comes to Venice to forget. But the city brings back dreadful memories, particularly to the husband (played by Donald Sutherland). Again and again, he sees a figure in a red coat running through the dark alleys, and believes he is seeing his child. The illusion finally leads the man, who has second sight without knowing it, to his death.

Playing with Death

The Comfort of Strangers is the name of a thriller filmed in 1990 by Paul Schrader and based on a novel by Ian McEwan. In this film, a couple travel to Venice to refresh their slightly stale love in the place where it once began. They too go astray, lose their way and run into the arms of a man played by Christopher Walken, who involves them in a game which in this city – by now this should be no surprise – can only lead to disaster. Once again, a movie plays on the mysterious, morbid atmosphere of Venice and ends in death.

19th and 20th Centuries

Since Venice had only limited space, expansion through the construction of new quarters, which was common in other cities, did not occur here in the 19th and 20th centuries. Little was built, and there were few major changes to the existing building fabric. A conspicuous feature of Giudecca is the large **Mulino Stucky** complex. Giovanni Stucky planned to build a mill and pasta factory, and commissioned the architect Ernst Wullekopf to provide designs. Construction began in 1896. Its historicizing neo-Gothic forms, castle-like character and brick construction reveal the north German origins of the architect. The pavilions on the site of the **Biennale** were designed by famous architects in the late 19th century and the 20th century. However, as their task was to represent individual nations in the pavilions, they did not relate to the Venetian style of architecture. **Carlo Scarpa** ran an architectural practice in Venice from 1927 and was particularly concerned with interior design. In 1952, he was entrusted with planning the restoration of the Accademia, in 1953–1960 that of the Museo Correr, and in 1961–1963 of the Galleria Querini Stampalia. Scarpa's feeling for scale and fine decoration can also be seen in the salesroom of Olivetti (1957/1958) on the north side of Piazza di San Marco. He sensitively designed the room around a central pillar, contrasted colours and materials, and skilfully combined the old with the new.

Early Printing

In the 15th century, Venice gained importance as a major centre of printing. In 1469, Johannes de Spira set up the first printing press in the city and introduced the Gutenberg press with moveable type. He obtained the exclusive right to carry out printing in Venice for five years. One year later, in 1470, de Spira died, whereupon his privilege became null and void. This was a stroke of luck for numerous competitors, who immediately opened their own print works and began to produce at a lively rate. Book printing in Venice rapidly developed from an art into an important sector of the economy. The fact that individual works could be protected with copyrights by obtaining a privilege encouraged this boom. For economic reasons, privileges as wide as that given to de Spira could no longer be granted. Rights therefore extended only to one book title and included printing as well as sales. Apart from many Venetian printers, the city attracted large numbers of **German printers**. The best known printer around 1500 was **Aldus Manutius** from Bassiano, founder of the Aldine Press. He had a flourishing establishment on Campo San Luca, still

Gianni Basso in his print shop

commemorated by an plaque today (at the side entrance of the savings bank). In 1495, he obtained a monopoly in Greek prints, which made large sales in Venice and elsewhere. Another significant printing press was headed by **Lucantonio Giunta**, who mainly printed liturgical works in Venice and worked closely with his brother in Florence, who specialized in humanist literature. Aside from religious works, classics in various languages, humanist literature, natural science textbooks, dictionaries and, from 1501, sheet music were published. The extensive collection of manuscripts left to the city by Cardinal Bessarion constituted an important resource for the printers. Venice was able to maintain its position as a printing city without loss of quality to the end of the 16th century.

Famous People

What linked Peggy Guggenheim, the »enfant terrible of the capitalist class«, or Giacomo Casanova, »master of the art of love and a frivolously cultivated lifestyle« to Venice? Read on for short tributes to well-known and lesser-known personalities who shaped the reputation of Venice or are associated with the city.

Jacopo, Gentile and Giovanni Bellini

Through stays in Florence and Rome and by working at the mar-   **Painters**
grave's court in Ferrara and in the university city of Padua, **Jacopo**
Bellini (c.1400 – c.1470/1471), as a student of Gentile da Fabriano,
learned the powerful naturalistic painting style of the early Renaissance and combined it with the Gothic elegance that was still typical
of Venice. He painted Madonnas in nuanced colours and soft lines.
His outstanding draughtsmanship reveals his study of antiquity,
while his narrative painting skills – a mixture of rich fantasy and depictions of reality – prepared the way for Venetian historical painting. His sons Gentile and Giovanni learned the art of painting from
their father, but were also influenced by their brother-in-law Mantegna and became internationally known masters.

Gentile (c.1429–1507) was the eldest son of Jacopo and a famous
portraitist, who always succeeding in depicting his subject in a psy-
chologically« empathetic manner. He stayed at the court of the sultan
in Constantinople in 1479–1481, among other things for the purpose
of portraying the Ottoman ruler. In Venice, his realistic views of the
city, his keen powers of observation in depicting rich and poor,
young and old, as well as the richness of his scenes, are impressively
shown in – among other works – the cycle on the miracles of the
true cross in the Accademia.

His younger brother **Giovanni** (c.1430–1516) is the main representative of early Venetian Renaissance painting. Few other artists of the
time possessed Giovanni's drawing style and palette of luminous colours, which was not least due to the new technique of oil painting
which he learned from Antonello da Messina. His often lyrical images, ranging from half-length Madonnas to mysterious allegories,
display both intimacy of emotion and admiration for nature. The
colour harmonies, the graduated light and the atmospheric quality
of his landscape backgrounds also fascinated Albrecht Dürer, who
met Giovanni Bellini in Venice in 1506 and asserted: »He is the best
in painting«. Excellent works by Giovanni can be seen in the Accademia as well as in the Frari church and in San Zaccaria.

Canaletto (Antonio Canal, 1697 – 1768)

Canaletto was one of the last great Venetian painters. Born in Venice,   **Painter**
he began as a theatre painter, then studied in Rome and turned to
natural observations. In Venice, he initially had great success with vedute, a style of painting in which cityscapes are painted in great detail. He was also known for working from nature instead of in studios, as was the custom then. But his work became so popular that
he later had to work from drawings due to lack of time. After his

← *Peggy Guggenheim on the roof of her Palazzo Venier dei Leoni on the
Canal Grande (1950s)*

second stay in Rome in 1742, he began to paint ideal landscapes. City views with authentic detail and full of atmosphere, in which people moved about in carnivals, festivals and processions, finally became his trademark. In the years 1746–1750 and 1751–1753, Canaletto stayed in England, where most of his works are today. In Venice, paintings by Canaletto can be admired primarily in the Accademia.

Giacomo Girolamo Casanova (1725 – 1798)

Man of Letters and the World The Venetian Giacomo Casanova , Chevalier de Seingalt – to give him the noble title he invented for himself – gained a legendary reputation as a master of the arts of love and a frivolously cultivated lifestyle. On his journeys throughout Europe in the service of various masters, he met famous contemporaries from the worlds of politics and literature, such as Frederick the Great and Voltaire, and never failed to break the hearts of ladies. Imprisoned in Venice in 1755 for atheism, Casanova successfully made an adventurous escape from the leaden chambers of the Palazzo Ducale in 1756. After a restless wandering life, he finally found a position as librarian to Duke Waldstein in Dux (Bohemia) in 1785. It was here that he wrote his famous memoirs, as well as a utopian novel and historical, mathematical and literary writings. As early as the mid-19th century, the adventurer, who is regarded to this day as the personification of seduction, became the subject of literature himself.

Peggy Guggenheim (1898 – 1979)

Bohemian and collector »I have always done what I want and never cared what others thought. Women's lib? I was a free woman long before the name existed.« Peggy Guggenheim lived a stormy life, personally and as a collector. In the early 1920s, the »enfant terrible of the capitalist class« joined Bohemian society in Paris and married painter and author Laurence Vail, which did not, however, prevent her from entering into close relationships with numerous artists such as Marcel Duchamp, Samuel Beckett and Max Ernst. She opened her first gallery »Guggenheim Jeune« in 1938 in London with a Cocteau exhibition. A meeting with writer and art historian Herbert Read was decisive for Peggy Guggenheim. With his aid, she wanted to open a museum in London, similar to the New York Museum of Modern Art. However, this failed due to the start of the Second World War. Instead, she returned to Paris and rapidly acquired the foundation of her collection – with the motto »Buy one painting every day.« She returned to New York in 1941. The most important events of the New York years were her marriage to Max Ernst, the founding of the legendary gallery »Art of this Century« and the discovery of Jackson Pollock. When her marriage to Max Ernst collapsed, Peggy Guggenheim moved to Venice in 1947. In 1948, she exhibited paintings from her collection in one of the Biennale pavilions, a breakthrough which brought her recognition as a collector. In 1949, she purchased Palazzo Venier dei Leoni, which still houses her collection, one of the main points of interest in the venerable city.

Claudio Monteverdi (1567 – 1643)

The music of Claudio Monteverdi was influential far beyond the 17th century. He was born in Cremona, studied composition in his home city until 1590, and then acted as court musician and conductor in Mantua until 1612. From 1613 until his death he held the position of musical director of St Mark's Basilica in Venice. Initially working in the polyphonic »a capella« tradition of the 16th century, Monteverdi developed increasingly free musical forms. The high points of his work are the operas *Orfeo* (1607) – which marks the beginning of opera as a genre – *Il Ritorno d'Ulisse in Patria* (1640) and *L'Incoronazione di Poppea* (1642), which influenced European opera up to the time of Richard Wagner.

Andrea Palladio (1508 – 1580)

When Venice sweltered in summer heat, nobles, rich merchants and clerics fled to the hinterland, where they built imposing country residences. One of the most popular architects was Andrea Palladio, the outstanding Renaissance architect, whose was a model for all of Europe. The rise of the stonemason Andrea di Piero from Padua began in 1538 with support from the Vicenza humanist Giangiorgio Trissi-

Architect

no, who encouraged him to study mathematics, music and Latin literature and gave him the second name Palladio – a play on the goddess of wisdom. Trissino took him to Rome in 1545. Here, Palladio studied the ancient ruins and particularly the Roman architect Vitruvius for two years. Shortly thereafter, in Vicenza, he won a competition for the redesign of Palazzo della Ragione. His idea was to surround the structure with arcades on both floors – an idea that made him famous. Palladio derived the proportions, which were oriented to those of the human body, from Roman architecture. Palladio also had a major influence on subsequent generations of architects through his architectural textbook, which was published in 1570 and spread Palladianism to England and North America. In Venice, Palladio is represented in three churches: in the façade of San Francesco della Vigna, an early work; in San Giorgio Maggiore in mature, classical and monumental forms; and in Il Redentore, a sublime late work.

Marco Polo (c.1254 – 1324)

Discoverer Marco Polo was the greatest adventurer of Venice and the most important European traveller in Asia in the Middle Ages. His experiences changed his contemporaries' view of the world and encouraged Europeans to explore far corners of the earth. In 1271, 16-year-old Marco Polo, with by his father Niccolò and his father's brother Matteo, two Venetian merchants, began a trading journey to Asia. The journey took 24 years. It first led via Anatolia through Persia and Turkmenistan to China. They reached Peking in 1275. Marco Polo worked for the local ruler Kublai Khan, grandson and successor of the legendary Genghis Khan, from 1275 to 1292. Kublai Khan sent

Marco Polo on extensive journeys to Asiatic countries and all the way to India. He learned much, among other things the Chinese art of porcelain manufacture and the processing of silk and cotton. He saw how trade was conducted in China with »flying« money, i.e. paper money instead of coins made from precious metals. In 1292, Marco Polo received permission to return to Europe. He journeyed back through the South China Sea, past the coasts of Vietnam, Malacca, Sumatra, Ceylon and western India to Hormuz, and on via Persia, Armenia and Trabzon to Constantinople, where he boarded a ship for Venice. He dictated the report of his travels to his fellow prisoner Rustichello da Pisa while imprisoned in Genoa (September 1298 to July 1299) and soon thereafter *Il Millione* (*The Wonders of the World*) was translated into other languages, and had a great influence on geographical ideas in the 14th and 15th centuries.

Sansovino (Jacopo Tatti, 1486 – 1570)

Architect

Few builders have influenced the appearance of Venice as strongly as Sansovino, a native of Florence whom the Venetians commissioned from 1527 onwards to redesign the city in the High Renaissance style. No fewer than 15 churches and public buildings were built wholly or partially by him, including St Mark's library, the mint (Zecca), the Loggetta next to the Campanile, the church San Francesco della Vigna and the Palazzo Corner. The statues of Mars and Neptune in the courtyard of the Doge's Palace and the vestry door of San Marco as well as the tomb of Doge Venier in San Salvatore also bear witness to his great talent as a sculptor.

Giambattista Tiepolo (1696 – 1770) and Giovanni Domenico Tiepolo (1727 – 1804)

Painters

As the outstanding painter of Venetian Rococo, Giambattista Tiepolo was commissioned by the doge and noble families to paint numerous altarpieces, murals and ceiling frescoes for churches, palaces and villas of the city and in other places in northern Italy. Further commissions led him to the residence of the Prince Bishop of Würzburg and the royal court in Madrid. Bold foreshortening and strong light effects in combination with a free, transparent application of colour are the hallmarks of his work, which can be seen, among other places, in the Accademia, in Sant'Alvise, the Scuola Grande dei Carmini and Palazzo Labia. Domenico learned the art of painting from his father and was an equal partner in the most significant commissioned works until his father's death. His style is generally more anecdotal, the colouration softer, and his paintings avoid the complicated figure composition of his father's works. In old age, Domenico increasingly devoted himself to genre paintings, and painted carnival and Pulcinello scenes.

Tintoretto (Jacopo Robusti, 1518 – 1594)

Tintoretto has a place in the history of Venetian art not only as a Mannerist painter with a rich variety of ideas and as a painter of the Counter-Reformation era, but also as an artist with significant commercial abilities. The son of a silk dyer (Tintore, the derivation of his pseudonym), he accepted every offer of work and tried to drive his numerous competitors out of business by quoting the lowest prices. Born in Venice, he only left the city of his birth once – a journey to Mantua in 1580 is proven –

but was nonetheless influenced by the major artistic trends of his time. Strong contrasts between light and dark, bold foreshortening and views from below, and unusual lighting effects are characteristic for his paintings, which frequently depict dramatically composed scenes from the Old and New Testaments. In Venice, many of his altar paintings are in the Accademia collection, in the Doge's Palace, in numerous churches (Madonna dell'Orto, San Giorgio Maggiore, San Marcuola, Santa Maria della Salute) as well as in the Scuola Grande di Rocco with fabulous wall and ceiling paintings.

Titian (Tiziano Vecellio, 1488/90 – 1576)

Painter From the Cadore valley in the Dolomites, Titian came to Venice in the early 16th century and received decisive impulses for his painting from Giovanni Bellini. After the great success of his commissioned works between 1510 and 1526, including the Assunta altarpiece and the Pesaro Madonna in Venice's Frari church, Titian rapidly rose to be a favourite painter at the courts of European princes. The d'Este, Gonzaga and Farnese showered commissions on him. François I of France held him in high esteem, and Charles V made Titian his court painter in 1533. In his late period, Titian worked almost exclusively for Philip II. Titian's extensive works, which could not have been carried out without a large atelier of assistants, include altar paintings, mythological works, nudes and allegories as well as a considerable number of portraits. Stylistically, Titian stands at the threshold from High Renaissance to Mannerism. Colour harmonies as well as strong contrasts between light and dark, dynamic diagonal compositions, atmospheric landscapes and the ability to satisfy the need of the ruling class for official representation are the essence of Titian's fascinating works. His technique and breadth of composition set an example for the following centuries.

Veronese (Paolo Caliari, 1528 – 1588)

Painter Paolo Caliari, also called Veronese, and born in Verona, was the brilliant chronicler of Venetian joie de vivre. Together with Tintoretto and Titian, he is regarded as the most important painter of late Renaissance Venice. From 1553, he worked in the city, where his sensual themes even gave him trouble with the Inquisition. He was able to handle the large number of orders only with the aid of a large atelier and assistants. His large-format compositions with numerous figures, among them magnificent celebrations and banquets, are conspicuous for their richness of colour and the lively depiction of persons. In Venice, works by Veronese are to be found in the church San Sebastiano (ceiling and wall paintings), in the Gallerie dell'Accademia (*Banquet in the House of Levi*) and in the Doge's Palace (ceiling and wall paintings; here is the climax of his late work, *The Triumph of Venezia*).

Antonio Vivaldi
(1678 – 1741)

The exceptionally gifted violinist Antonio Vivaldi was the most important Venetian composer, and his development of the solo concerto form made a major contribution to European music. In 1703, Vivaldi was ordained to the priesthood, and in the same year he became the maestro di violino at the Venetian girls' conservatory Ospedale della Pietà, where, with few interruptions, he also worked until 1740 as a conductor and house composer. Vivaldi's style influenced many composers, including Johann Sebastian Bach, who adapted several of Vivaldi's violin works for the organ. Aside from about 500 concerts, which excel through rich nuances of instrumentation, emotional melodies and lively rhythms, Vivaldi also composed more than 90 sonatas, 46 operas – of which 21 have survived – and three oratorios.

Practicalities

HOW DO YOU SAY »I NEED A ROOM« IN ITALIAN? WHICH FERRY GOES TO THE LAGOON? FIND OUT HERE – IDEALLY BEFORE YOUR TRIP!

Accommodation

Hotels Venice has a **wide range of hotels** in all categories from **five-star luxury** to **basic accommodation** with one star. The prices are above average for Italy and vary with the season. They are highest in August. The following hotels are divided into three categories. The prices refer to the least expensive double room.

Booking Since Venice has many visitors throughout the year, especially during the main season, for the carnival and for major events, it is recommended to make reservations in advance. Individual travellers can obtain help from the Associazione Veneziana Albergatori (AVA), Mo to Sat 9am–7pm, tel. 014 15 22 80 04, 04 15 23 80 32, fax 04 15 23 49 41, ava.ve@flashnet.it.

For further addresses, see www.venicehotels.com. Last-minute bookings can be made at tel. 800-84 30 06 (within Italy) or 00 39 / 04 15 22 22 64 (from abroad). AVA offices provide help **locally** when looking for a hotel, for example at the car park on Piazzale Roma (Garage Autorimessa and Garage S. Marco) at Tronchetto, in the railway terminal S. Lucia and at Marco Polo Airport.

> ! **Baedeker TIP**
>
> **Discounts**
>
> It can pay to book a hotel by internet. Many hotels offer special internet rates, often for last-minute bookings, at up to 35% below the normal room tariff. The Hotel Reservation Service, www.hrs.com is a reliable portal with countless special offers – but check the hotel website too, to be sure you get the best deal.

▶ RECOMMENDED HOTELS (**1, 2** see MAP p.98/99)

▶ **Price categories**
Luxury: double room more than €300
Mid-range: double room €150–250
Budget: double room up to €150

LUXURY: OVER €300

▶ ① **Cipriani**
Giudecca 10
Tel. 04 15 20 77 44
Fax 04 15 20 39 30; 98 rooms
www.hotelcipriani.it
One of the top addresses in Venice with gardens, a yacht harbour and private boat service.

▶ ② **Danieli**
Riva degli Schiavoni 4196, Castello
Tel. 04 15 22 64 80
Fax 04 15 20 02 08; 233 rooms

www.danieli.hotelinvenice.com
One of the most famous hotels in
the world in the 14th-century
palazzo of Doge Enrico Dandolo;
exquisite furnishings and perfect
service right on Piazza San Marco.
Diners in the much-lauded panorama restaurant have an unforgettable view across the lagoon to
San Giorgio Maggiore and the
Lido.

► ③ **Bauer – Il Palazzo e
Bauer Hotel**
Campo San Moisè 1465,
San Marco
Tel. 04 15 20 70 22
Fax 04 15 20 75 57; 219 rooms
info@bauervenezia.it
Luxury accommodation on the
Grand Canal a few steps from
Piazza San Marco, panorama res-
taurant.

► ④ **The Westin Europa & Regina**
Calle Larga XXII Marzo 2159,
San Marco, tel. 04 15 20 04 77
Fax 04 15 23 15 33; 199 rooms
www.westin.com
One of the most traditional city
hotels; favoured accommodation

for celebrities; the ultimate romantic experience is candlelight
dinner in the elegant Tiepolo
restaurant with a view of gondolas
gliding past the backdrop of Santa
Maria della Salute.

► **Excelsior**
Lungomare Marconi 41, Lido
Tel. 04 15 26 02 01
Fax 04 15 26 72 76; 222 rooms
Luxury oasis in neo-Moorish style
on the south side of the Lido; boat
transfer from the Lido to Piazza
San Marco.

► ⑤ **Gritti Palace**
Campo Santa Maria del Giglio,
San Marco 2467
Tel. 04 17 94 611
Fax 04 15 20 09 42; 96 rooms
The palace was built in the early
16th century for Doge Andrea
Gritti. In 1585, it was given to
Pope Sixtus V. Writers like Hem-
ingway described this legendary
hotel with the exclusive restaurant
Club del Doge.

► **San Clemente Palace**
Island of San Clemente
Tel. 04 12 41 34 84
Fax 04 12 45 800; 205 rooms
sanclemente@veniceby.com
Recently opened luxury hotel on a
private island, a few minutes by
boat from Piazza San Marco.

► **Des Bains**
Lungomare Marconi 17, Lido
Tel. 04 15 26 59 21
Fax 04 15 26 01 13; 195 rooms
High-class accommodation in the
belle époque style, made famous
by Thomas Mann's novella *Death
in Venice*, which Visconti filmed
here magnificently; the Liberty
restaurant has an exquisite menu;
boat transfer to Piazza San Marco.

MID-RANGE: €150-250

► ⑥ **Al Ponte Antico**
Calle dell'Aseo 5768, Cannaregio
Tel. 04 12 41 19 44
Fax 04 12 41 18 28; 6 rooms
www.alponteantico.com
Lovingly converted palazzo on the
Grand Canal with a view of the
Rialto bridge.

► ⑦ **Cavalletto & Doge Orseolo**
Calle Cavalletto, San Marco 1107
Tel. 04 15 20 09 55
Fax 04 15 23 81 84; 82 rooms
cavaletto@tin.it
Top address in the romantic loca-
tion of a gondola harbour behind
the Procuratie Vecchie.

► ⑧ **Luna Baglioni**
Calle Larga dell'Ascensione, San
Marco 1243
Tel. 04 15 28 98 40
Fax 04 15 28 71 60; 123 rooms
Oldest hotel in Venice, magnifi-
cent furnishings; perfect service.

► ⑨ **Londra Palace**
Riva degli Schiavoni, Castello 4171
Tel. 04 15 20 05 33
Fax 04 15 22 50 32; 71 rooms
Elegant four-star city hotel with a
British atmosphere; Tchaikovsky
composed his fourth symphony
here; view across the shore prom-
enade to the lagoon.

► ⑩ **Saturnia & International**
Calle Larga XXII Marzo,
San Marco 2398
Tel. 04 15 20 83 77
Fax 04 15 20 71 31; 109 rooms
www.hotelsaturnia.it
14th-century palace of a Venetian
admiral; beautiful inner courtyard
and roof terrace.

► ⑪ **Concordia**
Calle Larga, San Marco 367

Tel. 041 52 06 85 66
Fax 04 15 20 67 75; 56 rooms
venezia@hotelconcordia.it
Cosy comfortable hotel next to St
Mark's Basilica.

► **Hotel Villa Mabapa**
Riviera S. Nicolò 16,
Malamoco (Lido)
Tel. 04 15 26 05 90
Fax 04 15 26 94 41; 73 rooms
www.villamabapa.com
This villa combines four-star
comfort with plenty of 1930s
charm; 300m/330yd from the
beach and ten minutes by boat
from Piazza San Marco.

BUDGET: up to €150

► ⑫ **Accademia**
Fondamenta Bollani 1058
Dorsoduro

Tel. 04 15 21 01 88
Fax 04 15 23 91 52; 36 rooms
info@pensione.accademia.it
Popular accommodation with a
view of the canal or a romantic
garden.

▶ ⑬ **Bisanzio**
Calle della Pietà, Castello 3651
Tel. 04 15 20 31 00
Fax 04 15 20 41 14; 41 rooms
email@bisanzio.com
Elegant hotel in a 16th-century
building; only 300m/330yd from
Piazza San Marco.

▶ ⑭ **Flora**
Calle Larga XXII Marzo,
San Marco 2283a
Tel. 04 15 20 58 44
Fax 04 15 22 82 17; 43 rooms
info@hotelflora.it
Romantic hotel, wonderful
gardens.

▶ ⑮ **Giorgione**
Campo Santi Apostoli 4587
Cannaregio; tel. 04 15 22 58 10
Fax 04 15 23 90 92; 76 rooms
www.hotelgiorgione.com
Modern, comfortable hotel in a
15th-century palace.

▶ ⑯ **Metropole**
Riva degli Schiavoni, Castello 4149
Tel. 04 15 20 50 44
Fax 04 15 22 36 79; 64 rooms
www.hotelmetropole.com
Tip for romantics; stylish sur-
roundings in a former grain store.

▶ ⑰ **Ala**
Campo Santa Maria del Giglio,
San Marco 2494, tel.
04 15 20 83 33, fax 04 15 20 63 90;
78 rooms; info@hotelala.it
Pleasant middle-class hotel near
Piazza San Marco.

▶ ⑱ **Ateneo**
San Fantin, San Marco 1876
Tel. 04 15 20 07 77
Fax 04 15 22 85 50; 20 rooms
ateneo@ateneo.it
Small, pretty hotel with a family
atmosphere.

▶ ⑲ **Centauro**
Campo Manin, San Marco 4297
Tel. 04 15 22 58 32
Fax 04 15 23 91 51; 30 rooms
centauro@hotelcentauro.com
Rooms in the Venetian style, near
Piazza San Marco.

▶ ⑳ **Florida**
Calle Priuli 106/A
Cannaregio, tel. 041 71 52 53
Fax 041 71 80 88; 25 rooms
info@hotel-florida.com
Pleasant house, quiet situation
near the railway terminal.

▶ ㉑ **Pausania**
Fondamenta Gherardini,
Dorsoduro 2824
Tel. 041 52 22 08 36, 27 rooms
info@hotelpausania.it
Lovingly restored 14th-century
palace; begin the day restfully on
the breakfast veranda in the
garden.

▶ ㉒ **La Residenza**
Campo Bandiera e Moro, Castello
3608, tel. 04 11 28 53 15
Fax 04 15 23 88 59; 14 rooms
info@venicelaresidenza.com
Stylishly furnished patrician
palace.

▶ ㉓ **Rialto**
San Marco 5149
Tel. 04 15 20 91 66
Fax 04 15 23 89 58; 63 rooms
info@rialtohotel.com
Pleasant mid-category hotel next
to the Rialto bridge.

► ㉔ **Seguso**
Zattere 779, Dorsoduro
Tel. 04 15 28 68 58
Fax 04 15 22 23 40; 28 rooms
pensioneseguso@tiscali.it
Setting of Patricia Highsmith's
Those Who Walk Away, view of
the church of the Saviour, of La
Giudecca.

► ㉕ **Serenissima**
Calle Goldoni 4486, San Marco
Tel. 04 15 20 00 11
Fax 04 15 22 32 92; 37 Z.
www.hotelserenissima.it
The privately managed hotel (no
restaurant) is ideally located between the Rialto bridge and Piazza
San Marco. It has been in the
ownership of the Del Borgo family
for over 40 years. Modern art
hangs on the walls: the father of
the present-day owner was a pas-
sionate collector.

► ㉖ **Locanda Silva**
Fondamenta del Remedio 4423,
Castello
Tel. 04 15 23 78 92
Fax 04 15 28 68 17; 24 rooms
info@locandasilva.it
Between St Mark's Basilica and
Campo S. Maria Formosa on a
small canal; no elevator, spotless
rooms, friendly staff.

► ㉗ **Wildner**
Riva degli Schiavoni 4161, Castello
Tel. 04 15 22 74 63
Fax 04 15 26 56 15; 23 rooms
wildner@veneziahotels.com
Good price, central location.

**BEACH RESORTS OUTSIDE
VENICE**

► **Sole**
Sottomarina, Viale Mediterraneo 9
Tel. 041 49 15 05
Fax 04 14 96 67; 62 rooms
www.hotel-sole.com (budget)
Hotel directly behind the beach of
Chioggia seaside resort. Beautiful
rooms, ample breakfast buffet,
own garage.

► **Holiday park Pra' delle Torri**
Viale Altanea 201, Caorle
Tel. 080 01 81 39 14
Fax 04 21 29 94 45
www.pradelletorri.it (budget)
A paradise for families – every-
thing from a golf course to a car
racetrack and giant water slides.

► **Union Lido Park Hotel
Ca' di Valle s/n**
Cavallino
Tel. 04 12 57 51 11 or 12
Fax 04 15 37 03 55
www.unionlido.com (budget)
Perfect hotel for a high-class
family vacation, near the beach in
extensive holiday village.

► **Igea**
Via Ospedale 87, Padua
Tel. 04 98 75 05 77
Fax 049 66 08 65
www.hoteligea.it (budget)
Directly at the Ospedale Civile and
easy to find; the centre is within
walking distance.

Arrival · Before the Journey

Getting There

Travel by car is not recommended, since Venice has no room for cars **By car**
(except for the Lido). For those who do take their car to Italy (the
distance from London to Venice is
1,515km/940mi), the city is easily
accessible via the Italian autostrada
system: from the north from
Switzerland through the St Bernard
tunnel or from Austria across the
Brenner pass, from the west on the
European E70 route through the
Mont Blanc tunnel at Chamonix
and then eastwards via Turin, Milan and Verona. Use of most stretches of autostrada in Italy is subject to tolls (information is available from automobile clubs, at
border crossings and gas stations;
the **autostrada tolls** are paid in
cash, by credit card or with the
Viacard, which is available from automobile clubs, at main toll
stations and service stations).

! **Baedeker TIP**

Waiting times

The railway terminal buffet of Stazione Ferrovia
Santa Lucia in Venice is a good place to while
away waiting times. In Italy, it is customary to
pay for the drinks at the cash desk and then take
the scontrino (receipt) to the bar. Freshly
squeezed fruit juices and small snacks are
available, among other things. The pizza slices
are always fresh and highly recommended.
Open: daily 6am-9.55pm.

Parking fees are high (approx. €20). For safety reasons, it is recom- **Parking**
mended to leave the car in supervised parking lots. Illegally parked
vehicles are towed away. The nearly 40km/25mi-long »Freedom
Bridge«, Ponte della Libertà, leads straight into Venice. On the island
of Tronchetto, right after the railway station, or around the neighbouring Piazzale Roma, there are several car parks. They are open 24
hours, fairly expensive and often full. Next to them, there are docks
for water taxis as well as ferries (vaporetti), which provide a connection to the centre.

It is cheaper to park on the mainland near the Ponte della Libertà in
the car parks of San Giuliano and Fusina, or – for longer stays – in
Treporti, Punta Sabbioni or Mestre (here directly at the railway terminal) and enter the city by railway, bus or boat.

Various operators offer international bus or coach travel to Venice. **By bus or coach**
The Euroline buses which connect many European cities have no di-
rect link from London to Venice; with a change in Paris the journey
time to Venice is about 28 hours. Arrival by bus may be convenient
for travellers who are moving on to Rome from other parts of conti-
nental Europe. Even then, the journey can take some time: for example, the trip from Munich takes about 14 hours, changing in Milan.

By rail The train journey from London to Venice via Paris takes about 17 hours. There are also good direct connections to Venice from Germany, Austria and Switzerland (travel time from Munich, Zurich and Vienna approx. 8 hours). The railway terminal Stazione Santa Lucia lies at the north end of the Grand Canal, where it is possible to switch to a vaporetto or water taxi (► Transport). Information is available from the railway station and travel agencies.

Left luggage ► Temporary storage for luggage upon arrival or until departure: at platform 14, there are **lockers** (deposito bagagli; daily 4.30am to 0.30am). Luggage transport to or from hotels is handled, at set prices, by the **luggage carrier service**. It has various locations throughout the city (Cooperativa Trasbagli; tel. 04 15 20 30 70).

By air Venice's international **Marco Polo Airport** is 13km/8mi north-east in Tessera. Travel between the airport and the inner city (Piazza San Marco) is possible by **water taxi** (motoscafi) and **ferry** (vaporetti, Alilaguna line). The ferries depart hourly. Including the airport shuttle from the arrivals terminal to the quay (every 15 minutes, 5 minutes travel time), the total time to Piazza San Marco is 60 to 75 minutes. **Buses**, including the blue **airport buses** (aerobus), provide a connection from the airport to Piazzale Roma (opposite the railway terminal; tickets in the tabacchi store at the airport terminal; travel time approx. 20 min.).
Some airlines, such as Ryanair, use the small airport at Treviso, from where a bus service covers the 30km/19mi distance to Venice.

By ship Those who come on their own boat can head for the harbours of S. Elena or S. Giorgio. Venice, which is accessible by ship from all major Adriatic ports, is also a popular stop for cruises; the preferred moorings are Zattere and Riva degli Schiavoni.

Immigration and Customs Regulations

Personal documents Even as an EU citizen, do not travel to Italy without an identity card or passport. Children under the age of 16 years must have a children's identity card or be entered in their parents' passport.

Loss of documents If your travel documents are stolen or lost, the consulate of your country will help (►Information, p.106). However, the first place to go is the police, as nothing will proceed without a copy of the theft report. It is much easier to obtain replacement documents if you can show copies or access them from an electronic mailbox.

Vehicle papers What to bring: driving licence, the motor vehicle registration certificate and the International Green Insurance Card. Motor vehicles must bear the oval nationality identification sign unless they have a Euro licence plate. As usual, it is a good idea to photocopy all documents and keep them seperate from the originals.

Since 1 October 2004, persons wishing to bring pets (dogs, cats) to Italy require an EU pet ID issued by a veterinarian (with a rabies certification). Bring a muzzle and leash.

Pets

The European Union member states (including Italy) form a common economic area, within which the movement of goods for private purposes is largely duty-free. There are merely certain maximum quantities which apply (for example 800 cigarettes, 10 litres of spirits and 90 litres of wine per person). During random inspections customs officers must be convinced that the goods are actually intended for private use.

Customs regulations for EU citizens

For travellers from outside the EU, the following duty-free quantities apply: 200 cigarettes or 100 cigarillos or 50 cigars or 250g of tobacco; also 2 litres of wine and 2 litres of sparkling wine or 1 litre of spirits with an alcohol content of more than 22% vol.; 500g of coffee or 200g of coffee extracts, 100g of tea or 40g of tea extract, 50ml of perfume or 0.25 litres of eau de toilette. Gifts up to a value of €175 are also duty-free.

Customs regulations for non-EU citizens

Citizens of EU countries are entitled to treatment in Italy under the local regulations in case of illness on production of their **European health insurance card**. Even with this card, in most cases some of the costs for medical care and prescribed medication must be paid by the patient. Upon presentation of receipts the health insurance at home covers the costs – but not for all treatments. Citizens of non-EU countries must pay for medical treatment and medicine themselves and should take out private health insurance.

Health insurance

Since some of the costs for medical treatment and medication typically have to be covered by the patient, and the costs for return transportation may not be covered by the normal health insurance, additional travel insurance is recommended.

Private travel insurance

 USEFUL ADDRESSES

PARKING

► **Isola del Tronchetto**
Tel. 04 15 20 75 55
www.veniceparking.it

► **Piazzale Roma**
San Marco: tel. 04 15 23 22 13
Toderini: tel. 04 15 20 79 79
Communale: tel. 04 12 72 73 01
Sant'Andrea: tel. 04 12 72 73 04

www.asmvenezia.it and
www.urbislimen.it

► **Mestre**
Fusina: tel. 04 15 47 01 60
S. Giuliano: tel. 04 15 32 26 32
www.asmvenezia.it and
www.terminalfusina.it

RAILWAY TRAVEL

► In London
Rail Europe Travel Centre
178 Piccadilly
London W1V 0BA
Tel. 0870 8 37 13 71
www.raileurope.co.uk

► In Italy
Trenitalia, tel. 848 88 80 88
(toll-free)
www.fs-on-line.com
Stazione Ferroviaria
Santa Lucia di Venezia
Tel. 04 17 11 52 88

BY BUS

► Eurolines
Bookings online and in UK
through National Express
Tel. 087 05 80 80 80
www.eurolines.com and
www.nationalexpress.com

AIRPORTS

► Aeroporto Marco Polo
Information: tel. 04 12 60 92 40
and 04 12 60 92 50 (taped message,
arrivals and departures)
Tel. 04 12 60 92 60 (general information, Italian and English);
www.veniceairport.it

► San Giuseppe Airport, Treviso
Information:
Tel. 04 22 31 51 11
www.actt.it

► Aero Club G. Ancillotto
San Nicolò, Lido di Venezia; tel.
04 15 26 08 08 (small planes only)
Motor boat transfer from San
Nicolò to Riva degli Schiavoni

AIRLINES IN ITALY

► Air Canada
Tel. 06 650 11 462
www.aircanada.com

► Alitalia
Marco Polo Airport
Tel. 848 86 56 41
www.alitalia.it

► American Airlines
Tel. 06 660 53 169
www.aa.com

► British Airways
Tel. 199 71 22 66
www.britishairways.com

► Delta Air Lines
Tel. 800 47 79 99
www.delta.com

► easyjet
Tel. 848 88 77 66
www.easyjet.com

► Qantas
Tel. 06 524 82 725
www.qantas.com

► Ryanair
Tel. 899 67 89 10

Beaches

The nearest beach for swimming is on the ►Lido; however, the beaches here belong to hotels or commercial operators. For a fee, a

changing room (capanne), parasol and deck chair can be rented. There are public beaches at Alberoni or near the airport San Nicolò (on the south-west or north-east end of the Lido).

Beach life is most enjoyable in Lido di Jesolo (►Littorale del Cavallino) or in Sottomarina (►Chioggia). Information about water temperatures ► When To Go, p.137.

Children in Venice

With its crooked alleys, innumerable bridges, old palaces and the lagoon, Venice has many attractions for young visitors. And instead of using cars, locals and visitors alike travel on boats on the waterways. The trick is to find the right balance between culture and entertain-

For a »break from art«: sun, sand and sea

ment. Here are a few suggestions: aside from trips by vaporetto, traghetto or gondola, the highlights include counting stone lions, taking a boat trip to the islands of Burano and Murano to watch glass blowers at their work, or swimming on the Lido, Lido di Jesolo or Litorale del Cavallino. However, the 400 bridges are a major obstacle to parents with children in prams, and the canals without railings are a safety risk. There are numerous **discounts** for children in public transport (up to four years of age) and in museums. For teenagers and young adults, there is the **Rolling Venice** pass (▶Prices and Discounts p.121).

Electricity

The power network carries 220-volt alternating current. For three-pin plugs, an adapter (riduzione) is required, as the standard European 2-pin plugs are used in Italy.

Emergency

The emergency call numbers are on the first page of the telephone books (elenco telefonico) under the key word »Avantielenco«.

● EMERGENCY CALL NUMBERS

▶ **General emergency calls**
Tel. 113 (soccorso publico)

▶ **Police**
Tel. 112 (carabinieri)

▶ **Breakdown help**
Tel. 116 (soccorso stradale, ACI)

▶ **Fire department**
Tel. 115 (vigili fuoco)

▶ **Accident, ambulance**
Tel. 118 (emergenza sanitaria)

▶ **City hospital**
City hospital SS. Giovanni e Paolo
Tel. 04 15 29 45 16
and 04 15 29 45 17

▶ **Lost and found**
▶Information, p.106

Entertainment

Due to the high residential density and narrow alleys in which every sound echoes, as well as the increasingly elderly, noise-sensitive population, – not many younger people can afford the high rents or expensive real estate – Venice is not a destination for party people. Clubbers are better advised to go to the mainland (beach resorts on the Adriatic, Treviso). English-style pubs are in fashion. Unlike night cafes, lounges and in-bars, they are often overfilled. Most night-spots close no later than 1am, but there are some exceptions in the trendier quarter of Dorsoduro. A popular open-air meeting place in summer is the Campo Santa Margherita.

Venice – not a mecca for party people

CASINO

October to March:
Palazzo Vendramin-Calergi, Calle Larga Vendramin, Cannaregio 2040, tel. 041 72 00 44
(daily 4pm–4am)

April to September:
Palazzo del Casino on the Lido Lungomare G. Marconi 4
Tel. 04 15 29 71 11
(daily 4pm–3am)

SOME BARS AND NIGHT-CLUBS

► **Acropolis**
Lungomare Marconi 22, Lido Tel. 04 15 26 04 66 – popular place for disco fans.

► **Antico Martini e Martini Scala**
San Marco, Campo San Fantin 1983, tel. 04 15 22 41 21 – piano bar; snacks available until 3.30am.

► **Bacaro Jazz**
San Marco, Salizzada del Fontego dei Tedeschi 5546, tel. 041 28 52 49 – both the jazz music and the drinks are very popular – and expensive. Fortunately the bartenders know their business ...

► **Club Piccolo Mondo**
Dorsoduro, Calle Contarini Corfù 1056a, tel. 04 15 20 03 71 – stylish club with current hits.

► **Devil's Forest**
Rialto, Campo San Bartolomeo, tel. 04 15 23 66 51 – pub with live music.

► **Harry's Bar**
San Marco, Calle Vallaressa 1323, tel. 04 15 28 57 77 – restaurant

A legend: Harry's Bar

opened by Giuseppe Cipriani and Harry Pickering in 1931 and immortalized by the steadfast drinker Ernest Hemingway in his novel *Across the River and into the Trees*; the cocktail bar is open until 2am, and the gourmet restaurant on the first floor of the building attracts a famous clientele – so cocktails and snacks come at a price.

! *Baedeker* TIP

Where to meet Venetians

If you want to meet the locals, go to Margaret Duchamp, Dorsoduro, Campo Santa Margherita 3104, tel. 04 15 28 62 55. The club is popular amongst a mixed younger age-group, about 25 years old, of students, yuppies and others who are bent on partying until 2am at the earliest for a reasonable price in a relaxed and not exclusive atmosphere.

▶ **Taverna La Fenice**
San Marco 1938, tel. 04 15 22 38 56 – artists' favourite next to the Teatro La Fenice, with stylish dining.

▶ **The Fiddler's Elbow**
Cannaregio, Strada Nova 3847, tel. 04 15 23 99 30 – Irish music, rock or pop as an accompaniment to the Guinness.

▶ **Madigan's Pub**
Dorsoduro, Rio Terra Canal 3053/A, tel. 04 15 20 59 76 – always packed long after midnight, a hint of Irish character.

▶ **Paradiso Perduto**
Cannaregio, Fondamenta della Misericordia 2539, tel. 041 72 05 81 – student atmosphere, live music Sunday evenings, jazz Monday evenings.

Etiquette and Customs

What is acceptable in Italy and what isn't?

Bella figura, a beautiful appearance, is a deep-seated need for most Italians. Everyone who goes out in public likes to dress up, even for a trip to the post office or market, following Coco Chanel's motto: always be dressed to meet the love of your life. When there is a choice, money is always spent on fashion (and good food) rather than furniture or a coat of paint for the façade. Tourists who stroll into cathedrals with flip-flops on their feet, wear shorts to visit the art gallery, sit in a restaurant in sandals or even dare to stroll through the old city with a naked chest – something not even the tifosi, soccer fans from Juventus Turin, Lazio Roma or Sampdoria Genoa, would consider – are looked down upon with amusement or a complete lack of comprehension.

Bella figura can also be admired in the baristi, who truly play the leading role in the hundreds of thousands of bars up and down the country: to prepare steaming espresso they usually wear smart waiter's jackets and snappy little caps; they are the sovereign rulers of the public standing before them, who hand out foamed cappuccini, freshly-baked cornetti and of course glasses of fresh water with matchless elegance. Compared to this performance, a sit-down breakfast in other countries is boring. Break out of the hotel routine for a change, and treat yourself to a colazione all'italiana. And leave a few coins as a tip for the boys behind the counter – service professions are often low-paid.

Bella figura also makes life easier for photographers. Most Italians are happy to get in front of a lens – this reveals their love of theatre. Take the opportunity for a chat which can quickly develop into a spontaneous casting session. Often the next-door neighbour will want to join in, the children wave over their entire class for the photo session and the padrone insists that the entire brigade of waiters gets into the picture. A photo is always a public event, an expression of vitality, of being chosen.

Italians are also spontaneous behind the wheel. Although the government of Silvio Berlusconi decided to introduce a points system for traffic offences in 2004, southern Italians in particular constantly prove their mastery of the art of living, airily attempting to overtake on the wrong side or parking their Fiats three deep – how nice it is when the chaos then unsnarls and as many people as possible join in with all the gestures at their command. Then the street becomes a

Torcello, with the alps in the background

Everyday Venetian life outside the tourist areas, e.g. in Castello, Santa Anna

living piazza, the machine-like routine of day-to-day life is interrupted. The purpose of all this is to communicate, and only rarely to be proved right, a fact proven by the Italians' courtesy towards pedestrians, which is a pleasing contrast to other Mediterranean countries.

To enjoy life in Italy, approach individual Italians and let them know through a smile or a gesture just how much you appreciate and enjoy dealing with such a competent and winning counterpart. Do not hesitate to ask for the waiter's first name, and call out a »bravo«, »grande« or »bello« too many rather than one too few. And if things are not working out, bring the ancient Italian art of »arriangiarsi« into play. With Venetians, Romans and Milanese, a sympathetic compliment is usually more effective than a threatening attitude, which – you guessed it – are detrimental to the bella figura. This is a nation which prefers to be adored than to be told what to do.

Festivals, Holidays and Events

Holidays

1 January: New Year's Day (Capo d'anno)
6 January: Epiphany (Epifania)
Easter Monday (Pasqua)
25 April: Liberation Day 1945 (and the day of San Marco)
1 May: Labour Day (Festa del primo maggio)

15 August: Ascension of the Virgin (Ferragosta; family holiday, the climax of Italian summer holidays)
1 November: All Hallows (Ognissanti)
8 December: Immaculate Conception (Immaculata Concezione)
25/26 December: Christmas (Natale)

Information about events, opening times etc. is provided by the dailies *Il Gazzettino* and *La Nuova Venezia* as well as the Italian-English brochures *LEO Bussola, Venezia News, Un Ospite di Venezia* (www. unospitedivenezia.it), *Venezia da Vivere* (www.veneziadavivere. it) and *Meeting Venice* (www.meetingvenice.it), which are found at all APT offices (▶Information) and in hotels.

Event listings

 ## CALENDAR OF FESTIVALS

JANUARY

Early in the morning of 1 January, people gather on the beach of the Lido – brave souls even take their first swim of the year.

▶ **Regate delle Befane**
»Witches' Regatta« on the Grand Canal on 6 January, the day of Epiphany (Epifania).

FEBRUARY

▶ **Carnevale di Venezia**
Carnival begins 14 days before Ash Wednesday and lasts until Shrove Tuesday. The burning of Pantalone on a pyre symbolizes the end of carnival. Then revellers go to Riva degli Schiavoni to the church of Santa Maria della Pietà, where the Ash Wednesday concert (Concerto delle Ceneri) takes place at midnight – the only concert where it is allowed to wear masks.

MARCH

▶ **Su e Zo per i Ponti**
Marathon for all age groups across the city on a Sunday in mid-March.

 Memorable festivals

- Carnival in Venice: the city holds the most impressive and famous carnival in Italy
- Festa di San Marco: festival in honour of the city patron with a traditional gondola regatta on the Grand Canal
- Regata storica: historic gondola regatta in remembrance of a great maritime past

▶ **Easter: Benedizione del Fuoco**
The »blessing of the flame« on the late afternoon of Maundy Thursday is a highlight of Holy Week. In the complete darkness of St Mark's Basilica, the holy flame is first lit in the atrium, then the procession walks through the basilica and lights all candles until the whole church is bathed in light.

APRIL

▶ **Festa di San Marco**
Feast of the city patron on 25 April. At the time of the republic, this was a state ceremony with solemn processions. Today, high mass is celebrated in St Mark's Basilica. In the afternoon, the gondoliers hold their Regatta dei

*Old and young fools
at the carnival in Venice*

MADCAP DAYS

January and February are not usually the most popular months in which to travel, not even for Italy. But Venice makes an exception. Because: The first few weeks of the year are also the most crazy ones – carnival!

It is Sunday morning, still ten days before the start of Lent. A dense crowd on St Mark's Plaza stares up to the Campanile, to the large dove that, according to ancient tradition, is pulled up from its belfry to the upper arcades of the doge's palace. Right on the dot at 12 noon, it begins: Colourful balloons rise into the sky and gaudy confetti rains down on the crowd – the Venice carnival is underway once again.

There are concerts and costume competitions on stages around the city; the international art scene shines in the theatres and palaces; and on the floating raft in front of the Piazzetta, the Venetian past is reawakened to life. The celebrations continue in the alleys and on the canals of the city on the lagoon until far into the night – until Shrove Tuesday, when a gigantic fireworks display ends the foolishness for another year.

Feasting Before the Fast

The first documented record of the Venetian carnival comes from the year 1094. The original heathen purpose of the ceremony was to celebrate the arrival of spring after a long winter. The term carnival from the Latin carne vale (= flesh fare well), which arose along with Christianity, initially referred to the last meal before Lent but soon represented all carnival celebrations before Ash Wednesday, since all meat, butter and eggs had to be used up before the fast. Oxen were butchered, sword fights were carried out and masterful acrobatic achievements were performed on St Mark's Plaza in the presence of the doge, high dignitaries and foreign state guests; and of course there was ample gambling which was only permitted during the carnival period, although this lasted almost six months due to special laws.

The processions on the water with beautifully decorated gondolas were especially elaborate. When the last doge stepped down in 1797 and the French entered Venice, Napoleon banned the infamous Carnevale.

a black hood made from velvet or silk that left the face exposed, was also permitted for special festivities. The Bautta was worn with the tricorn (tricorno) and a long black coat (tabarro). The actual mask was white

»This beautiful celebration harbours the most irrepressible joy along with the sweetest melancholia«

Rebirth

Nearly two centuries passed before resourceful tourism managers rediscovered the legendary masked celebration and revived it in 1979. Venice quickly became a bastion of the carnival. The nearly extinct trades of costume creator and mask-maker experienced a real Renaissance. The masks made from paper-mâché, ceramics, or leather have long since become a symbol of the city.

Traditional Costumes

Wearing masks probably originated mainly from contact with the orient and Muslim attire. Strictly speaking, masks were only permitted during the carnival; however, the elegant Bautta,

or black and hid the top half of the face; for those who wanted to remain completely incognito, a lace handkerchief on the lower edge of the mask also covered the mouth and chin. The domino, a white cloak similar to a monk's cowl that completely hid its wearer from view, was of Spanish origin. The moretta, a small oval velvet mask, was only worn by women. The mattacini, colourful fool's costumes with large feather hats, were very popular. The medico della peste was created as a result of the devastating plague epidemics repeatedly visited upon Venice. With this costume, the coarse plaid and a slouch hat drawn low over the face left only the eyes exposed; the mask with the

characteristic over length hooked nose was supposed to filter the mephitic air, and the long staff allowed patients to be examined from a safe distance.

Arleccino and Co.

The carnival scene was enriched by the figures of the Commedia dell'Arte, the most famous among them being the Arlecchino in a colourful costume who is known for his antics. Arlecchino and the imaginative servant Brighella perform as the two Zanni. The female counterpart is Colombina, an adroit maid, while Pulcinella from the back country of Naples embodies the braggadocio. The symbol of the clever Venetian businessman is the Pantalone with a goatee, clad in red knee-breeches, red doublet and a black coat, the beloved moneybag on his belt.

The Dottore, a jurist with a hammer nose, is regarded as the parody of intellectual vanity. A special role plays the Capitano with his colourful striped uniform, sword, and wide-brimmed feather hat as a symbol of the revolution against foreign rule and the epitome of the carnival freedom to speak one's mind. Although a lot Venetians flee to the mainland to get away from the turbulence of the carnival, many continue to participate in the lively activities; others get together for private balls while the official masked spectacle takes place on and around St Mark's Plaza as a media event. Every carnival has a different motto, and it remains a fixed part of the Venetian calendar in spite of any criticism. The best thing to do is to just go along with it and indulge in the ancient longing to slip into the role of another.

A climax of the Festa del Redentore: the fireworks

Traghetti on the Grand Canal. According to an ancient tradition, Venetians give their sweetheart a rosebud, the so-called bocolo.

MAY

▶ **Sposalizio col mare**
In accordance with tradition, the symbolic marriage of the Serenissima to the sea is celebrated on the Sunday after the Ascension of Christ. Until the end of the republic in 1797, the doge had himself rowed out from the Lido, where he tossed a gold ring into the waters. A 14-day fair attracted merchants from all over Europe; the festivities ended with a banquet for the diplomatic representatives. Today, there is a historic procession on Piazza San Marco, with the mayor as the doge, accompanied by representatives of the church and armed forces. From Riva degli Schiavoni, thousands observe the crossing of the fleet to the Lido, where a simple laurel wreath is now symbolically dropped into the water.

▶ **Vogalonga**
Rowing regatta on the Sunday after the Ascension of Christ, starting at 8.30am in the Bay of San Marco, via various islands in the lagoon – Sant'Erasmo – San Francesco del Deserto – Burano – Mazzorbo – and returning to the bay of San Marco.

JUNE

▶ **Biennale d'Arte**
International art exhibition
▶Baedeker Special, p.207

▶ **Sagra di San Pietro di Castello**
In the last week of June, small booths are set up in the piazza before San Pietro, serving wine and Venetian specialities; the Sunday ends with a large prize draw.

! *Baedeker* TIP

A good view

To get a good view of the regatta, do not fail to make a reservation well in advance through a travel agent for a seat in a stand, on a balcony or in a window on the Grand Canal.

JULY

▶ **Festa del Redentore**
The festival of the Saviour on the third Sunday commemorates the end of the plague epidemic in 1576. It begins on the previous evening with a parade of decorated boats on the Canale della Giudecca and a great firework display. On Sunday, believers cross a temporary bridge to the island of Giudecca, where mass is held in the Redentore church. Traditional dishes are served on the boats and in the alleys. The celebration ends in the early morning hours on the beach of the Lido, where sunrise is greeted with singing and dancing.

AUGUST

▶ **Mostra Internazionale d'Arte Cinematografica**
International film festival on the Lido, a media event with lots of celebrities from the world of cinema.

▶ **Concerto dell'Assunta**
Concert on 15 August, the day of the Assumption of the Virgin, in the Basilica Santa Maria Assunta on Torcello.

SEPTEMBER

▶ **Regata Storica**
The historic gondola regatta on the Grand Canal on the first Sunday in September is a reminder of the great days of Venetian maritime power. Historic figures such as the doge, his wife the dogaressa, the queen of Cyprus and ambassadors take part in a magnificent procession before the start. Four different races take place between 2.30pm and 7pm: the youth regatta, the women's regatta, the regatta with caorlina (type of boat from the neighbouring Caorle) and a regatta with small gondolas. The goal is the Ca' Foscari, where the victors are also honoured. On the second Sunday in September, the boats of the historic regatta are paraded on the Brenta canal.

▶ **Sagra del Pesce di Burano**
On the third Sunday, fish and wine stands are set up in Burano before the Burano regatta takes place.

▶ **Festival di Musica Contemporaneo**
Festival for contemporary music, until October.

OCTOBER

▶ **Festival del Teatro**
Theatre festival throughout the city

▶ **Sagra del Mosto di Sant'Erasmo**
Wine festival of the island St Erasmus on the first Sunday with new wine (mosto) and snacks,

music, dancing and the only regatta in which women and men participate jointly.

▶ Marathon in Venice
On the second Sunday: the starting point is Strà on the mainland. The route crosses the Ponte della Libertà to the finishing line Riva dei sette Martiri (info: www.venicemara thon.it).

NOVEMBER

▶ Festa dei Morti
On the first Sunday of the month, lovers give their sweethearts so-called fave – small, coloured cakes of shortcrust pastry.

▶ Festa di San Martino
On 11 November, St Martin's day, children parade through the city. They drum on pots with wooden spoons and sing about the good deeds of St Martin. They are given a small tip for their performance – or more often, to get them to stop. Bakeries sell St Martin on horseback in the form of a pastry with coloured sugar glaze.

▶ Festa della Madonna della Salute
To commemorate salvation from

Regata storica, a historic rowing regatta

the plague epidemic of 1630, a large procession of pilgrims goes from St Mark's Basilica over a pontoon bridge on the Grand Canal at the level of Campo Santa Maria del Griglio to the church Santa Maria della Salute on 21 November. The traditional dish on this day is castradina, made from mutton and savoy cabbage.

Food and Drink

La cucina italiana

Although Italian food has conquered the world, it always tastes best in its place of origin. And the imaginative cucina veneziana, with its preference for oriental spices and unusual recipes, was once regarded as the finest cuisine in the world. It also mirrors the long history of the city: many simple dishes have also been preserved in Venetian food – the ingredients, such as rice, corn and many kinds of vegetables, come from the fertile hinterland.

Trattoria, osteria, ristorante?

Venice has a wide selection of places to eat. They range from exquisite gourmet restaurants to boring »calorie filling stations« for tourist groups. The variety in prices is just as great – the restaurants in less-visited city quarters such as Dorsoduro, Cannaregio or in the north and east of Castello are less expensive than those around Piazza San Marco. Since Venice is almost always busy, timely reservations are recommended. Some places offer tourist menus (menu turistico) at fixed prices. There are different types of restaurants: apart from the ristorante, there is the more popular **trattoria** and **osteria** and of course the **pizzeria**, where the waiter will not look askance if you ask for the bill, »il conto per favore«, after only a pizza and a glass of beer. For a snack or a cup of coffee in between, go to a **caffè** or stand at the counter of a **bar** or a bacaro.

Dining habits

Regardless of the locality, there are some ways in which Italian dining habits differ from those in other countries. For instance, it is not the custom in Italian restaurants to choose your own table. Wait until the waiter directs you to a table. In some cases, the price for service (servizio) as well as the bread and place setting (pane e coperto) are additionally billed.

Italians do not eat breakfast in the true sense. In the morning, it is »un caffè e via«, a strong coffee and let's get going. Most hotels do now offer breakfast (**colazione**). However, this is usually insubstantial (and somewhat costly). For a much more interesting environment, go to a bar and order a bun or sandwich (panino or tramezzino) –

Popular place for a break: café on the Campo Santo Stefano

the »normal« Italian types of coffee are better than the tourist coffee in most hotels. Lunch (**pranzo**) is usually available between 12 noon and about 2.30pm, while dinner (**cena**) is available from 7pm to about 10pm.

The order of the dishes on the menu is always the same: lunch or dinner consists of cold or warm antipasti (hors d'oeuvres), primo piatto (first course of pasta, rice or soup), secondo (main course of meat or fish) with vegetables (contorno) or salad (insalata). Then there is a choice between cheese (formaggio), dolce (dessert), frutta (fruit) or gelato (ice cream). An espresso rounds off the meal. Some order it as a »corretto« (»corrected« with grappa, cognac, Amaro or Sambuco).

In hotels and restaurants, service is included in the price; however at least 5 to 10% of the invoice amount is expected as a tip. In bars or cafés, service is frequently not included. In such cases, 10 to 15% is given as a tip. For taxi trips, round up the sum.

Tips mancia

►Language

Menu

A Selection of Venetian Dishes

In Venice, the range of fish and seafood is particularly generous. The city is also known for its risotti – rice dishes. Alla veneziana on the menu means »cooked with onions«, a centuries-old tradition.

Alla veneziana

Brodetto di pesce: Venetian fish soup of sea fish with onions, tomato juice, white wine, parsley, bay leaf and oil
Broèto: eel soup
Panada veneziana: bread soup with olive oil, garlic, bay leaf and parmesan
Risi e luganega: rice soup with Venetian pork sausages

Soups

Arancino: rice balls filled with minced meat or ham, breaded and fried in fat
Bovoleti: snails with garlic and parsley
Bruschetta: toasted bread with olive oil, garlic and tomatoes
Castraure: young artichokes cooked in oil and garlic
Cicheto: tasty pieces of small octopus, meat balls or pickled sardines
Gnocchi alla Fontina: gnocchi (small semolina dumplings) with grated Fontina cheese
Riso e bisi: rice with fresh peas, diced bacon and ham
Risotto de peoci o de cape: rice with seafood
Soppressa: minced pork sausage, especially tasty variations are spiced with pepper, garlic, white wine or even grappa.

Hors d'oeuvres

LIQUID SHADOWS

The Bacari (the 1st syllable is stressed) are part of everyday Venetian life: Simple stand-up bars where one can enjoy a few snacks, the genuine Cicheti, along with a glass of the normally open house wine from mid-morning until late into the night.

The name »Venetians« is a derivation of »Enetians« (Greek Enos = wine). Bacari, reminiscent of the sensuous god of wine Bacchus, is what the typical Venetian wine taverns are called. Here one can enjoy a glass of wine at an ancient wooden counter; mainly fresh, light selections such as a Pinot Bianco, Tocai, Chardonnay, or Merlot. This is accompanied by simple Cicheti, appetizing titbits which are usually home-made according to traditional recipes; croquettes with tuna, stockfish and herb canapés, fried rice and meatballs, anchovy rolls and pickled calamari, stuffed olives, grilled eggplant and artichokes as well as pickled sardines with onions, raisins and pine nuts, the typical Venetian Sarde in saor.

The wine is served »in the shade« of a 100ml/3.5fl oz glass called an Ombra. It is said that the wine used be sold on the Piazza San Marco, and that the wine sellers always followed the shade (= Ombra) of the Campanile in order to keep the wine cool. A Bacaro is an extremely democratic event. Here, one guest is as good as another and differences in social standing do not apply; there are no language problems, nobody gives you a hard time, but there is lots of communication. Make sure to take advantage of the Bacari when exploring Venice on one of the Baedeker walking tours.

Giro de ombre

Here some addresses for an Ombre tour (the taverns are usually closed on Sundays; numbers refer to the map on page 92):

37 Al Bacaretto, San Marco, Calle delle Botteghe 30124; with much sought after tables inside and outside; mixed crowd; imaginative Cicheti

39 Al Mascaron , Castello, Calle Lunga Santa Maria Formosa 5225; one of the most inventive wine taverns. Recommended: Spaghetti with mantis crabs and the traditional Castradina con verze sofegae (= smoked mutton with braised savoy cabbage and bacon)

40 Al Volto, San Marco, Calle Cavalli 4081; a popular place for Venetian youth; well-stocked wine cellar and excellent selection of Crostini

41 Da Codroma, Dorsoduro, Fondamenta Briati 2540, closed on Thursdays. Traditional Osteria which is popular with students as a hangout and for graduation parties, with various snacks and Panini

42 Antico Dolo, San Polo, Ruga Vecchia San Giovanni 798. Bruno Ruffini's extremely cosy wine tavern at the Rialto market has three tables; the tiny kitchen conjures up local delicacies, including a hefty Tripa rissa and pickled sardines.

43 Bancogiro ►Tip page 244

44 Cantinone ►Tip page 253

45 Da Alberto, Castello, San Lio 6015. Beautiful Bacaro with first-rate pea risotto and irresistible Baicoli

46 Do Mori, San Polo, Calle dei do Mori 429. One of the oldest and best Bacari on the Rialto market; try the tingly layered prosecco Cartizze and select from up to 90 different delicacies such as steamed artichoke hearts and stockfish mezzini.

47 Do Spade, San Polo, Sottoportego del le Do Spade 860. The ancient wine tavern »To the Two Swords« is also located next to the Rialto market; it is said that in 1744, Casanova spent an unforgettable night of love with a local beauty in the room of the Bacaro with the same name during the carnival; try the stuffed pig's feet, smoked bull's neck filet, or the spicy Tramezzini

29 Fiore, San Marco, Calle delle Botteghe 3461. Rich selection of Cicheti, including spicy meatballs and fried fish

Spaghetti con cozze/peoci: spaghetti with mussels
Spaghetti alle vongole: spaghetti with clams

Meat dishes Bracialo alla veneziana: pork chop braised in cider vinegar
Castradina: mutton cooked with savoy cabbage
Fegato alla veneziana: calf liver in the Venetian style with onion rings, steamed in oil
Museto: pig's head sausages, usually with lentils and mashed potatoes
Trippa: tripe

Fish dishes Bacala: cod, fried, boiled or as a ragout
Bacala mantecato: foamy cod puree with polenta
Bisato (Venetian dialect): eel, which is available in many forms, as an antipasto, risotto or main dish
Caparossoli, vongole: clams
Cape sante: scallops
Caragoli: sea snails
Coda di rospo ai ferri: grilled monkfish
Filetti di San Pietro fritti: fried fillets of John Dory, breaded in eggs and flour
Go: Venetian lagoon fish
Granceola: spider crabs spiced with pepper, oil and lemon
Mansanete: crabs fried in oil
Molèche col pien: crabs fried in egg dough
Polpetti: small boiled octopus with lemon juice, olive oil and parsley
Risotto nero: risotto with squid (black due to the ink)
Sarde in saor: fried sardines which were previously marinated in vinegar, onions, olive oil, raisins and pine nuts
Seppioline: small squid
Seppie al nero: squid, cooked in the ink, with polenta
Sogliola alla casseruola: sole steamed with mushrooms

Sweets Baicoli: Venetian speciality – thin, sweet rusk which can be dipped into coffee or hot chocolate
Buraneli: ring-shaped egg-dough cookies from Burano which are dipped in wine before eating
Bussolai ciosoti: ring-formed egg-dough cookies from Chioggia (similar to those from Burano)
Croccantini: a caramel-almond mixture which is eaten with sweet wine and crackers
Crostoli: carnival pastry
Fritole: carnival doughnuts with raisins and pine nuts
Fugassa: cake of yeast dough
Nicolota: crackers with raisins and aniseed
Persegada: quince bread served on St Martin's Day
Pinsa: similar to fruit bread, made for the day of the Three Wise Men, or Epiphany

Spriz, an aperitif of white wine, Campari, Aperol and sparkling water, is a Venetian speciality. The best-known white wines from Venetia are the dry Breganze Bianco, Bianco di Conegliano and Gambellara; the fragrant Barbarano Bianco, Tocai and Verduzzo; the medium-dry Soave; and Reciotto, a dessert wine. The dry red wines of the Veneto include Barbarano Rosso, Breganze Rosso, Cabernet di Treviso, Friularo, Bardolino, Merlot, Ricioto Amarone and Valpantena, while Redioto Rosso, Rubino della Marca and Rubino del Piave have a rather flowery bouquet. The sweet Moscato di Arqua is a dessert favourite. Table wines are served open in litre, half-litre and quarter-litre carafes (un litro, mezzo litro, un quarto) and by the glass (un bicchiere). Do not fail to try Prosecco di Valdobbiadone e Conegliano, an outstanding aromatic product of the Venetian wine region.

Drinks
Wines

Throughout Italy, meals end with caffè espresso. However, foreign visitors to Venice favour cappuccino, a caffè with plenty of hot milk and the famous milk foam on top, or latte macchiato (»spotted milk«, that is, a lot of milk and not much caffè). The focal point of the caffè bar is an espresso machine. Seating is rare – customers stand at the counter – furnishings are sparse, but choosing the right coffee is a science. Espresso, which is simply referred to as »caffè« in Italy, is available as double (doppio), corrected (corretto) with grappa, cognac or bitters, and even weak and diluted (ristretto). A simple milky coffee is caffè latte or macchiato (spotted).

Caffè and
cappuccino

 RECOMMENDED RESTAURANTS (see map p.98)

▶ **Price categories**
Expensive: more than €50
Moderate: more than €30
Inexpensive: up to €30 for a three-course menu (not tourist menu) without drinks

EXPENSIVE

▶ ① **Antico Martini**
San Marco
Campo San Fantin 1983
Tel. 04 15 22 41 21
A favourite amongst artists and intellectuals since the opening of the adjacent opera house La Fenice; in 1921, the Baldi family took over this elegant restaurant with the wine bar Vino Vino and the piano bar Martini Scala.

▶ ② **Alla Borsa**
San Marco, Calle delle Veste 2018
Tel. 04 15 23 54 34
Top-level gourmet restaurant, exclusive atmosphere.

▶ ③ **La Caravella**
San Marco, Calle Larga XXII Marzo 2397, tel. 04 15 20 89 01
Gourmet meeting place with excellent risotto and heavenly fish specialities; for romantics, candlelight dinner between ships' figureheads and models of three-masted ships.

▶ ④ **La Colomba**
San Marco, Piscina Frezzeria 1665
Tel. 04 15 22 11 75

Venice Hotels and Restaurants

Restaurants
1 Antico Martini
2 Alla Borsa
3 La Caravella
4 La Colomba
5 Corte Sconta
6 Harry's Bar
7 Harry's Dolci
8 Da Franz
9 Da Arturo
10 Antiche Carampane
11 Fiaschetteria Toscana
12 Da Fiori
13 Dalla Marisa
14 Haig's
15 Da Ignazio
16 Alla Madonna
17 Ai Coristi
18 Quattro Ferri
19 Da Alberto
20 Poste Vecie
21 Antica Pizzeria La Corte
22 Alla Botte
23 Pizzeria Due Colonne
24 Ai Gondolieri
25 Al Mondo Novo
26 Boldrin
27 Canottieri
28 L'Olandese Volante

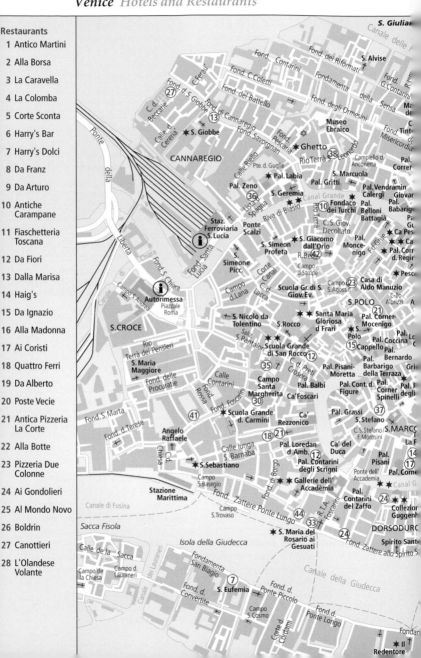

Torcello, Burano, S. Erasmo,
Murano, S. Francesco

S. Michele
in Isola

N

Cimitero S. Michele

200 m

©Baedeker

★ Isola di S. Michele

rini Sacca della
affo Misericordia

Canale delle Fondamente Nuove

Abbazia
d. Mis.   ★ I Gesuiti

S. Caterina   Campo
d.Gesuiti

Fondamenta Nuove

R. d. Pozzi

Rio Terrà
B. Fruttarol

S. Lazzaro
dei Mendicanti

Sofia (15)
Pal.   ✝ SS. Apostoli
Valmarana
(26) ★★ S. Maria dei
Ca da Mosto Miracoli   Ex Scuola Grande
Fabbriche   d. S. Marco
Vecchie (11)   (19)   ★★
★ Pal. d. (6)   Monumento   ★ Santi Giovanni
Camerlenghi   Colleoni   e Paolo • S. Zanipolo
★ Fondaco d. (6)   Barbaria d. Tole   ★ S. Francesco
Ponte   Tedeschi   Campo d.   d. Vigna
di Rialto   Campo d.   S. Marina   Campo d.
(28) ★ S. Lio   Confraternita
(22)   (25)   Calle del   Campo d.
S. Maria   Paradiso (39)   Celestia
d. Fava   ★ S. Maria
★ S. Salvador   Formosa   Campo
Pal. Dolfin Manin   ★ Fondazione   S.Lorenzo   ★ Scuola d. S. Giorgio
(32)   Ponte   Querini-   d. Schiavoni
Barateri   Stampalia
(26)   S. Giorgio   ★
rini   (11)   d. Greci
ovolo   S. Giovanni   C. d. Arco
(7)   Proc. Vecchie   Nuovo   Campo
(4)   ★★ ★ Piazza   ✝ S. Zaccaria (13)   Bandiera
San Marco   ★★ S. Marco   e Moro
Napoleonica   Ala (29)   ★★ Pal.   Pal. Dandolo (27)   (22)   ★ S. Giovanni
(3)   Proc. Nuove   Ducale (2)   (9)   in Bragora
(8)   (31)   Riva   S. Maria degli   Campo d.
(6)   Molo   d. Pietà (16)   Schiavoni   Arsenale
★ Museo
ntarini   Storico Navale
an   Punta della   ★ S. Francesco
Dogana   ✝ S. Biagio   di Paola
Dogana   Riva dei Sette Martiri
da Mar
aria   Salute   Canale   di San   Marco

Canale di S. Giorgio

Campo
S. Giorgio
★ S. Giorgio
Maggiore
Fondazione
Cini

Teatro Verde   Isola di S. Giorgio
Maggiore

ella Croce
C. drio la Croce   ✝ Le
Zitelle (1)

Canale della Fondamenta Nuove

Fondamenta Nuove

Fondamenta Nuove

Hotels

1 Cipriani
2 Danieli
3 Bauer
4 The Westin
   Europa & Regina
5 Gritti Palace
6 Al Ponte Antico
7 Cavalletto &
   Doge Orseolo
8 Luna Baglioni
9 Londra Palace
10 Saturnia &
   International
11 Concordia
12 Accademia
13 Bisanzio
14 Flora
15 Giorgione
16 Metropole
17 Ala
18 Ateneo
19 Centauro
20 Florida
21 Pausania
22 La Residenza
23 Rialto
24 Seguso
25 Serenissima
26 Locanda Silva
27 Wildner

Works of Carrà, Chagall, De Chirico, Oskar Kokoshka and others grace the walls of the restaurant; the owner, who had an interest in art, let the artists, who were little known at that time, pay him in paintings instead of lire – to the benefit of later visitors.

In the Trattoria da Ignazio

► ⑤ **Corte Sconta**
Castello, Calle del Pestrin 3886
Tel. 04 15 22 70 24
Fish in all variations, particularly popular in the moleche season.

► ⑥ **Harry's Bar,** ⑦ **Harry's Dolci**
►p.81 and Baedeker Tip p.209

► ⑧ **Osteria da Franz**
Castello, Fondamenta San Giuseppe 754
Tel. 04 15 22 08 61
Creative cuisine; recommendation: scallops au gratin, spaghetti with rocket and mantis crabs.

► ⑨ **Trattoria da Arturo**
San Marco, Calle de la Verona 3656
Tel. 04 15 28 69 74
A tiny gem of a restaurant with matchless fillet of beef.

MODERATE

► ⑩ **Antiche Carampane**
San Polo, Rio Tera delle Carampane 1911
Tel. 04 15 24 01 65
Extremely cosy. Don't miss the clam soup and the croccantini with sweet wine.

► ⑪ **Fiaschetteria Toscana**
Cannaregio, San Giovanni Crisostomo 5719, tel. 04 15 28 52 81
Tasty lagoon fish and wonderful zabaglione.

► ⑫ **Da Fiori**
San Polo, Calle del Scaleter 2202
Tel. 041 72 13 08
Traditional dishes such as mantis crabs, cod puree and breaded artichokes.

► ⑬ **Dalla Marisa**
►Baedeker Tip p.247

► ⑭ **Haig's**
San Marco, S. Maria del Giglio 2477, tel. 04 15 23 23 68
Warm food into the early hours of the morning.

► ⑮ **Trattoria da Ignazio**
San Polo, Calle Saoneri 2749
Tel. 04 15 23 48 52
The typically Venetian riso e bisi tastes as good here as the squid rings cooked in their own ink. Ignazio offers Venetian and international dishes and is very popular with local customers.

► ⑯ **Trattoria alla Madonna**
San Polo, Calle della Madonna 594
Tel. 04 15 22 38 24
Very popular old restaurant which specializes in fish, two minutes from the Rialto bridge (market side).

Simple and good: Osteria a la Campana

► ⑰ **Osteria ai Coristi**
San Marco, Campo S. Fantin 1995
Tel. 04 15 22 66 77
Traditional restaurant in the
Venetian style with a magical inner
courtyard near the Teatro La
Fenice.

► ⑱ **Quattro Ferri**
Dorsoduro
Campo S. Barnaba 2754/b
Tel. 04 15 20 69 78
Pleasant trattoria with typically
Venetian dishes, including fish
lasagna, stuffed clams or innards.

► ⑲ **Osteria da Alberto**
Cannaregio, Calle Giacinto Gallina
5401; tel. 04 15 23 81 53
At Alberto Ferrari, heavy copper
pans hang from the ceiling, pot-
bellied wine bottles line the walls,
and only traditional Venetian
dishes are served.

► ⑳ **Poste Vecie**
Rialto, Pescheria
Tel. 0 1 72 18 22
The oldest trattoria in the city,
with an enchanting garden and
stylish dining room.

INEXPENSIVE

► ㉑ **Antica Pizzeria La Corte
Ex Birreria**
San Polo, Campo San Polo

Tel. 04 12 75 05 70
Very good pizza, modern furnish-
ings. In the summer, tables on the
Campo.

► ㉒ **Alla Botte**
San Marco, San Bartolomeo 5482
Tel. 04 15 20 92 99
Superb pizza from a wood-burn-
ing oven; imitates a grotto.

► ㉓ **Pizzeria Due
Colonne**
San Polo
Campiello S. Agostin 2343
Tel. 04 15 24 06 85
Excellent pizza; in summer, there
are also tables on the quiet piazza.

► ㉔ **Ai Gondolieri**
Dorsoduro, Fondamenta Zorzi
Bragadin, San Vio 366
Tel. 04 15 28 63 96
Well stocked wine cellar; try the
liver paté, the venison fillet in
Madeira and the homemade
sweets.

► ㉕ **Al Mondo Novo**
Castello, Salizzada San Lio 5409
Tel. 04 15 20 06 98
Comfortable with a little garden;
fish specialities.

i Special recommendations

- Alla Madonna: specializes in fish, always busy
- Da Ignazio: good value for money
- Pizzeria Due Colonne: excellent pizza; outdoor tables in summer
- Harry's Dolci on Giudecca: magnificent view and slightly lower prices than its »big brother«
- Al Ponte del Diavolo on Torcello: the shady terrace is especially beautiful

Upscale address: Locanda Cipriani on Torcello

▶ ㉖ **Boldrin**
Cannaregio, Salizzada San
Canziano
Tel. 04 15 23 78 59
Popular enoteca with culinary
delicacies.

▶ ㉗ **Canottieri**
Cannaregio, Fondamenta del Ma-
cello 690
Tel. 041 71 54 08; C
Delicious pasta dishes; cabaret on
Tuesdays, concerts on Thursdays.

▶ ㉘ **L'Olandese Volante**
Castello, Campo San Lio 5658
Tel. 04 15 28 93 49
Sit on the small campo with an
aperitif or a beer – they have a
giant selection – and eat one of the
creative sandwiches, salads or
pasta dishes.

BURANO

▶ **Galuppi**
Via B. Galuppi 468?470
Tel. 041 73 00 81 (moderate)
Excellent fish dishes and local
specialities.

▶ **Al Gatto Nero**
Fondamenta della Giudecca 88
Tel. 041 73 01 2 (expensive)
Cosy trattoria on the other side of
the canal at the fish market; special
recommendation: risotto alla bur-
anella with seafood.

MURANO

▶ **Antica Trattoria Muranese**
Fondamenta Cavour (at the glass
museum)
Tel. 01 73 96 10 (inexpensive)
Pleasant trattoria with a lovely
garden.

TORCELLO

▶ **Al Ponte del Diavolo**
▶Baedeker Tip p.277

▶ **Locanda Cipriani**
Tel. 041 73 01 50 (expensive)
Giuseppe Cipriani's gourmet restaurant attracts an internationally
famous clientele.

CAORLE

▶ **Pizzeria Enotria**
Campo Sponzetta 4

Tel. 042 18 41 63 (inexpensive)
Popular pizzeria right in the old
centre of Caorle.

CAVALLINO

► **Da Achille**
Piazza S. Maria Elisabetta 16
Tel. 041 96 80 05 (moderate)
An institution in Cavallino – no
wonder, for the restaurant has
been run by the Scarpa family
since 1948. Wonderfully fresh fish
and clams, nothing but the best.
Seasoning and preparation are always based on old Venetian recipes.

CHOGGIA

► **Ristorante and Trattoria Eden**
Calle Airoldi 152/B

Tel. 04 15 50 04 25 (inexpensive)
Simple restaurant in a side alley of
Corso del Popolo. Fish dishes at
moderate prices.

JESOLO

► **Antica Jesolo**
Piazza 1 Maggio 2, Jesolo Paese
Tel. 04 21 95 14 70 (moderate)
Inexpensive restaurant with so-
phisticated cuisine, popular with
the locals.

► **Alla Grigliata**
Via Buonarroti 17
Tel. 04 21 37 20 25 (inexpensive)
Small, simple trattoria at the water
park Aqualandia. Speciality: grilled
meats.

Cafés and ice cream parlours

The first person to speak, or rather write, about coffee in Italy was
Gian Francesco Morosini, who was the ambassador of the Serenissima to the sultan of Constantinople from 1582 to 1585: »In Turkey,
they drink a black water made from a seed called 'cave'; it is said that
it can keep people awake.« The **first caffè** of the city is said to have
served the bittersweet Turkish beverage as early as 1647. Drinking
coffee became very fashionable; in the 18th century, there were eight
coffee houses on Piazza San Marco alone. In Venice today there is a
caffè bar on every major piazza, with a large selection of beverages
ranging from coffee and tea to juices and beer, aperitifs and wine.
Snacks are often sold as well – freshly baked goods in the morning,
buns or sandwiches at noon, cream tarts, biscottini and other sweets
in the afternoon.

CAFES AND ICE CREAM PARLOURS

► ㉙ **Florian, Lavena and Quadri**
The three famous, but also expensive cafés around Piazza San
Marco are still among the most
beautiful in the world.

► ㉚ **Causin**
Dorsoduro
Campo S. Margherita 2996
Irresistible ice cream varieties.

► ㉕ **La Boutique del Gelato**
Castello

Salizzada S. Lido 5727
Small selection of carefully prepared ice cream flavours.

▶ ㉛ **Chioggia**
San Marco, Piazzetta 11
With a view of the Doge's Palace.

▶ ㉜ **Dal Col**
San Marco, Calle dei Fabbri
On Saturdays, aromatic strudels
and warm croissants are served.

▶ ⑦ **Harry's Dolci**
▶Baedeker Tip p.209

▶ ㉝ **Nico**
Dorsoduro
Zattere ai Gesuati 922
Inimitable ice cream specialities.

▶ ㉞ **Rosa Salva**
San Marco
Campo San Luca 4589
A must for cappuccino fans and
everyone with a sweet tooth.

INTERNET CAFES

▶ ㉟ **Caffè Noir**
Dorsoduro
Calle San Pantalon 3805
Daily 7am–2am
This cyber-café is where Venice's
internet fans meet for surfing or
next door for a cup of hot
chocolate, tea or a beer.

▶ ㊱ **Casanova Internet Café**
Cannaregio 158/a
Lista di Spagna
Mon–Sun 9am–4pm
www.casanova.it

▶ ㊲ **Net House**
San Marco 2967/2958
Campo Santo Stefano/Calle de le
Botteghe; open daily
www.venicepages.com

▶ ㊳ **Planet Internet**
Cannaregio 1519
Rio Terrà San Leonardo
Open daily

Café Florian on Piazza San Marco

Health

MEDICAL AID

City hospital Santi Giovanni e
Paolo: tel. 04 15 29 45 16 or
04 15 29 45 17; health care centre
on the Lido: tel. 04 15 26 17 50.

EMERGENCY DOCTOR

Tel. 118

PHARMACIES

Pharmacies (farmacia) are open
Mon–Fri 9am–12.30pm and
4pm–7.30pm. They close on
Wednesdays and Saturdays alternately. A listing of the emergency
service pharmacies (farmacie di
turno) is on display at all pharmacies.

Information

USEFUL ADDRESSES

► **Italian National Tourist Office
ENIT
(Ente Nazionale Italiano per
il Turismo)**
www.italiantourism.com

IN AUSTRALIA

► **Italian Government Tourist
Office**
Level 4, 46 Market Street
NSW 2000 SIDNEY
Tel. 02 92 621 666

IN CANADA

► **Italian Government Tourist
Office**
175 Bloor Street E, Suite 907
Toronto M4W 3R8
Tel. 416 925 48 82

IN UK

► **Italian State
Tourist Board**
1 Princes Street
London W1B 2AY
Tel. 207 408 12 54

IN USA

► **Italian State Tourist Board**
630 Fifth Avenue, Suite 1565
10111 New York
Tel. 212 245 48 22

IN VENICE

► **Venice**
Azienda di Promozione Turistica
di Venezia (APT)
(for written inquiries):
Castello 5050
I-30122 Venezia
www.turismovenezia.it

Uffici informazioni
(information offices) in the city:
Tel. 04 15 29 87 11
Fax 04 15 23 03 99
San Marco all'Ascensione
S. Marco 71/f (daily 9am–3.30pm)
Pavilion Ex Giardini Reali
(daily 10am–6pm)
Stazione Ferrovie (railway termi-
nal)
daily 8am–6.30pm)
Piazzale Roma (Garage ASM)
(daily 9.30am–6.30pm)
Aeroporto (airport)
Marco Polo (daily
9.30am–7.30pm)

► **Lido di Venezia**
Gran Viale 6
Tel. 04 15 26 57 21
Fax 04 15 26 57 20

► **Chioggia e Sottomarina**
Lungomare Adriatico 101
30019 Sottomarina – Venezia
Tel. 041 40 10 68
Fax 04 15 54 08 55
www.chioggiatourism.it

► **Lido di Jesolo**
Piazza Brescia 13
I-30017 Lido di Jesolo
Tel. 04 21 37 06 01
Fax 04 21 37 06 08
www.jesolo.it

► **Hello Venezia**
Tel. 041 24 24
The English-speaking operators
regard themselves as a first contact
for visitors in all questions con-
cerning vacation in Venice.

CONSULATES

► **Australian Consulate**
Nearest consulate is in Milan
Via Borgogna 2
Milano
Tel. 027 770 42 27
www.italy.embassy.gov.au

► **British Consulate**
Piazzale Donatori die Sangue 2
Mestre
Tel. 041 505 59 90
www.britishembassy.gov.uk

► **Canadian Consulate**
Nearest consulate is in Padua
Riviera Ruzzante 25
Padua
Tel. 049 876 48 33
www.canada.it

► **Irish Consulate**
Nearest consulate is in Milan
Piazza S. Pietro in Gessate 2
20122 Milano
Tel. 025 518 88 48
www.ambasciata-irlanda.it

► **New Zealand Consulate**
Nearest consulate is in Milan
Via Guido d'Arezzo 6
20145 Milano
Tel. 02 499 02 01
www.nzembassy.com

► **United States Consulate**
Nearest consulate is in Milan
Via Principe Amadeo 2/10
Milano
Tel. 02 29 03 51
www.usis.it

LOST PROPERTY OFFICES • UFFICI OGGETTI SMARRITI

► **City Lost Property Office**
c/o Vigili Urbani
Piazzale Roma
Tel. 04 15 22 45 76

► **City transport operators**
Tel. 04 12 72 21 79
(ACTV, Vaporetti)

Fisherman in the lagoon of Venice

► **Stazione Santa Lucia**
Railway terminal, tel. 041 78 52 38

► **Aeroporto Marco Polo**
Airport, tel. 04 12 60 64 36

INTERNET ADDRESSES

► **www.turismovenezia.it**
Website of the Venetian tourism office in English with current themes and a lot of information

► **www.comune.venezia.it**
Italian website of the city of Venice

► **www.actv.it**
Useful information, fares and vaporetti schedules of the Venetian transport company ACTV

► **www.venicecard.it**
Info about the Venice Card

► **www.hellovenezia.it**
Plenty of practical information (transport, sights etc.) in English

► **www.veniceby.com**
English website with a lot of practical information

► **www.venezia.net**
Large amounts of information about Venice; currently only in Italian, but the English translation of the website is in progress.

► **www.meetingvenice.it**
Tourism portal with a calendar of events and a lot of other information.

▶ **www.veneziacultura.it**
Calendar of events

▶ **veniceexplorer.net**
A great deal of useful information, including hotels, restaurants, shops, schedules

▶ **www.gondolavenezia.it**
History of and stories about the gondola

▶ **www.venicebanana.com and www.veneziadavivere.it**
Event information and other tips for young visitors to Venice

▶ **www.promovetro.com**
About glass art

Language

| Italian | Italian developed from Latin and is the closest to it of all the Romance languages. Due to the earlier political division of the country, among other reasons, numerous dialects developed, of which the Tuscan dialect prevailed and is the official written language to this day. |
| Venetian dialect ▶ | Venetian is regarded as the softest dialect in Italy; the words themselves are changed, e.g. frari instead of frati (brothers), ca' instead of casa (house), anzelo instead of angelo (angel), pesse instead of pesce (fish). |

SHORT PHRASE BOOK

At a glance

Sì/No	Yes/No
Per favore/Grazie	Please/Thank you
Non c'è di che	You're welcome
Scusi!/Scusa!	Excuse me!
Come dice?	Excuse me? (as in: what did you say?)
Non La/ti capisco.	I can't understand you.
Parlo solo un po' di ...	I only speak a little ...
Mi può aiutare, per favore?	Can you please help me?
Vorrei ...	I would like ...
(Non) mi piace	I like that/do not like that (non=not)
Ha ...?	Do you have ...?
Quanto costa?	How much does it cost?
Che ore sono?/Che ora è?	What time is it?
Come sta?/Come stai?	How are you doing?
Bene, grazie. E Lei/tu?	Thank you. And you?

Mr/Mrs	Signora/Signor(e)
Buon giorno/Buona sera	Good day/good evening
Buona notte	Good night
Arrivederci/Ciao	Goodbye/Hello, see you later

On the move

a sinistra/a destra	left/right
diritto	straight ahead
vicino/lontano	close/distant
Quanti chilometri sono?	How far (in kilometres)?
Vorrei noleggiare ...	I would like to rent ...
... una macchina	... a car
... una bicicletta/una barca	... a bicycle/a boat
Scusi, dov'è ...?	Excuse me, where is ...?
la stazione centrale	the main railway terminal
l'aeroporto	the airport
all'albergo	to the hotel
Ho un guasto.	I have a breakdown.
Mi potrebbe mandare un carro-attrezzi?	Would you send me a tow truck?
Scusi, c'è un'officina qui?	Is there a workshop here?
Dov'è la prossima stazione di servizio?	Where is the nearest gas station?
benzina normale	Normal gasoline
super/gasolio	Super/diesel
deviazione	detour
senso unico	one-way street
sbarrato	blocked
rallentare	drive slowly
tutti direzioni	all directions
tenere la destra	drive on the right side
zone di silenzio	no honking
zona tutelata inizio	start of no-parking zone
aiuto!	Help!
attenzione!	Attention!
Chiami subito ...	Please quickly call ...
... un'autoambulanza/la polizia	... an ambulance/the police

Going out

Scusi, mi potrebbe indicare ...?	Where is ...?
... un buon ristorante?	... a good restaurant?
... un locale tipico?	... a typical restaurant?
C'è una gelateria qui vicino?	Is there an ice cream parlour here?

Può riservarci per stasera un tavolo per quattro persone?	Can I reserve a table for four persons for tonight?
Alla Sua salute!	To your health!
Il conto, per favore.	My bill, please.
Andava bene?	Was it good?
Il mangiare era eccellente.	The food was excellent.
Ha un programma delle manifestazioni?	Do you have a calendar of events?

Shopping

Dov'è si può trovare ...?	Where can I find ...?
... una farmacia	... a pharmacy
... un panificio	... a bakery
... un negozio di articoli fotografici	... a photo store
... un grande magazzino	... a department store
... un negozio di generi alimentari	... a grocery store
... il mercato	... the market
... il supermercato	... the supermarket
... il tabaccaio	... the tobacco shop
... il giornalaio	... the newspaper seller

Overnight accommodation

Scusi, potrebbe consigliarmi ...?	Can you please recommend me ...?
... un albergo	... a hotel
... una pensione	... a bed and breakfast

Ho prenotato una camera.	I have reserved a room.
È libera ...?	Do you still have ...?
... una singola	... a single room
... una doppia	... a two-bed room
... con doccia/bagno	... with shower/bath
... per una notte	... for one night
... per una settimana	... for one week
... con vista sul mare	... with sea view
Quanto costa la camera ...?	What does the room cost ...?
... con la prima colazione?	... with breakfast?
... a mezza pensione?	... with half board?

Doctor and pharmacy

Mi può consigliare un buon medico?	Can you recommend a good doctor?
Mi puo dare una medicina per ...	Please give me medication for ...
Soffro di diarrea.	I have diarrhoea.
Ho mal di pancia.	I have abdominal pain.
... mal di testa	... headache
... mal di gola	... sore throat
... mal di denti	... toothache
... influenza	... flu
... tosse	... cough
... la febbre	... fever
... scottatura solare	... sunburn
... costipazione	... constipation

Numbers

zero	0
uno	1
due	2
tre	3
quattro	4
cinque	5
sei	6
sette	7
otto	8
nove	9
dieci	10
undici	11
dodici	12
tredici	13
quattordici	14
quindici	15

sedici	16
diciassette	17
diciotto	18
diciannove	19
venti	20
ventuno	21
trenta	30
quaranta	40
cinquanta	50
sessanta	60
settanta	70
ottanta	80
novanta	90
cento	100
centouno	101
mille	1000
duemille	2000
diecimila	10 000
duecento	200
un quarto	1/4
un mezzo	1/2

Menu

Prima colazione	*Breakfast*
caffè, espresso	small coffee without milk
caffè macchiato	small coffee with a little milk
caffe latte	coffee with milk
cappuccino	coffee with foamed milk
tè al latte/al limone	tea with milk/lemon
cioccolata	chocolate
frittata	omelette/pancake
pane/panino/pane tostato	bread/bun/toast
burro	butter
salame	sausage
prosciutto	ham
miele	honey
marmellata	marmalade
iogurt	yoghurt

Antipasti	*Hors d'oeuvres*
affettato misto	mixed cold cuts
anguilla affumicata	smoked eel
melone e prosciutto	melon with ham
vitello tonnato	cold veal roast with tuna mayonnaise

Primi piatti	*Pasta and rice dishes, soup*
pasta	pasta
fettuccine/tagliatelle	ribbon noodles
gnocchi	small potato dumplings
polenta (alla valdostana)	polenta (with cheese)
agnolotti/ravioli/tortellini	filled pasta
vermicelli	thin round noodles
minestrone	thick vegetable soup
pastina in brodo	meat broth with fine noodles
zuppa di pesce	fish soup

Carni e pesce	*Meat and fish*
agnello	lamb
ai ferri/alla griglia	from the grill
aragosta	crayfish
brasato	roast
coniglio	rabbit
cozze/vongole	mussels/clams
fegato	liver
fritto di pesce	small baked fish
gambero, granchio	shrimp
maiale	pork
manzo/bue	beef
pesce spada	swordfish
platessa	plaice
pollo	chicken

rognoni	kidneys
salmone	salmon
scampi fritti	fried crayfish
sogliola	sole
tonno	tuna
trota	trout
vitello	veal

Verdura	*Vegetables*
asparagi	asparagus
carciofi	artichokes
carote	carrots
cavolfiore	cauliflower
cavolo	cabbage
cicoria belga	chicory
cipolle	onions
fagioli	white beans
fagiolini	green beans
finocchi	fennel
funghi	mushrooms
insalata mista/verde	mixed/green salad
lenticchie	lentils
melanzane	eggplant/aubergine

patate	potatoes
patatine fritte	French fries
peperoni	peppers
pomodori	tomatoes
spinaci	spinach
zucca	pumpkin

Formaggi	*Cheese*
parmigiano	parmesan
pecorino	sheep's milk cheese
ricotta	type of cream cheese

Dolci e frutta	*Desserts and fruit*
cassata	ice cream slice with candied fruit
coppa assortita	mixed ice cream
coppa con panna	ice cream cup with cream
tirami su	lady's fingers with mascarpone cream
zabaione	foamed egg cream
zuppa inglese	liquor soaked sponge cake with vanilla cream

Bevande	*Drinks*
acqua minerale	mineral water
aranciata	orangeade
bibita	refreshing drink
bicchiere	glass
birra scura/chiara	dark/light beer
birra alla spina	beer from the keg
birra senza alcool	alcohol-free beer
bottiglia	bottle
con ghiaccio	with ice
digestivo	digestive
gassata/con gas	carbonated
liscia/senza gas	uncarbonated
secco	dry
spumante	sparkling wine
succo	fruit juice
vino bianco/rosato/rosso	white/rosé/red wine
vino della casa	house wine

LEARN ITALIAN IN VENICE

DID YOU KNOW ...?

- Don't be surprised to hear strange weights named while you are shopping. The term »pound« is completely unknown in Italy (454 g), instead they talk about »mezzo chilo" (a half kilo). And with smaller quantities, do not ask for 100g but un etto, and for 200g, 300g etc. due etti, tre etti, etc.
For lengths and other measurements Italy, like the rest of Europe, uses the metric system.

► **Italian Courses Istituto Venezia**
Dorsoduro 311/a
Campo S. Margherita
Tel. 04 15 22 43 31
Fax 04 15 28 56 28
www.istitutovenezia.com

► **Venice International University**
Isola di San Servolo
Tel. 04 12 71 95 11
www.acitve.com
A range of undergraduate courses, but also Italian courses and Venetian culture

Literature

Venice must be one of the most described and photographed cities in the world. The following provides a small selection of recommended reading.

History and culture

Paolo Barbaro: *Venice Revealed: An Intimate Portrait.* Souvenir Press, 2002. A poetic description by a gifted writer with a profound knowledge of the city.

Christopher Hibbert: *Venice – Biography of a City.* Norton, 1989. Well-written and informative chronicle by the biographer of Florence, Rome and London.

Jan Morris: *Venice.* Faber & Faber, 1993. Classic portrait of the city by one of the best British travel writers of recent times.

Giovanna Scire Nepi and Alberto Prandi: *Treasures of Venetian Painting: The Gallerie Dell'Accademia.* Arsenale, 2006. A sumptuous volume showing the development of Venetian painting through works in the main art gallery of the city.

John Julius Norwich: *A History of Venice.* Penguin Books, 2003. A highly readable account of the thousand-year history of the Venetian republic.

Philip Rylands and Robert Krens: *Peggy Guggenheim Collection.* Guggenheim Museum, 2004. An informative guide to 20th-century art in the Palazzo Venier dei Leoni.

Luca Campigotto: *Venice – The City by Night.* Thames and Hudson, 2006. Atmospheric black-and-white images of the canals and city.   Photo books

Tudy Sammartini: *The Decorative Floors of Venice.* Merrell, 2000. Numerous detailed photographs of the often overlooked stone floors of 59 Venetian buildings.

Tudy Sammartini, Daniele Resini: *Venice from the Bell-Towers.* Merrell, 2002. The photographer climbed the church towers and took dizzyingly beautiful photographs.

E. M. Forster: *Where Angels Fear to Tread.* Penguin Books, 2001. A   Novels young English widow shocks her conservative family by marrying an Italian.

Ernest Hemingway: *Across the River and into the Trees.* Scribner Classic, 1998. First published in 1950, the novel tells the story of the last days of a retired American army officer, who hunts duck in the lagoon and seduces a beautiful young contessa.

Henry James: *Aspern Papers.* Oxford Classics, 1994, a darkly ironic tale, first published in 1888, by a master of the psychological novel, and *The Wings of the Dove* (Penguin Books, 2001), in which Venice is the setting for the attempts of a penniless man to secure the fortune of an heiress.

Donna Leon: The incorruptible Commissario Guido Brunetti battles against a corrupt, avaricious society which – behind the mask of Venice – will stop at nothing to defend its privileges. The successful American author has made Venice her home and the backdrop for a series of thrillers including *The Anonymous Venetian* and *Death at Le Fenice.*

Thomas Mann: *Death in Venice,* Vintage 2001 (see Baedeker Special, p.56.)

Ian McEwan: *The Comfort of Strangers,* Picador 1982 (see Baedeker Special, p.56.

William Shakespeare: *Merchant of Venice,* Oxford 1998. Shakespeare's classic trgic comedy – or comic tragedy, if you prefer – is set in the Venice of the Middle Ages. While the story doesn't say much about Venice itself, it shows that humannature hasn't chnaged much, and that certain topics – racism, love, friendship and female ingenuity – never become irrelevant.

Media

Newspapers English-language newspapers and magazines are sold at the bus and railway stations and at news stands all over the city. The most important Italian dailies are *Corriere della Sera*, *La Stampa* and *La Republica*. Local newspapers include *La Nuova Venezia* and *Gazzettino di Venezia*. Both always include useful telephone numbers and addresses as well as information about ►Festivals, Holidays and Events.

Money

Euro The euro has been the official currency in Italy and eleven other European Union countries since 1 January 2002.

Foreign exchange regulations Citizens from EU member countries are allowed to import and export any amount of EU currency.

Banks The usual opening hours of banks are Mon–Fri 8.30am–1pm, afternoons approx. 2.30pm–3.30pm. Banks close at 11.20am on days preceding holidays.

i **Exchange rates**

- 1 € = 1.35 US$
- 1 US$ = 0.74 €
- 1 £ = 1.47 €
- 1 € = 0.68 £

Travellers **cheques** can be cashed at banks. However, some Italian financial institutions charge high fees for cashing them!

The numerous **cash machines** (ATMs; in Italian: bancomat) provide problem-free access to money with credit cards and/or bank cards around the clock.

The common international **credit cards** are accepted almost everywhere. Usually a credit card is required to rent valuable items such as a car, or a deposit has to be made.

In Italy, purchasers are obliged to ask for and keep the **cash register receipts** (ricevuta fiscale or scontrino). You may be asked to show the receipt after leaving a shop – this is intended to make tax fraud more difficult.

Opening Hours

Most stores are open 9am–12.30pm and 4pm–7pm. Nearly all are closed on Saturday afternoons and Sundays, some also on Monday mornings.

Retailers

Viewing times of the 15 Chorus churches (► p.120): Mon–Sat 10am–5pm, Sun from 1pm; I Frari, Mon–Sat 9am–6pm, Sun from 1pm. The churches are closed on Sundays in July and August with the exception of the Frari church.

Chorus churches

Pharmacies ►Health
Banks ►Money
Post offices ►Post and Communications

Further
information

Post and Communications

The post offices handle mail and postal banking services (Mon–Fri 8.25am–1.45pm and Sat to 12 noon). The main post office is in ► Fondaco dei Tedeschi. **Stamps** (francobolli) are also available in tobacco shops, which are identified with a »T« sign (tabacchi). Postcards and letters (up to 20g/7oz) within Italy and to European foreign countries cost €0.62 (posta prioritaria).

Mail

◄ Postage

COUNTRY CODES

► **From Italy**
to other countries: 00 followed by the country code, e.g.
to UK: 0044
to USA: 001

► **From other countries
to Italy:**
+39

CITY AREA CODES

The local area codes are part of the Italian telephone numbers. Both in local calls and when calling from foreign countries, the area code including the 0 must also be dialled.

TELEPHONE DIRECTORY INQUIRIES

In Italy tel. 12,
Abroad tel. 4176

FEES

Lower fees are charged daily from 10pm to 8am and on weekends.

Telephoning International direct dialling is possible from public long-distance telephones with an orange telephone receiver symbol. They operate with telephone cards (carta / scheda telefonica), which are available in bars, at news stands or in tobacco shops. Remove the marked cor-

Mobile phones ▶ ner before using for the first time. The use of mobile telephones (telefonino, cellulare) from other European countries is normally trouble-free in Italy. The two densest mobile broadcast networks are maintained by the telephone companies Telecom Italia Mobile (access number 2 22 01) and Omnitel Pronto Italia (access number 2 22 10).

Prices and Discounts

Chorus Many churches in Venice can only be viewed for an entry fee, which goes towards the maintenance of the church. Chorus is an association of currently 15 churches which can be viewed with the Chorus ticket (approx. €9). The ticket is available in the churches and from the APT office (www.chorus-ve.org).

Museum pass The museum pass for approx. €18 applies to the museums on Piazza San Marco (among others, the Palazzo Ducale, Museo Correr, Museo Archeologico), Ca' Rezzonico, Palazzo Mocenigo, Casa Goldoni as well as the museums on the islands of Murano and Burano (information: tel. 04 15 20 90 70).

Venice Card See Venice and save money with the 1, 3 or 7-day Venice Card which is available for young and old in two versions. The **blue Venice Card** applies to all public transport and **public washrooms**, while the orange Venice Card also includes entry to city museums (in some museums reduced admission charge with the Venice card). The card

Advance can be pre-ordered no later than 48 hours before arrival in Venice
purchase ▶ (on the internet at www.venicecard.it or under tel. 041 24 24). A reservation number is issued for a card which can be picked up and paid for in Venice, from locations including the VELA sales offices,

▶ WHAT DOES IT COST?

Simple dbl room
€10

Simple meal
from €12

Espresso
from €1,50

Vaporetto journey
€5 (Canal Grande)

open 7am/8am and 8pm/9pm at the airport, Piazzale Roma, railway terminal, Tronchetto or Punta Sabbioni as well as the Alilaguna/ATVO Ticket Office.
The Venice Card is also available without pre-ordering from the VELA sales offices (see above), at the local tourist information offices (►Information, p.105) as well as at InterParking Italia.

◄ Local purchase

With this pass (€3 euros), those aged 14 to 29 years receive more discounts (information: tel. 04 12 41 39 08, rollingvenice@venicecard.it; sales offices ►above, Venice Card).

Rolling Venice

Shopping

Venice is famous for its masks, fine Burano lace and artistic glasswork from Murano. There is also a wide range of unusual textiles, in some cases made to old designs (Fortuny, ►Baedeker Tip p.237), but also to modern designs (Rubelli). Numerous boutiques offer exclusive fashion, high-quality leather wares and unique old and new jewellery. Fans of antiques and delicacies (from all over Italy) will also find what they like. Typically Venetian: paper made using old methods, as well as beautiful carvings and cast metal items, two arts which were at their peak in Venice during the Renaissance and can still be admired on many house doors today. The city is expensive. This is especially true in the stores around Piazza San Marco, the so-called Mercerie between the Rialto and Piazza San Marco, as well as in Calle Larga XXII Marzo. With some luck, it might be possible to find a good deal along one of the less luxurious shopping streets such as Lista di Spagna or Strada Nova. However, it is useful to know that many of the goods on offer are no longer produced in native studios, but in countries with low wages.

 VARIOUS SHOPPING ADDRESSES

ANTIQUES

► Antiquus
San Marco, Calle del Botteghe 2973, tel. 04 15 21 01 06
High-quality Murano antiques, also rarities from England and France.

► Casellati
San Marco, Calle Larga XXII Marzo, tel. 04 15 23 09 66
Largest antique dealer in the city.

! *Baedeker* TIP

Lanterns from Venice

They are a unique product – traditional Venetian lanterns of glass and wrought iron frames whose production demands great skill. A unique souvenir from Venice as well as a testimony to ancient craftsmanship, available solely from La Fucina del Ferro Battuto, Cannaregio, Strada Nova 4311, tel. 04 15 22 24 36.

► **Frezzati**
San Marco, Calle Larga XXII
Marzo 2070, tel. 04 15 22 77 89
Venetian painting from the 14th to
19th centuries.

► **Francesco Saverio Mirate**
San Marco, Calle della Verona
1904, tel. 04 15 22 76 00
Beautiful picture frames and vases.

► **Grafica Antica**
San Marco, Calle Larga XXII
Marzo 2089, tel. 04 15 22 71 99
Old engravings and historic city
views of Venice.

► **Scarpa**
San Marco, Calle Larga XXII
Marzo 2089, tel. 04 15 22 71 99
Old Italian masters.

► **Luisa Semanzato and Patrizia
Walcher**
San Marco, Marcaria San Zulian
732, tel. 04 15 23 14 12
Engravings, majolica and porce-
lain.

► **Veneziartigiana**
San Marco, Calle Larga San Marco
412/413, tel. 04 15 23 50 32
In a former pharmacy, various
dealers offer traditional masks, old
glass and antique jewellery.

ART GALLERIES

► **Il Capricorno**
San Marco, San Fantin 1994
Tel. 04 15 20 69 20
Renowned avant garde.

► **Cavallino**
San Marco, Frezzeria 1725
Tel. 04 15 21 04 88
Modern Italian artists, art library,
theatre, music.

► **Contini**
San Marco, Campo S. Stefano
2765, tel. 04 15 20 49 42
Classic modern and contemporary
art.

► **Naviglio**
San Marco, Calle della Piscina
1652, tel. 04 15 22 76 34
Modern classics.

► **Santo Stefano**
San Marco, Campo Santo Stefano
2953, tel. 04 15 23 45 18
Venetian masters, including De
Chirico.

► **Totem – Il Canale**
Dorsoduro, Accademia 878/b
Tel. 04 15 22 36 41
Contemporary art from northern
Italy.

► **Il Traghetto**
San Marco, Campo Santa Maria
del Giglio 2460
Tel. 04 15 22 11 88
Modern art from Italy and North
America.

ARTISTS' SUPPLIES

► **Arcobaleno**
San Marco 2968, Calle delle Bot-
teghe, Campo S. Stefano
Tel. 04 15 23 68 18

► **Testolini**
San Marco
Fondamenta Orseolo 30124
Tel. 04 15 22 92 65

BOOKS

► **Arsenale Punto Libri**
Santa Croce, Calle dei Vinanti 29
Tel. 04 15 22 94 95
Good selection of art and archi-
tecture books.

Treasures from the past or kitsch: sometimes, the line is blurred

▶ **Bertoni**
San Marco, Calle della Mandola
3637b, tel. 04 15 22 95 83
Secondhand.

▶ **Fantoni Libri d'Arte**
San Marco, Salizzada San Luca
4121, tel. 04 15 22 07 00
Art books, catalogues and magazines.

▶ **Goldoni**
San Marco, Calle dei Fabbri 4742,
tel. 04 15 22 23 84
Venice literature.

▶ **Sansovino**
San Marco, Bacino Orseolo 84, tel.
04 15 22 26 23
Venice books and antiquities.

▶ **Santi Giovanni e Paolo**
Castello, Campo Santi Giovanni e
Paolo 6358,
tel. 04 15 22 96 59
English-language literature.

▶ **Toletta**
Dorsoduro, Sacca della Toletta
1214, tel. 04 15 23 20 34
Attractive special offers.

CARNIVAL

▶ **Bac Art Studio**
San Marco, Campo San Maurizio
2663, tel. 04 15 22 81 71
Beautiful prints about the carnival.
▶Masks and costumes

DEPARTMENT STORE

▶ **Coin**
Cannaregio, Fontego Salizzada San
Crisostomo 5787 (at the Rialto)
The only department store; a
stylish range of goods.

FABRICS

▶ **Mario Bevilacqua**
San Marco, Fondamenta Canonica
337b, tel. 04 15 28 75 81
Brocade fabrics, tapestries and
finest scarves.

▶ **Camiceria**
Top-quality shirt fabrics, ▶p.124

▶ **Color Casa**
San Polo 1990, tel. 04 15 23 60 71
Glorious fabrics.

▶ **Frette**
Calle Larga XXII Marzo 2070, tel.
04 15 22 49 14
Bed-linen to die for.

A talisman from Venini – a beautiful souvenir

▶ **Rubelli**
San Marco 3877, Palazzo Corner
Spinelli, tel. 04 15 23 61 10
Wondrous designer fabrics.

FASHION

▶ **Laura Biagiotti**
San Marco, Calle Larga XXII
Marzo, tel. 04 15 20 34 01
Extravagant and playful fashion.

▶ **Borsato**
San Marco, Calle Vallaresso 1318,
tel. 04 15 22 55 25
Selected haute couture.

▶ **Camiceria San Marco**
San Marco, Calle Vallaresso 1340,
tel. 04 15 22 14 32
First-class tailored shirts and finest
fabrics.

▶ **Paola Carraro**
Dorsoduro 869, tel. 04 15 20 60 70

Handknit items with Picasso and
Matisse patterns.

▶ **La Coupole**
San Marco, Frezzeria 1674, tel.
04 15 20 60 63, and Calle Larga
XXII Marzo 2366, tel.
04 15 22 42 43
Unusual items from Rena Lange,
Kenzo and Valentino.

▶ **Elite**
San Marco, Calle Larga San Marco
284, tel. 04 15 23 01 45
Classic items for her and him.

▶ **Elysée**
San Marco, Calle Goldoni 4485,
tel. 04 15 23 69 48
Stylish items by Giorgio Armani.

▶ **Elysée Due**
San Marco, Frezzeria 1693, tel.
04 15 33 30 20

Designs by Armani, Cerrutti and Versace.

► **Gianfranco Ferre**
San Marco, Calle Larga San Marco 287, tel. 04 15 22 51 47
Current fashions.

► **Fiorella Show by Fiorella Mancini**
San Marco, Campo San Stefano 2806, tel. 04 15 20 92 28
Unusual fashions. The androgynous doge figures as window dummies are a curiosity.

► **Giuliana Longo**
San Marco, Calle del Lovo 4813, tel. 04 15 22 64 54
Interesting hat creations.

► **Maricla**
San Marco, Calle Larga XXII Marzo 2401, tel. 04 15 23 22 02
Wonderful undergarments.

► **Valentino**
San Marco, Salizzada San Moisè 1473, tel. 04 15 20 57 33
Elegant wear by a top designer.

► **Versace**
San Marco, Calle Larga XXII Marzo 2359, tel. 04 15 23 21 62
Stylish and sporty.

► **Volpe**
Rialto, Sant'Aponal 1228, tel. 04 15 23 80 41
Dolce & Gabbana, Moschino jeans, shirts from Le Garage.

► **ZetaSport**
San Marco, Calle dei Fabbri 4668, tel. 04 15 22 07 18
Sportswear from Fila, Ellesse and Sergio Tacchini.

FOOD AND DRINK

► **Mascari**
►Baedeker Tip p.244

► **Aliani Gastronomia**
San Polo, Ruga Rialto 654
Tel. 04 15 22 49 13
The displays are a joy to the eye – ham and biscotti, pasta and other delicacies, nothing but the best.

► **G. Rizzo**
Cannaregio, Calle S. Giovanni Crisostomo 5778, tel. 04 15 22 28 24
High-quality foods.

► **Rizzo**
San Marco, Calle dei Fabbri 933/A
Tel. 04 15 22 33 88
A treasure trove of culinary traditions of Venice; giant selection of specialized bakery items.

► **San Marco**
Calle Fiubera 951 and Campo San Luca 4589
Castello, Campo Santi Giovanni e Paolo 6779 – perhaps the best confectioner in town.

GLASS

► **Barovier & Toso**
Murano, Fondamenta dei Vetrai 28, tel. 041 73 90 49
The workshops of the famous glass blowers use traditional techniques and modern designs.

► **Cenedese**
Piazza San Marco 139
Tel. 04 15 22 93 99
Traditional and modern Murano glass.

► **Ferro & Lazzarini**
Murano, Fondamenta Navagero 75, tel. 041 73 92 99
Lamps and chandeliers.

▶ **I Lirici**
Piazza San Marco 114
Tel. 04 15 22 72 23
Creative Murano design.

▶ **Angelo Mantin**
San Marco, Calle Fiubera 953, tel.
04 15 23 81 07
Venetian glass beads.

▶ **Mazzega**
Murano, Fondamenta Da Mula
147, tel. 041 73 68 88
Beautiful glass art – ancient and
modern.

▶ **Murrina**
Murano, Fondamenta Cavour 17,

tel. 041 73 92 55
Sumptuous chandeliers and lamps.

▶ **Salviati**
San Marco, Piazza San Marco 78,
tel. 04 15 22 42 57
Traditional design and magnificent
chandeliers.

▶ **Paolo Scarpa**
San Marco, Mercerie San Salvador
4850, tel. 04 15 28 68 81
Glass beads from Murano.

▶ **Venini**
San Marco, Piazzetta Leoncini 314,
tel. 04 15 22 40 45
Murano vases and other items by
Carlo Scarpa and Tapio Wirkkala.

GONDOLA ROWLOCKS

The traditional forcole, as the rowlocks of Venetian gondolas are called
(▶ Baedeker Special, p.254), are sold
at:

▶ **Carli S.d. Brandolisio**
Castello, Calle Rotta 4725
Tel. 04 15 22 41 55

▶ **Spaziolegno**
Castello, Fondamenta del Tintor
3865, tel. 04 15 22 56 99

▶ **Saverio Pastor**
Dorsoduro, Fondamenta Sorenzo
detta Fornace 341 (between the
Collezione Guggenheim and the
Salute church), tel. 04 15 22 56 99;
www.forcole.com

HERBS

▶ **Il Melograno**
Campo S. Margherita 2999
Tel. 04 15 28 51 17
Oldest and best-stocked herbalist
in Venice.

An ancient tradition:
handmade marbled paper

JEWELLERY

▶ **Chimento**
San Marco, Campo San Moisè
1460, tel. 04 15 23 60 10
Top address beside the luxurious
Bauer-Grünwald Hotel.

▶ **Il Mercante**
Cannaregio, Strada Nova 2223
Tel. 041 71 60 84
Unusual jewellery and lamps in
the Fortuny style.

▶ **Nardi**
Piazza San Marco 69
Tel. 04 15 22 57 33
Select haute couture.

▶ **Salvadori**
San Marco, Mercerie San Salvador
5022, tel. 04 15 23 06 09
Exclusive jewellery since 1857.

▶ **Paropamiso**
San Marco, Frezzeria 1701
Tel. 04 15 22 71 20
Unusual jewellery, including
foreign items.

LACE

▶ **Jesurum**
Piazza San Marco 60/61
Tel. 04 15 22 98 64, and
Mercerie del Capitello 4856
Tel. 04 15 20 60 85
The best place to get first-class
lace.

▶ **Kerer**
Castello, Calle Canonica 4328a
Tel. 04 15 23 54 85
A famous shop.

▶ **Maria Mazzaron**
Castello, Fondamenta dell'Osmarin 4970, tel. 04 15 22 13 92
Finest Burano lace.

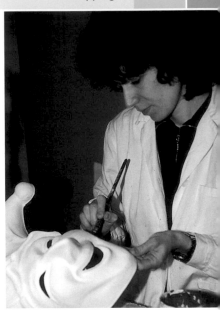

▶ **Merletto Antico**
Burano, Via Galuppi 215,
Tel. 0 1 73 00 52
Exquisite lace and a museum.

LEATHER GOODS AND SHOES

▶ **La Bauta**
San Marco, Marzaria San Zulian
729, tel. 04 15 22 38 38
Prada, Granello and Henry Beguelin and more.

▶ **Bottega Veneta**
San Marco, Calle Vallaresso 1338
Tel. 04 15 22 84 89
Braided leather dreams.

▶ **Casella**
San Marco 5048, tel. 04 15 22 88 48
Fashionable footwear.

▶ **Rolando Segalin**
San Marco, Calle dei Fuseri 4365
Tel. 04 15 22 21 15

?   DID YOU KNOW ...?

■ To make leather masks, a wooden model is needed; for paper masks, a plaster model. The model is stuffed with many layers of papier machè, which has been soaked in glue.

Visitors to Alberto Sarria's shop can watch how he and his colleagues produce traditional and modern masks (San Polo, Ruga Rialto 777, where the small theatre is occasionally used for performances; and Santa Croce 1807, near S. Stae vaporetto stop, tel. 04 15 20 72 78, www.masks venice.com).

The best made-to-measure shoes, since 1932.

▶ Fratelli Rosetti
San Marco, Calle San Moisè 1477, tel. 04 15 22 08 19
Fashionable and elegant footwear.

MARBLED PAPER

▶ Carta
San Marco, Calle dei Fabbri 831, tel. 04 15 22 98 01
Lovely paper and unusual inkwells.

▶ Carta Venezia
S. Croce, Calle del Cristo 2125
Tel. 04 15 24 12 83
Handmade paper.

▶ Legatoria Piazzesi
San Marco, Campiello della Feltrina 2511, tel. 04 15 22 12 02
Imaginative paper prints and puppet theatres.

▶ Paolo Olbi
Campo S. Maria Nuova, near the church S. Maria dei Miracoli; Calle Bandi 5478 and in Calle della Mandola 3653, San Polo.
In addition to handmade paper, there are also beautifully bound books and albums.

MARKETS

The largest market is open Mon–Sat 7am–1pm (fish market also closed on Mondays) around the *Rialto bridge.* In the Castello district, in *Via Garibaldi,* fruit, vegetables, fish and household goods are sold on weekdays from 7am. Smaller markets with vegetable, fish and flower stands are open in the mornings in Cannaregio on the *Ponte delle Guglie,* in Dorsoduro on *Campo Santa Margherita* and in the San Marco quarter on *Campo Santa Maria Formosa.* On *Campo San Barnaba,* fruit and vegetables are sold from boats.

MASKS AND COSTUMES

▶ Il Ballo del Doge
San Marco 1823, tel. 04 15 22 68 59
Wonderful masks, marionettes and Rococo costumes.

► **Alberto Sarria**
Studio and shop, ►Baedeker Tip
p.128

► **Cartapesta & Co.**
Castello, Barbaria delle Tole 6656,
tel. 04 15 22 31 10
Classic masks and tasteful picture
frames.

► **Laboratorio Artigiano Maschere**
Castello, Barbaria delle Tole 6657,
tel. 04 15 22 31 10
Masks patterned by old engravings.

► **La Mano**
Five artists' studios:
Castello, Calle Longa Santa Maria
Formosa 5175; Cannaregio, Rio
Terra dei Birni 5415; Castello,
Barbaria delle Tole 6468; San Polo,
Ruga Rialto 1032; San Marco,
Calle Fiubera 818.

► **Tragicomica**
San Polo, Calle dei Nomboli 2800,
tel. 041 72 11 02
Gualtiero dall'Osto makes masks
and costumes, for the Arena in
Verona or the Teatro San Carlo in
Naples among others.

► **Mondonovo**
Dorsoduro, Rio Terra Canal 3063,
tel. 041 52 84 73 44
Out-of-the-ordinary creations.

► **La Venexiana**
Castello, Ponte Canonica 4322, tel.
04 15 23 35 58
Magnificent theatre and carnival
masks.

METAL GOODS

► **Valese**
San Marco, Calle Fiubera 793, tel.
04 15 22 72 82
Gondola irons and old door
knockers.

► **Renato Burelli**
Dorsoduro, Calle Lunga San Bar-
naba 2729, tel. 041 52 243 09
Brass mountings and paints.

SOAP

► **Lush**
Cannaregio, Strada Nova 3822, tel.
04 12 41 12 00
Soap, bathing essences and body
lotions in all colours and shapes –
as a piece of cheese, chocolate bar
or apple that foams wildly when
put into water.

WOOD ART

► **Livio de Marchi**
Livio de Marchi, San Marco, San
Samuele 3157a, tel. 04 15 28 56 94,
www.liviodemarchi.com
Everything wooden – from cur-
tains to furniture, from cars to
books.

Sports

For sporting activities after a leisurely stroll through the city and re-
laxing cultural programmes, go to the Lido, where water sports such
as water skiing and sailing are offered, as well as opportunities for

Sports offerings

horse riding, tennis and golf (Circolo Golf Venezia, Alberoni, Via del Forte, tel. 041 73 13 33, Fax 041 73 13 39, www.circologolfvenezia.it).

Football (calcio) The city Stadio P.L. Penzo is located on the island of Sant'Elena in the far south-east of Venice. Information: tel. 04 15 23 99 99.

Theatre • Concerts

Music

Concerts Concert performances take place year-round in Venice. They are often an opportunity to get a look at the interior of city palaces which are usually not accessible. The festival for contemporary music (Festival di Musica Contemporaneo) has been held annually in September since 1930.

Collegium Ducale This chamber orchestra performs Baroque, Classical and Romantic works year-round. Venues include the Palazzo delle Prigione (beside the Doge's Palace) as well as the churches Santa Maria Formosa and San Lio. Information and tickets: tel. 041 98 42 52 and www.collegiumducale.com.

Interpreti Veneziani Internationally successful musicians who regularly play in the church San Vidal, particularly Baroque works by Vivaldi, Bach, Tartini etc. Information: tel. 04 12 77 05 61 and www.interpretiveneziani.com.

▶ THE MAIN VENUES

▶ **Teatro La Fenice**
San Marco, Campo S. Fantin 1965
►Sights from A to Z
Opera and ballet.

▶ **Teatro Malibran**
Tel. 041 78 67 64
www.teatrolafenice.it
Opera, ballet, concerts.

▶ **PalaFenice**
Theatre tent on the car-parking island of Tronchetto, tel. 041 78 65 11 www.teatrolafenice.it
Advance ticket sales: Mon–Sat 8.30am–6.30pm in Calle dei Fuseri, tel. 04 12 41 80 29, and at

Piazzale Roma, tel. 04 12 72 22 49, or from approx. 1 hour before the performance in the theatre tent. Originally the alternative quarters until the re-opening of La Fenice.

▶ **Teatro Goldoni**
San Marco, Calle Goldoni 4650
Tel. 04 12 40 20 11
www.teatrostabileveneto.it.
Comedies, particularly by Goldoni.

▶ **Teatro Avogaria**
Dorsoduro, Campo San Sebastiano 1617, tel. 04 15 20 61 30
Fax 04 15 20 92 70
Experimental and dialect theatre.

New Year's concert on 1/1/2004 in the sold-out newly opened Teatro La Fenice

Gondola trips with music on the Grand Canal and the other canals are the essence of romantic Venice. However, this has its price (information at the tourist office ►Information).

Gondola serenades

Information about events, opening times etc. is provided by the dailies *Il Gazzettino* and *La Nuova Venezia* as well as the Italian-English brochures *LEO Bussola, Venezia News, Un Ospite di Venezia* (www.unospitedivenezia.it), *Venezia da Vivere* (www.veneziadavivere.it) and *Meeting Venice* (www.meetingvenice.it). The latter are found at all APT offices (►Information) and in the hotels.

Programme information

Time

Italy uses Central European time (= GMT +1 h). From the end of March to the end of October, Central European Summer Time applies (= GMT +2 h).

Tours and Guides

Guided tours Authorized English-language tourist guides (guide turistiche) are provided – it is best to make an appointment in advance – by the Associazione Guide Turistiche, San Marco 750, tel. 04 15 20 90 38, fax 04 15 21 07 62, guide@guidevenezia.it.

Competent guided tours are offered, among others, by »Walk Inside Venice« (www.walksinsidevenice.com, tel. and fax 04 15 20 24 34).

On your own No visit to Venice is complete without at least one trip around the city by vaporetto, the »water bus«. Lines 1 and 82 travel the Grand Canal (►Sights, Grand Canal) in both directions between Piazza San Marco and the railway terminal. Line 1 serves all stops, Line 82 only the most important ones. There is enough time on the way to see the patrician palaces and churches or take a break at a station.

Line 52 Line 52 goes around the centre of Venice in approx. two hours. It starts at Riva degli Schiavoni east of the Doge's Palace. The route is through the Arsenale to Fondamenta Nuove, where a side trip past the cemetery island San Michele to the islands of Murano, Burano and Torcello is possible, then rounds the district of Cannaregio with the basilica Madonna dell'Orto and through the Canale di Cannaregio to the north end of the Grand Canal, leaving it again at Piazzale Roma to head through the western harbour to the Guidecca Canal on the island La Guidecca, reaching the Piazza San Marco again opposite San Giorgio Maggiore.

Gondola trips ►Baedeker Special p.254

Excursions into the lagoon A special feature of Venice is the lagoon, a labyrinth between the ocean and the land with canals, salt marsh and gardens, islands and islets. Excursions, some with sail and motor boats or the ACTV ferries, are offered by the **environmental cooperative RiVivi natura**. For instance, a day trip into the northern lagoon has the theme »the arts of lace, glass and cooking« (l'arte fra merletti, preziosi vetri e buona cucina). Another is dedicated to archaeology in the lagoon, and includes historic fortifications and salt vegetable gardens. Contact: RiVivi natura, San Marco, Calle Vitturi 2923, tel. 04 12 77 41 89, fax 04 15 21 28 31, www.rivivi natura.it; info@rivivinatura.it.

Transport

By water Boats are the most important means of transport in Venice. Two different types of »water bus« of the city transport service (ACTV) provide connections within the city and to the lagoon islands: the **vapo-**

retto, which is high in the water, and the smaller **motoscafo**. They generally run between 6am and 11pm, some – like Line 1 – all night, even though they only run once hourly after 1am. In very narrow canals, Venetians use **gondolas** (►Baedeker Special p.254). **Traghetto** is the name for a gondola ferry without seats which transports Venetians and tourists across the Grand Canal for little money (there are several standing spaces). The two-deck **motonavi** run between Venice, the Lido and the lagoon islands. Since they only make a few stops, they are much faster than the vaporetti. All other routes have to be covered on foot.

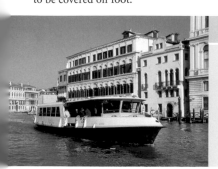

! **Baedeker** TIP

Venice Card

To keep down the costs of travelling on the vaporetti ferries, and as a more convenient way to pay than continually buying single tickets, it is worth buying the blue Venice Card. It is valid for all ferry lines and also gives admission to the public toilets, which otherwise cost money (►Prices and Discounts, p.120).

Timetables

Information about routes and schedules – there is a differentiation between festiva (Sunday) and feriale (weekdays) – is available from the ACTV offices on Piazzale Roma and Piazza San Marco (Ponte dei Fuseri) as well as under www.actv.it and www.hellovenezia.it.

Tickets
Venice Card

Tickets (individual ticket without Grand Canal currently €3.50; 24-hour ticket €10.50) are available at the ticket booths (or from the uniformed boat operators). When staying several days, it is worth buying a Venice Card ►p.120.

Grand Canal
City centre

The most used vaporetto lines in the city centre are no. 1 from the Piazzale Roma/railway terminal through the Grand Canal (stops at all stop locations) to the Lido and back, and no. 82 from Tronchetto via the Piazzale Roma, railway terminal, Rialto, Vallaresso, S. Zaccaria and back through the Giudecca canal.
Lines 41/42, 51/52, 61/62 run right around the old city, both clockwise and counter-clockwise.

◄ *Island round trip*

Linee Lagunari

The so-called Linee Lagunari travel into the lagoon to Chioggia as well as Treporti and Punta Sabbioni. Line 17, a **car ferry**, operates between Tronchetto and the Lido.

Gondola trips
Traghetti

Aside from the three pedestrian bridges, there are gondola ferries for crossing the Grand Canal: railway terminal – Fondamenta S. Simeon,

S. Marcuola – Fondaco dei Turchi, S. Sofia/Ca' d'Oro – Pescheria, Riva del Carbon – Riva del Vin (Rialto), Ca' Garzoni – San Tomà, S. Samuele – Ca' Rezzonico, S. Maria del Giglio – Palazzo Genovese.

Gondolas The very essence of romance is a trip on one of the approximately 400 sleek black **gondolas,** the most famous symbols of Venice (▶Baedeker Special p.254). The fares for gondola trips are regulated: an hour currently costs about €120.

Gondola quays
Bacino Orseolo, San Marco, tel. 04 15 28 93 16
Calle Vallaresso, San Marco, tel. 04 15 20 61 20
Campo San Moisè, San Marco, tel. 04 15 23 18 37
Campo Santa Sofia, Cannaregio,
tel. 04 15 22 28 44
Danieli, Riva degli Schiavoni,

Castello, tel. 04 15 22 22 54
Ferrovia, San Simeon Piccolo,
Santa Croce, tel. 041 71 85 43
Molo, San Marco,
tel 04 15 20 06 85
Piazzale Roma, tel. 04 15 22 05 81
Riva del Carbon, Rialto,
tel 04 15 22 49 04
Santa Maria del Giglio, San Marco,
tel. 04 15 22 20 73
San Tomà, San Polo,
tel 04 15 20 52 75
Tronchetto, tel. 04 15 23 89 19

Motoscafi (water taxis) are now the most used transport apart from the ferries. They charge fixed rates which are posted at the various stops, such as **Marco Polo Airport**, tel. 04 15 41 50 84, the **railway terminal** Stazione Santa Lucia, tel. 041 71 76 72 86, **Fondamenta Nuove**, tel. 04 15 23 73 13, the **Lido**, Viale S.M. Elisabetta, tel. 04 15 26 00 59, **Piazzale Roma**, tel. 041 71 69 22, **Rialto**, tel. 04 15 23 05 75, **San Marco**, tel. 04 15 22 97 50 and **Tronchetto**, tel. 04 15 21 14 44

Buses Venice is linked to the mainland by bus: Piazzale Roma – Aeroporto
Line 5 Marco Polo
Lines 2, 4, 7, 12 Piazzale Roma – Mestre
Line 6 Piazzale Roma – Marghera
Line 19 Piazzale Roma – Favaro

At the Lido At the Lido, buses connect the Santa Maria Elisabetta quay with the casino at Lungomare Marconi and Via Colombo (Line A) as well as

S. Maria Elisabetta station with Malamocco and the stop S. Nicolò (Line B) as well as Alberoni (Line C). There is also a link from S. Maria Elisabetta to Alberoni, S. Pietro in Volta, Pellestrina and Chioggia (Line 11).

In the car-free lagoon city, car taxis only go as far as Piazzale Roma (radio taxi, tel. 04 15 23 77 74), on the route to the mainland to Mestre and Marghera (radio taxi, tel. 041 93 62 22) and at the Lido (radio taxi, tel. 04 15 26 59 74, 04 15 26 59 75). **Taxis**

Traffic Regulations

The use of the highway (autostrada) is usually subject to tolls in Italy (pedaggio). The autostrada toll can be paid in cash, by credit card or Viacard. It is available in Italy at the automobile clubs, at ACI offices at the border crossings or the most important autostrada entries, in tobacco shops as well as at petrol stations. **Highway**

The import and transport of petrol in canisters is prohibited. There is unleaded petrol (95 octane, benzina senza piombo or benzina verde), super (97 octane) and diesel fuel (gasolio). Petrol stations are generally open from 7am to noon and 2pm to 8pm. There is usually 24 hour service on an autostrada. On the weekends, increasingly also during lunch hour and at night, many petrol stations only have fill-ups available at automatic pumps. **Petrol stations**

The following speed limits apply in Italy: cars, motorcycles and motor homes up to 3.5 t: 50kmh/30mph in towns, 90kmh/55mph outside towns, 110 kmh/70mph on highways with two lanes in each direction, 130kmh/80mph on an autostrada. **Speed limits**

Vehicles over 3.5 t: 80kmh/50mph outside towns, 80kmh/50mph on highways and 100kmh/60mph on an autostrada. There are heavy fines for speeding.

Parking in Venice ▶Arrival, p.75 **Parking parking**

The limit for alcohol in the blood lies at **50mg per 100ml**. Outside towns, dipped headlights must be on while driving in the daytime (since June 2003). In towns with good street lighting, parking lights are permitted. Helmets are required on motorcycles above 50cc. A breakdown jacket is also mandatory when travelling to Italy. Private towing on the autostrada is prohibited in Italy. **Other regulations**
In the event of a breakdown, call ▶Emergency. If the vehicle is a total write-off, the Italian customs authorities must be notified, since it is otherwise import duties may be charged for the damaged vehicle. In Italy, telephoning in cars is only permitted with a hands-free system.

CAR RENTALS

▶ **Avis**
Tel. 018 05 / 55 77 55
Marco Polo Airport:
Tel. 04 15 22 58 25
www.avisautonoleggio.it

▶ **Hertz**
Tel. 0 18 05 / 33 35 35
Airport: tel. 04 15 41 60 75
www.hertz.de

▶ **Europcar Italia Inter Rent**
Airport: tel. 04 15 41 56 54 and
Tel. 04 15 41 50 92
www.europcar.it

▶ **Sixt**
Tel. 0 18 05 / 25 25 25
Piazzale Roma:
Tel. 8 00 90 06 66 and
Tel. 04 15 28 95 51
www.e-sixt.de

Rental Cars

For trips to the mainland, it is best to rent a car at Piazzale Roma, in Mestre or at the airport. Local telephone books list renters under »Autonoleggio«. To obtain a rental car, it is necessary to have a minimum age of 21 years, hold a national driving licence and a credit card, and have one year of driving experience. With international car rental companies, bookings can be made from the home country.

Travellers with Disabilities

Venice is a difficult city for handicapped travellers, not just because of the more than 400 bridges and the use of water taxis (vaporetti are easier to get into). Information about the few wheelchair aids

INFORMATION FOR THE DISABLED

IN VENICE

▶ **Disabled assistance office**
By platform 4, Stazione di
Santa Lucia
Daily 7am–9pm

USA

▶ **SATH (Society for the
Advancement of Travel
for the Handicapped**
347 5th Ave., no. 610

New York, NY 10016:
Tel. (21) 4 47 72 84
www.sath.org

UNITED KINGDOM

▶ **RADAR**
12 City Forum, 250 City Road,
London EC1V 8AF
Tel. (020) 72 50 32 22
www.radar.org.uk

and mobility in the city: APT (▶ Information), which has a map marking areas of the city accessible without bridges, and from Informahandicap, tel. 04 15 34 17 00.

Some public transport has wheelchair access: vaporetto lines 1 and 82, the larger ferries to the lagoon, and the following bus lines:

No. 2, Piazzale Roma to Mestre railway station
No. 4, Piazzale Roma to Corso del Popolo, Mestre
No. 5, Piazzale Roma to Marco Polo Airport
No. 6, Piazzale Roma to mainland
No. 15, Marco Polo Airport to Mestre

When To Go

Venice has a moderate Mediterranean climate, meaning cool, occasionally even cold, foggy winters and sunny, hot summers, but without the typically Mediterranean dry period.

Best times for visiting: April–June and September–October

The lagoon city is worth a trip at any time, but the unpleasant weather between November and March with many foggy days (an average of 20 in December), rain and even snow dissuades many travellers from winter trips. The weather improves from April. The downside: the feared Genoa low is particularly active in spring. It makes itself felt about every third to fourth day with showers and thunderstorms into June. High summer brings a lot of sun and sweaty temperatures. In July and August, the thermometer usually rises at least to 28°C, while night-time temperatures drop to a balmy 18°C. And with hot southerly winds from Africa (sirocco), temperatures may even climb above 35°C. Little wind and high air humidity make the summer muggy at times. Then the Lido offers a welcome chance to cool off with water temperatures around 24°C.

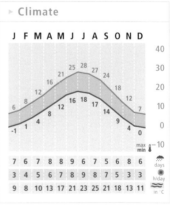

▶ Climate

September is also an excellent month for travelling. This is due to the more moderate daytime temperatures of 24°C, the low number of rainy days (only 5, the lowest in the year) and the still-warm sea. The beautiful late-summer weather frequently lasts into the first week of October. Then autumn comes with lower temperatures, severe thunderstorms and sometimes torrential rainfall.

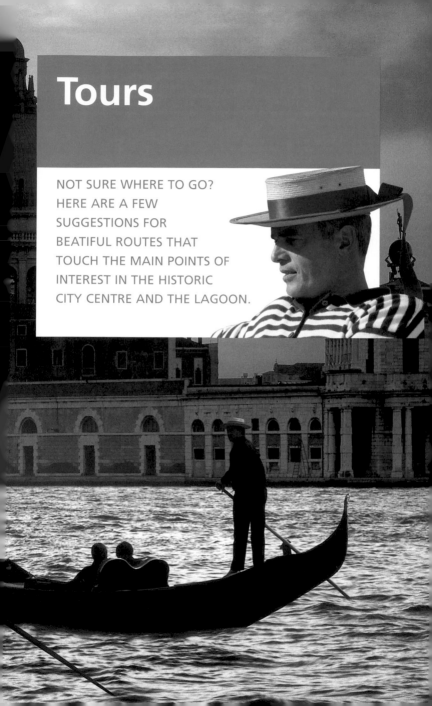

Tours

NOT SURE WHERE TO GO?
HERE ARE A FEW
SUGGESTIONS FOR
BEATIFUL ROUTES THAT
TOUCH THE MAIN POINTS OF
INTEREST IN THE HISTORIC
CITY CENTRE AND THE LAGOON.

TOURS THROUGH VENICE

Four tours on foot and a small excursion by boat will take you to the lagoon and the main attractions of Venice.

S. Giuliano

Canale delle

Aeroporto, Padua

Palafenice

Fusina

Isola del Tronchetto

Isola del Tronchetto

Ponte della Liberta

Stazione Marittima Merci

Bacino Stazione Marittima

Stazione Marittima

Sacca Fisola

Isola della Giudecca

Canale di Fusin

Canale Scomenzera

C. d. al Magazzini

Fond. S. Marta
S. Teresa
S. Nicolò
Fond. d. Terese

Angelo Raffaele
C. d. Chiesa

S. Sebastiano

Campo S. Basegio

Stazione Marittima

Fond. Zattere Ponte Lungo

Campo S. Trovaso

S. Maria del Rosario ai Gesuati

Beccarie
Calle d. Celeria

S. Giobbe

Calle d. Cannaregio
Fond. Savorgnan

CANNAREGIO

Calle Riello
Pte. d. Guglie

Pal. Zeno

Fond. Pescaria

Fond. dei Riformati

Contarini

Fondamenta della Sensa

Fond. degli Ormesini

S. Alvise

Fond. G. Contarini

Museo Ebraico

Ghetto

Rio Terrà S. Leonardo
Campiello d. Anconetta

Pal. Labia
Pal. Gritti

S. Marcuola

S. Geremia

Canal Grande

Fondaco dei Turchi

C.S. Giov. Decollato

S. Giacomo dall'Orio
R. Bella
Campo d. Strope

S. Simeon Profeta

Staz. Ferroviaria
S. Lucia

Ponte Scalzi

Riva di Biasio

Fond. Santa Lucia

Fond. S. Chiara

S. Simeone Picc.

Conte Canal

Campo d. Lana

Lacca

Campo S. Andrea

Autorimessa
Piazzale Roma

S. CROCE

Rio Terrà dei Pensieri

S. Maria Maggiore

Fond. delle Procuratie

S. Nicolò da Tolentino

Sala S. Pantalon

Scuola Grande di San Rocco

S. Rocco

Santa Maria Gloriosa dei Frari

C. d. Preti Crosera

Pal. Pisani-Moretta

Calle Contarini

Fond. Rossa

Fond. Foscarini

Campo Santa Margherita

Pal. Balbi

Ca' Foscari

Pal. Cont. d. Figure

Scuola Grande d. Carmini

Pal. Zenobio

Ca' Rezzonico

Pal. Grassi

Calle lunga S. Barnaba

Pal. Loredan d. Amb.

Ca' del Duca

Pal. Contarini degli Scrigni

Calle di Borgo

Gallerie dell'Accademia

Ponte dell'Accademia

Pal. Contarini del Zaffo

Collezione Guggenh.

DORSODURO

Spirito Sant

Campo S. Agostin

Casa di Aldo Manuzio

C-llo Albrizzi

S. POLO

Pal. Corner-Mocenigo

S. Polo

Pal. Coccina

Pal. Cappello

Pal. Bernardo

Pal. Barbarigo della Terrazza

Pal. Corner Spinelli

S. Stefano

C. S. Stefano
F. Morosini

S. MARCO

La F

Pal. Pisani

Pal. Corner

Canal G

Rio Terra

Pal. Vendramin Calergi

Pal. Belloni Battagià

Pal. Moncenigo

Pal. Babarigo

Ca' Pes

Ca'

Pal. Corner d. Regin

Pes

Museo Ebraico

Pal. Correr

Fond. Tint

Fond. Misericordia

TOUR 1 — Sestiere di San Marco
Start and and finish at the Piazza San Marco … ► **page 143**

TOUR 2 — Sestiere di San Polo e Santa Croce
Venetian local local colour … ► **page 145**

Torcello, Burano, S. Erasmo, ↙
Murano, S. Francesco

S. Michele
in Isola

N

200 m

© *Baedeker*

Cimitero S. Michele

★ *Isola di S. Michele*

TOUR 3 **Sestiere Cannaregio**
In Cannaregio life is still normal … ► page 148

TOUR 4 **Sestiere Dorsoduro**
From fishing wharfs to high-end residences… ► page 151

Out and About in Venice

How long to stay Is a day trip to Venice worth it? Of course! But it only provides a first impression – no more, no less. Two to three days are the minimum for a short visit. One week is recommended – this allows time to get to know **the different sides of the city**. Palaces, museums and churches with more than 1000 years of architecture, sculpture and painting display **the cultural side of** Venice. At the Biennale and film festivals, the city hosts the »jet set«. And in quieter corners, away from the main tourist routes, the **everyday world** of Venice is waiting to be discovered. To see what makes this city unique, a quick trip to the **lagoon** and the islands is a »must«. One week also leaves enough time for trips further afield. Depending on tastes and interests, the options include a **leisurely boat trip** on the Brenta canal, an ancient waterway with long idyllic stretches. For sun, sea air, **sandy beaches** and a swim in the Adriatic, go to the Lido or on the peninsula of Litorale del Cavallino.

 ## DON'T MISS

- A trip by vaporetto on the Grand Canal
- Piazza San Marco at the south end of the Grand Canal, the heart of the city
- Have a look from the Campanile; it offers a unique view across the city and the lagoon.
- Basilica di San Marco & Palazzo Ducale
- Sample the legendary coffee houses around Piazza San Marco.
- Walk through the Mercerie, the shopping paradise between Piazza San Marco and the Rialto.
- Gallerie dell'Accademia, a treasure chest of Venetian painting
- Boat trip to the lagoon and islands

A compact city Venice is a compact city that can comfortably be crossed on foot in about an hour. Before or after viewing the **main sights**, allow **chance** take over for a while: »It's all right to get lost in Venice – you won't get far in any case. The worst thing that can happen is that you will find the edge and end up looking at the lagoon.« (Tiziano Scarpa, *Venice is a fish)*. It is not possible to get lost. Venice grew out of numerous small islands with their own core consisting of a church, campanile and campo (piazza). Find your way either by the city map, or after searching briefly at a corner for a yellow sign or arrow giving the direction to »Rialto«, »San Marco«, »Ferrovia« (railway station) or »Accademia«, or allow a friendly Venetian to show you the way.

Tour 1 Sestiere di San Marco

Start and finish: Piazza San Marco   **Duration:** 1 day

The start and finish of this first tour is Piazza San Marco (St Mark's Square), probably one of the most famous squares in the world. The Sestiere San Marco, the »sixth of the city« that surrounds it, has been the heart of Venice since its foundation. Its luxury hotels, restaurants and shops make it the tourist centre of Venice.

Start at the busy ❶ ✳ ✳ **Piazza San Marco**, the »most beautiful salon in the world« (Napoleon). To get your bearings, take the elevator to the top of the ✳ **Campanile**, which provides a marvellous view across the older part of the city and the lagoon. Next, visit the ✳ ✳ **Basilica di San Marco** and ✳ ✳ **Palazzo Ducale**, centre of power for centuries.

Now leave Piazza San Marco and slowly walk west along the elegant shopping street ❷ ✳ ✳ **Calle Larga XXII Marzo** to ❸ **Campo San Maurizio**. Surrounded by proud patrician palaces, ❹ ✳ **Campo Santo Stefano**, one of the most spacious squares in the city with numerous cafes, bars and restaurants, is the next stop and a good place for

Pala d'Oro, goldsmith masterpiece in St Mark's Basilica

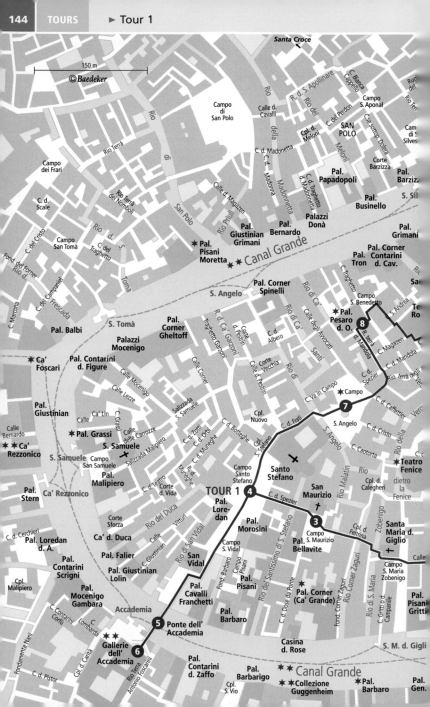

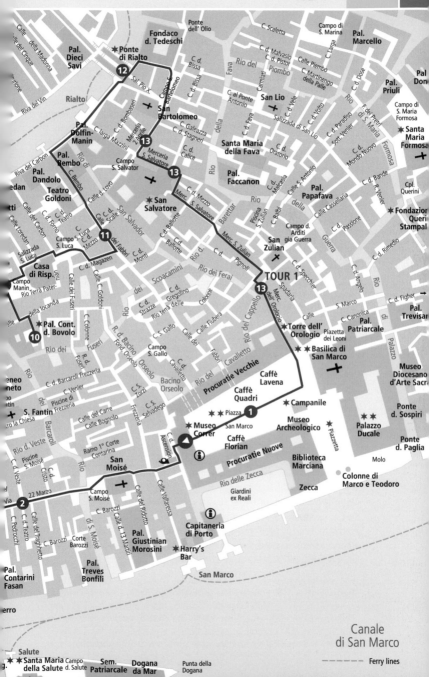

Calle della Madonna
Calle del Cinque
Pal. Dieci Savi
✷ Ponte di Rialto
12
Rialto
Riva del Vin
Pal. Dolfin-Manin
Pal. Bembo
Pal. Dandolo
Teatro Goldoni
11
Casa di Risp.
Campo Manin
Rio Terra Pater-
✷ Pal. Cont. d. Bovolo
10
Rio dei
✷ S. Fantin
la Chiesa
2
22 Marzo
Via
Pal. Contarini Fasan
Pal. Treves Bonfili

Ponte dell' Olio
Fondaco d. Tedeschi
C. Scaletta
Campo di S. Marina
Pal. Marcello
C. Larga
Rio del Piombo
Calle Piembo
C. d. Pistor
Pal. Priuli
Pal. Don
C. d. Dose
C. d. Bissa
Rio del
Carimati
Martinengo della Palle
San Lio
Campo di S. Maria Formosa
✷ Santa Maria Formosa
San Bartolomeo
13
Mercerie 2 Aprile
C. Galeazza
C. d. Stagneri
Santa Maria della Fava
C. d. Oratorio
C. d. Paradiso
Sott. Venier
C. d. Mondo Nuovo
Campo S. Salvator
Merceria S. Salvatore
13
Rio
Pal. Faccanon
C. d. Bande
R. Venier
Cpl. Querini
✷ San Salvatore
Merc. S. Salvatore
Pal. Papafava
✷ Fondazion Queri Stampal
San Zulian
TOUR 1
13
Merc. Orologio
S. Marco
C. d. Figher
Pal. Trevisar
✷ Torre dell' Orologio
Piazzetta dei Leoni
Pal. Patriarcale
✷✷ Basilica di San Marco
Museo Diocesano d'Arte Sacra
Procuratie Vecchie
Caffè Lavena
Caffè Quadri
✷✷ Piazza **1**
San Marco
✷ Museo Correr
Caffè Florian
Procuratie Nuove
✷ Campanile
Museo Archeologico
Palazzo Ducale
Ponte d. Sospiri
Ponte d. Paglia
Biblioteca Marciana
San Moisé
Rio delle Zecca
Giardini ex Reali
Zecca
Molo
Colonne di Marco e Teodoro
Campo S. Moisé
Capitaneria di Porto
Pal. Giustinian Morosini
✷ Harry's Bar
San Marco

Salute
✷✷ Santa Maria della Salute
Campo d. Salute
Sem. Patriarcale
Dogana da Mar
Punta della Dogana
Canale di San Marco
– – – – Ferry lines

a diversion to the south. A wooden bridge, **❺Ponte dell'Accademia**, leads across the Grand Canal to the **❻✷ ✷ Gallerie dell'Accademia**, the most significant collection of Venetian paintings. In the Palazzo Venier dei Leoni, slightly down the canal, the **✷ ✷ Collezione Peggy Guggenheim** has a fine exhibition of modern art. The museum café is a convenient place to take a break. Return to Campo Santo Stefano, past the church of the same name to the pretty **❼Campo Sant'Angelo** and **❽✷ Palazzo Pesaro degli Orfei**, where there is a museum about Mario Fortuny, the last resident and creator of sensual dreams in plissé. At **❾Campo Manin**, where a monument to the patriotic lawyer Daniele Martin stands, it is worth taking a quick walk to **❿✷ Palazzo Contarini del Bovolo**, where the inner courtyard has a lovely spiral staircase dating from around 1500.

Via Campo San Luca, walk past the stores on **⓫Calle dei Fabbri** to the Grand Canal or the **⓬✷ Ponte di Rialto**, which was the only bridge across the canal until the 19th century. Return to Piazza San Marco along the **⓭✷ ✷ Mercerie**, which lure passers-by into shopping heaven. Everything is available here – fashionable clothing stores, carnival masks and costumes, the finest Burano lace, artistic Murano glass as well as jewellery. At the end, relax in one of the cafes around **❶✷ ✷ Piazza San Marco** and listen to the house musicians over a cappuccino or aperitif while enjoying the unforgettable atmosphere of the square.

Tour 2 Sestiere di San Polo e Santa Croce

Start: Santa Lucia railway station **Duration:** 6 hours
Finish: Piazza San Marco

The second walk leads through the city districts of San Polo and Santa Croce, which are more down-to-earth than San Marco and lie in the upper loop of the Grand Canal. This area contains not only the economic heart of Venice – the Rialto market – but also the fantastic Frari church and the Scuola Grande di San Rocco. Narrow alleys, homes and workshops existing side by side, and many campi and campielli are features of both districts.

The starting point is the Grand Canal footbridge, **❶✷ Ponte di Rialto**, between **✷ Fondaco dei Tedeschi** (left bank, Sestiere San Marco) and the lovely **❷Palazzo dei Camerlenghi** (San Polo). On weekdays from the early morning, **❸✷ the Rialto market** with its colourful fruit and vegetable stands begins right behind the bridge. A visit to the market is one of the most enjoyable experiences in

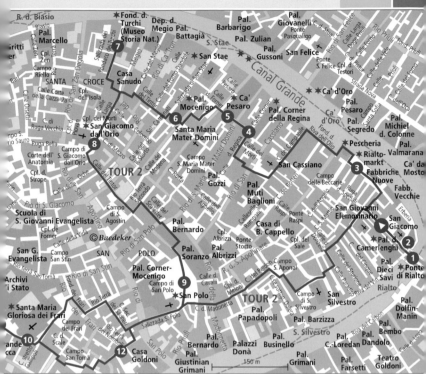

Venice. Around the Rialto market there are numerous reasonably priced Bacari which offer a chance to sample Venetian wines and Cicheti, Venetian snacks. The church of San Giacomo di Rialto at the busy Ruga degli Orefici is said to be the city's oldest church. Continue past the Fabbriche Nuove to the **Pescheria**, where fishermen offer their wares every morning except Sunday and Monday. Head across Campo S. Cassiano and past the mighty Baroque palace ➍ ✶ **Corner della Regina** to the imposing ➎ ✶ **Ca' Pesaro**, where the ground floor houses the **Galleria d'Arte Moderna** and the third storey the **Museo d'Arte Orientale**. Only a few steps farther, ➏ **Palazzo Mocenigo** presents a collection of precious fabrics and costumes. Information about the flora and fauna of the lagoon is found in the Museum of Natural Science in the ➐ ✶ **Fondaco dei Turchi**. Next go south along narrow canals to the church ➑ ✶ **San Giacomo dell'Orio** with its impressive ceiling. At noon, the piazza of the same name is like a playground; its inviting cafés are a good place for a break. The next goal is Campo San Polo, one of the largest squares in Venice, which is named after St Paul. In summer it is a venue for open-air cinema. ➒ ✶ **San Polo** church, for which the piazza is named, has a *Last Supper* by Tintoretto.

Baedeker TIP

Off Piazza San Marco

The Comune di Venezia along with the Touring Club Italiana has put together a couple of walking tours in order to present some of the less well-knwon treasures of the city on the lagoon. The map with descriptions is available at the tourist offices. The following tour is based on the tour »From Santa Lucia railway station to the Fondamenta Nuove«.

A visit to the famous Frari church, properly called ⑩ ✳ ✳ **Santa Maria Gloriosa dei Frari**, with masterpieces by Titian, Bellini and Donatello, is a must for art lovers. At 70m/ 233 feet, its bell tower is one of the highest in Venice.

In the immediate neighbourhood is the ⑪ ✳ ✳ **Scuola Grande di San Rocco** with paintings by Tintoretto, also a main point of interest in Venice.

The return route to the **Ponte di Rialto** passes ⑫ ✳ **Casa Goldoni**, once the residence of the illustrious comic poet. A ✳ ✳ **gondola trip** through the canals is a wonderful end to the day. Or simply stroll through the crooked alleys, across the innumerable bridges and magical piazzas, and let the special charm of Venice away from the main tourist track cast its spell on you.

Tour 3 Cannaregio

Start: Santa Lucia railway station
Finish: Fondamenta Nuove

Duration: 3 hours

This walk leads through Cannaregio in the north-western part of Venice. Before the construction of the railway bridge, this sestiere was the main entrance to the city. Here, visitors still find the everyday world of Venice, some handsome churches, palaces and the oldest ghetto of the world.

❶ **Santa Lucia railway station** (1954; it bears the house number 1 of this city quarter) stands on the site of two monasteries which were destroyed to build Ponte della Libertà (the construction of this connection between the mainland and the city began in 1841). They are commemorated in the church **Santa Maria degli Scalzi** (1654; B. Longhena). Follow Rio Terrà Lista di Spagna to Campo Santa Geremia; here stands the magnificent ❷ ✳ **Palazzo Labia** (mid-17th century), today the seat of RAI, the state radio and television institution. On **Ponte delle Guglie**, cross the Canal di Cannaregio and on the opposite side, walk through Sottoportego del Ghetto into the first and oldest ❸ ✳ ✳ **ghetto** in Europe (►Baedeker Special p. 202). Leaving Campo Ghetto Nuovo, cross Rio della Misericordia and turn left into Calle Turlona. Continue across Rio della Sensa to Palazzo Michiel (16th century), left again into Calle dei Riformati to Fondamenta dei Riformati and the former Carmelite nunnery (ex Monas-

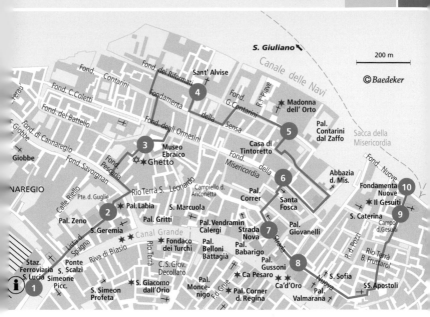

tero delle Carmelitane Scalze) and ❹**Sant'Alvise** church. Zigzag
(across Rio di S. Alvise into Calle di Capitello, left into Fondamenta
della Sensa and Calle Loredan), to Fondamenta Madonna dell'Orto.
Immediately after crossing Rio Madonna dell'Orto, you reach the
small Corte Cavallo, *horse court*, the former site of the foundry in
which Verrocchio had his equestrian monument of Bartolomeo Colleoni cast in 1496. Slightly east, the former Scuola dei Mercanti (remodelled in 1570 by Palladio) and the beautiful brick church ❺ ★
Madonna dell'Orto, a place of pilgrimage for Tintoretto fans, lie on
Campo della Madonna dell'Orto. Cross Campo dei Mori, the »piazza
of the Moors« named after the four statues on the house walls, pass
the house where Tintoretto died and reach Campo dell'Abbazia with
the Chiesa S. Maria della Misericordia, founded in the 10th century,
and the Scuola Vecchia, the former meeting house of the silk weavers' guild. Across Rio dell'Abbazia, pass the Scuola Nuova della Misericordia, built in 1583 by Sansovino but not completed, and Palazzo Lezze (1670; Longhena) to the little church of San Marziale
(1721) with a richly decorated Baroque interior. From here, cross
two bridges to ❻**Campo Santa Fosca**, where a monument (1892)
commemorates Father Paolo Sarpi, a supporter of Venetian independence. Here is the lively ❼**Strada Nova**, which was laid out in
1868–1878 parallel to the Grand Canal as a link between the railway
station and the centre of Rialto. Palazzo Correr Contarini at the very
beginning of Strada Nova dates from the 15th century; just a little
further, on the opposite side of the street in a walled garden, is Palaz-

zo Giovanelli (15th century). From Rio di Noale there is a beautiful view of its façade; the outside stairway dates from the 19th century. At the Renaissance church of **San Felice** with its five domes (one of Tintoretto's oldest paintings, *St Demetrius and a Donor from the Ghissi Family* hangs inside); continue to the elegant ❽ ✳ ✳ **Ca' d'Oro**. Strada Nova joins **Campo dei Santi Apostoli**, where the church has an eye-catching campanile. This is a convenient place for a short detour to the church of **Santa Maria dei Miracoli**. Behind the choir of Santi Apostoli church the street called first Rio Terrà dei Santi Apostoli, then Salizzada Seriman that leads to Campo dei Gesuiti. On the left, take a look at Palazzo Zen (1534, ascribed to S. Serlio, while the Oratorio dei Crociferi with a significant cycle of paintings by Palma the Younger (1583–1591; viewing times: Apr-Oct Fri, Sat, 3.30–6.30 pm) and the Jesuit church ❾ ✳ **I Gesuiti** are further along on the right. A short side trip across Calle Larga dei Botteri (just behind I Gesuiti) leads to the home and workshop of Titian (behind a brick

Santa Maria dei Miracoli, masterpiece from the early Renaissance

wall). Take **Salizzada degli Specchieri** to ❿**Fondamenta Nuove**, the »new quay« founded in 1589, to look across at the cemetery island **San Michele** and ✱ ✱ **Murano**. Boats to the lagoon islands also depart from here.

Tour 4 Dorsoduro – »hard back«

Start: Santa Lucia railway station   **Duration:** 3 hours
Finish: Zattere

Unlike the other sestiere of Venice, Dorsoduro, the district between the Grand Canal (north-east) and the Canale della Giudecca, stands not on tree-trunk piles, but on solid island soil. It has a varied character. The western part was originally occupied by fishermen, sailors and workers. Some of the industrial or church buildings here now house parts of the university. Campo Santa Margherita is a favourite meeting place. East of the Accademia, Dorsoduro has become one of the most popular (and most expensive!) residential areas.

This tour also starts from ❶**Santa Lucia railway station**. Past the Chiesa degli Scalzi, cross the bridge of the same name to the south bank of the Grand Canal. Following the signs for »Frari«, first walk along a narrow alley and then along a canal to the south-east. After several changes of direction, you will reach a church decorated with paintings by Titian and named ❷✱ ✱ **Santa Maria Gloriosa dei Frari**. Another highlight is close by – the ❸✱ ✱ **Scuola Grande di San Rocco** with paintings by Tintoretto. Follow Scuola Grande and Calle San Pantalon to the extensive ❹**Campo Santa Margherita**, one of the most popular piazzas in the city with many cafes and bars, where there is a small fruit and vegetable market in the mornings. The ❺✱ **Scuola Grande dei Carmini** at its southern tip is worth visiting for the ceiling painted by Giambattista Tiepolo. Now follow the canal on the rear side of the Scuola (Fondamenta Briati). At the beautiful ❻**Palazzo Zenobio**, cross the canal and follow Fondamenta Briati. It becomes Fondamenta Barbarigo and joins Corte Maggiore. Cross the canal again. From Fondamenta della Teresa there is a view of the so-called **Case Tron** opposite, 18th-century townhouses with seven chimneys. This is the start of the old workers' quarter Santa Marta, which dates from the first decades of the 20th century. Slightly farther west, the route ends at a cotton-spinning factory, today part of the architectural college. Here stands one of Venice's oldest churches, ❼**San Nicolò dei Mendicoli**, in its present form dating from the 16th century. Return via Fondamenta Lizza and a bridge to the church San Angelo Raffaele. It is decorated by a lovely scene

from the legend of Tobias by Franceso Guardi (1750). For the Renaissance church ❽ **San Sebastiano**, Veronese, who is also laid to rest here, created a major cycle of paintings. From Campo San Sebastiano, cross the canal of the same name and go south a short distance on Fondamenta San Basilio. Turn left into the narrow Calle della Chiesa, follow Fondamenta Ognissanti and Rio Ognissanti to Campo ❾ **San Trovaso** with San Trovaso church and the Squero di San Trovaso, Venice's oldest gondola workshop. Only a few minutes' walk farther south, a view opens up across the Canale della Giudecca onto the island of **Giudecca** with the conspicuous Mulino Stucky and the Redentore church. Here is ❿ ✳ **Zattere**, Venice's »sun promenade« with numerous bars, ice cream salons and restaurants. From here, it is approximately 1.5km/1mi to the **Punta della Dogana** at the eastern tip of Dorsoduro.

Tour 5   By ferry to the lagoon

Start: Fondamenta Nuove   **Duration:** 1 day
Finish: S. Zaccaria

It is the lagoon that makes Venice unique. Here are suggestions for an »exploration« by ferry. Up-to-date ferry timetables are available at the ferry terminals; Fondamenta Nuove (Cannaregio) and San Zaccaria (San Marco) are the most important. Various lines can be combined (for further information see the websites www.act-v.it, www.comune.venezia.it and www.venicecard.it; click on »Itinerari«).

The well-known islands of Murano, Torcello and Burano can be reached by public ferry. The boat LN (Laguna North) passes the cemetery island ✳ **San Michele** towards ✳ ✳ **Murano**, home to a glass-blowing workshop since 1291. Continuing to Mazzorbo, the boat also passes uninhabited islands such as San Giacomo in Paludo, where pilgrims stopped on their way to the Holy Land from the 11th century, and Madonna del Monte, seat of a 14th-century Benedictine monastery. **Mazzorbo**, which was probably settled as early as the 6th century, still has 350 inhabitants. Of the former five churches and six monasteries, only Chiesa di Santa Caterina (late 13th century) remains. It is possible to walk to the neighbouring island of Burano from here via a wooden bridge.

Next, the boat visits the fishing island of ✱ ✱ **Burano**, whose colourful houses glow from afar. To visit ✱ ✱ **Torcello**, it is necessary to change boats here. The adjacent island, which is now home to less than 50 people, was once the most important settlement in the lagoon. Now you can return from Burano via Mazzorbo and Murano directly to Fondamenta Nuove. However, it is also possible to go from Burano via Treporti and Punta Sabbioni, two stops on the Cavallino peninsula, to the ✱ **Lido**, returning to Venice (San Zaccaria quay) from there.

Cathedral S. Maria Assunta on Torcello the mosaic »The Final Judgement«

The typical brightly painted façades of houses on Burano

Line 13 (from Fondamenta Nuove, ending in Treporti; connection ►
above) is the route to the »vegetable islands« of the lagoon, **Le Vignole** and **Sant' Erasmo**.
✳ **San Francesco del Deserto**, the small island to the north-east
ahead of Sant'Erasmo, is accessible only by water taxi or private boat,
e.g. from Sant'Erasmo.

Excursions

! *Baedeker* TIP

Excursions to the lagoon

Venice »swims« in a lagoon which is approximately 25 miles long. Organized tours, for
whole or half days, by vaporetto, motor and
sailing boat and with expert guidance, are
offered, among others, by RiViviNatura (►p.
132). The trips provide introductions to the
islands, their history, culture and arts as well as
the lagoon ecosystem.

For visitors with time and interest, here are some suggestions
for further trips outside Venice.

The islands of ✳ **Giudecca** and
✳ **San Giorgio Maggiore** are also worth a trip. From the campanile of San Giorgio Maggiore,
there is a wonderful view over
the city and the lagoon. For perfect sunbathing go to the sandy
beaches of the ✳ **Lido**, where
world-class films and actors are

awarded the Golden Lion at the Palazzo del Cinema every year in early August. Beach-lovers flock to the nearly 20km/12mi-long peninsula ✳ **Litorale del Cavallino** and the Lido di Jesolo, which have excellent camping and bathing areas (there are bus and boat connections between Piazzale Roma, San Zaccaria and Jesolo and Cavallino/Treporti).

Baedeker TIP

A quiet lunch

A place to eat lunch away from the busy tourist areas: Trattoria Alla Maddalena, directly by the quay for Mazzorbo (daily except for Thursdays, 12.30–3pm; tel. 041 73 01 51). On Sundays, it is best to make a reservation if you would like to sit on the terrace or in the garden.

The splendour of past days comes to life on a boat trip along the Brenta canal to the most beautiful **villas of Venetia**. From March to October, various operators run boats between Venice and Padua (information in the tourist offices of Padua and Venice). Barely 40km/25mi inland, the lively old university town of **Padua** with its art treasures is also worth a longer visit. It is reached most quickly and easily by train or bus (information: APT Padua, Riviera Mugnai 8, I-35137 Padova, Stazione Ferrovie, tel. 04 98 75 20 77, fax 04 98 75 50 08, www.turismopadova.it).

Sights from A to Z

ST MARK'S BASILICA, THE MAGNIFICENT DOGE'S PALAC THE PALACES OF NOBLES ON GRAND CANAL – THESE ARE ONLY A FEW OF THE HIGHLIGHTS OF VENICE.

Arsenale

Location: Rio dell'Arsenale   **Quay:** Arsenale

A fort in the middle of the city

From the beginning, the power of Venice was based on the arts of shipbuilding and navigation. Consequently the arsenal, the shipyard, was an important symbol of the maritime republic. It was founded in 1104. In the following centuries, it was constantly expanded and fortified. Aside from merchant ships with capacious holds and long, nimble war galleys, it also produced slinging machines, catapults and later, cannon. At its height, the shipyard employed up to 16,000 workers. As keepers of secrets, the arsenalotti enjoyed high regard and such privileges as an old age pension and free housing. The organization of the work was reminiscent of conveyor-belt production. This made it possible, as early as 1188, to produce up to 100 new galleys for the high seas within half a year. In 1571, the year of a battle against the Turkish fleet, 100 galleys were built in 60 days. Until the

Ingresso di Terra, ground entrance into the arsenal. The »workshop« of the trade metropolis was probably the first industrial operation in the middle ages.

end of the 18th century, the Arsenale was regarded as one of the largest and most productive shipyards in the world, admired by visitors almost as much as St Mark's Basilica or the Doge's Palace.

The Dante bust commemorates the visit of the Florentine poet **Dante Alighieri**, who immortalized the Arsenale in his *Divine Comedy*: »As the Venetians in the Arsenale boil the thick tar in wintertime in order to seal their leaking ships which are no longer seaworthy, while one builds a new ship and another tightens the ribs of a ship which has made numerous journeys, one hammers on the bow and one on the stern, one carves paddles whilst another twists ropes, yet another repairs top and mizzen sails, it is there that not through fire, no, but through the art of God, a thick black porridge boils, rendering the stony banks sticky all around.« (XXI Canto; the verses are inscribed on a marble plate to the left of the entrance).

! Baedeker TIP

In the Arsenale
The Arsenale, an area of 32 ha/13 acres owned by the Italian navy, is not open to the public. Only during the Biennale is it possible to get a look inside: the oldest international festival for contemporary art takes place every two years, and the venues include the Arsenale (see p.207).

The Arsenale was a forbidden area, accessible only through one sea and one land entrance. The land entrance, a large gate in the form of an ancient triumphal arch (1460), is one of the first Renaissance monuments in the city. The two lions were brought from Greece as spoils of war by Francesco Morosoni in the 17th century. The sitting lion originally guarded the port of Piraeus, the recumbent lion came from Delos and was once set up on the Sacred Way between Athens and Eleusis.

Ingresso di Terra

In the maritime museum, the former grain store of the Arsenale opposite the church of San Biagio, much can be learned about the history of Venice as a sea power. Exhibits include spoils from the innumerable maritime wars of the republic, many different models of ships, navigation instruments, uniforms and documents about shipbuilding and types of ships. One of the main items of interest is the gondola collection, including a 17th-century Bucintoro – the magnificent state galley of the doge burned out in 1798.

★
Museo Storico Navale
⏲
Opening hours:
Mon–Sat
9am–1.30pm

Behind the bridge is the start of the unusually wide Via Garibaldi, built in 1808 under Napoleon. On the very first house, a marble plate commemorates Giovanni and Sebastiano Caboto, who discovered Newfoundland, Labrador and Greenland in 1497. The street, which is lined by many small shops and cafés and barely touched by tourism, leads to Isola di San Pietro with the cathedral ▶San Pietro di Castello. Halfway there is the entrance gate of the ▶ Giardini Pubblici.

Via Garibaldi

✱✱ Basilica di San Marco

G/H 12

Location: Piazza San Marco

Quay: Vallaresso S. Marco., San Zaccaria

⏱
Opening hours:
Mon–Sat
9.30am–5pm
Sun from 2pm

The unique Basilica di San Marco (St Mark's Basilica) with its five domes, traceried arches and windows, the core which goes back 1000 years, is the church of the doge, the state church of the republic, the monumental shrine for St Mark and, since 1807, a cathedral too. The magnificent décor of the basilica is partly the result of a law of Doge Domenico Selvo, who ordered the entire city to participate in adorning St Mark's Basilica in 1075: he required everyone who came home from a voyage to bring a precious ornament for the »house of Saint Mark«. This explains the numerous architectural fragments and ornaments from the orient – columns, reliefs, sculptures and jewellers' work from a large variety of materials.

Building history
Today's building is the third on the site. The first St Mark's Basilica was built after the arrival of the relics of St Mark, which two sailors took from Alexandria in 828 (►History p.34). The church was destroyed by a fire in the Doge's Palace in 976, and rebuilt. This building was torn down in the 11th century and replaced by the existing church. Its initiator was Doge Domenico Contarini (1043–1070), for which reason it is often known as the **Contarini church**. The layout was that of the preceding buildings: a Greek cross with two aisles, with a dome above the crossing and four smaller domes over the arms of the cross. In 1094, the basilica was consecrated in the presence of Holy Roman Emperor Henry IV and made the state church. After the conquest of Constantinople in 1204, the domes were raised, the north vestibule added and the west front designed as a columned façade. The brick building, which had been nearly undecorated until then, was richly adorned inside and out with marble, mosaics and innumerable pieces of booty. A last construction phase, the Gothicization of St Mark's Basilica, began in the second half of the 14th century and lasted into the 16th century. On the exterior the upper storey, in particular, was altered (windows were embellished with tracery, arches with decorative gables and tabernacles with statues, etc). Inside, additional structures such as the Cappella Mascoli and the Cappella Zeno were built.

DON'T MISS

- the stone floor of San Marco (most of it is unfortunately hidden under carpets) and the mosaics
- the Pala d'Oro behind the high altar
- the four horses of San Marco on the loggia of the basilica
- attending one of the infrequent concerts or mass (e.g. on Sunday every hour from 7am to 10am), in order to appreciate the unique acoustics of San Marco

Outside Appearance

St Mark's Basilica has three façades: the main façade to Piazza San Marco, the southern façade to the Piazzetta and the sea, and the north façade to Piazzetta dei Leoncini.

Two round-arched portals decorated with mosaics in deep niches dominate the west façade. Precious spolia columns in various colours are arranged on the sides of the portal in two rows, one above the other. The larger central portal penetrates the balustrade of the terrace, on which bronze copies of the horses of Saint Mark stand. The central arch is emphasized by its size and the angel stairway which leads to the statue of Saint Mark. The mosaics of the lunettes in the side niches of the portals show the story of St Mark's relics, beginning on the far right with the removal of the body from Alexandria, veneration of the relics and their arrival in Venice – all work of the 17th and 18th centuries. The only mosaic from the 13th century is above the outer left portal, the Porta di San Alippio. It shows the transfer of the saint's body into St Mark's Basilica and the external appearance of the church in the 13th century before it was altered in the Gothic style.

★ ★
West façade

Detail of the heavenly staircase above the centre arch

The lunette of the main portal shows Christ as the judge of the world with the Judgment Day (1836). The mosaics of the upper storey depict scenes from the passion of Christ to his ascension (17th century). The inner surfaces of the arches are ornamented with Byzantine-Roman reliefs. The central arch shows many different crafts (mid-13th century). The reliefs in the spaces of the outer arcade arches depict scenes from the legend of Hercules (13th century).

The three **flagstaffs** of cedar wood before the west façade were placed there in 1376. In 1505, they received fine iron bases from the workshop of Alessandro Leopardi. The reliefs of the central pedestal show Justice between elephants (a symbol of strength and wisdom) and Pallas (symbol of plenty). The southern pedestal depicts nereids

Basilica di San Marco *Plan*

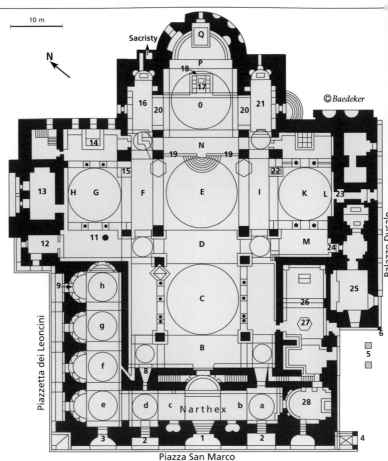

10 m

Sacristy

N

© Baedeker

Piazzetta dei Leoncini

Piazza San Marco

1 Main door
2 Iron grille by Venetian master Bertuccius (c. 1300)
3 Porta di S. Alippio
4 Pietra del Bando
5 Pilastri Acritani
6 Sculpture: the tetrarchs
7 To Museo Marciano
8 Porta di San Pietro
9 Porta dei Fiori
10 Altar of the Annunciation
11 Romanesque holy water basin with angels (12th century)
12 Capella dei Mascoli
13 Capella di Sant' Isidoro

14 Capella della Madonna Nicopeia
15 Altare di San Paolo
16 Capella di San Pietro
17 High altar
18 Pala d'Oro
19 Iconostasis
20 Reliquary shrines
21 Capella di San Clemente
22 Altare di San Giacomo
23 Connection to Doge's Palace
24 Entrance to treasury
25 Treasury (tesoro)
26 Baptistery
27 Baptismal font (1546)

28 Capella Zeno (for Cardinal G. B. Zeno, † 1501)

MOSAICS

a Genesis
b Noah's ark
c Story of Noah and the Tower of Babel
d Story of Abraham
e-g Story of Joseph
h Story of Moses

A Paradise
B Apocalypse
C Whitsun

D Scenes of Christ's passion
E Ascension of Christ
F St Michael with sv
G Life of St John
H Life of the Virgin
I Washing of feet, Temptations in the wilderness
K St Leonard's dome
L Four miracles of Je
M Legend of St Mark
N St Peter, resurrecti etc
O Choir mosaics
P Lamb of God
Q Christ as Pantocra'

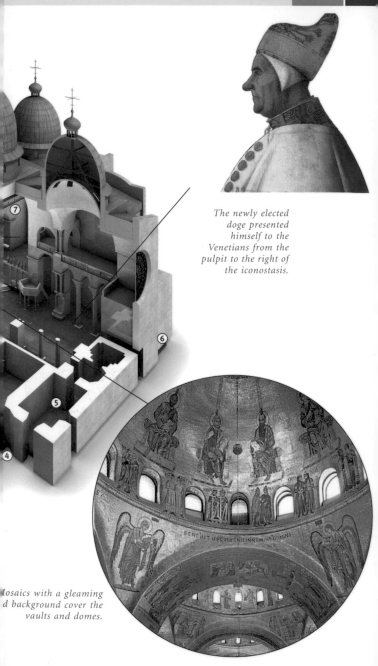

The newly elected
doge presented
himself to the
Venetians from the
pulpit to the right of
the iconostasis.

Mosaics with a gleaming
gold background cover the
vaults and domes.

Detail of the angle staircase that leads up to the statue of St Mark's.

8

... four bronze horses ... e from Greece. They ... decorated the ... nphal arch of Emperor ... an in Rome. The origi- ... are on display in the ... eo Marciano. Copies ... t visitors to San Marco ... the centre entrance.

2

1

3

© Baedeker

g|

and begin in the southern arch of the west vestibules with scenes from Genesis, and continue in the following arches with the stories of Noah, Abraham, Joseph and Moses.

Some niches contain doges' tombs from the 12th century. The southern Porta San Clemente is particularly noteworthy. Its bronze door, which originated in Constantinople, reached Venice in the 11th century. A copy of it was used as a central portal in the 12th century. The grille door which separates the Cappella Zeno from the narthex is also from Byzantium.

Interior

** **
Mosaics

The spatial effect of the interior is determined by the five domes which rest on massive columns and are connected to wide barrel vaults. San Marco has more mosaics than any other church in the West. They cover an area of 4,240 sq m/45,640 sq ft and mainly date from the 12th and 13th centuries, but were partly replaced between 1500 and 1750 according to new designs by Titian, Tintoretto, Veronese and Tiepolo, among others. The main themes are developed between the apse and the exit, beginning with Christ as Pantocrator in the east and closing with the apocalypse in the west. Between them are the events from the passion to the ascension of Christ. The wall surfaces of the north and south arms of the transept show stories of saints and the parents of Jesus.

Pentecost Dome

Closest to the main entrance is the Pentecost Dome, probably the oldest in the church (late 12th century). The Holy Spirit floats at its centre as a dove, sending fiery tongues over the twelve apostles enthroned at the lower edge of the dome.

Passion Vault

In the Passion Vault, between the Pentecost Dome and the Ascension Dome, the capture and crucifixion of Christ and Christ in limbo are shown (around 1200).

Ascension Dome

In the central dome (12th century), Christ floats in a circle of stars borne by angels, below it the Virgin at prayer with two angels and twelve apostles separated by olive trees. The pendentives are occupied by the four evangelists.

Choir dome

The dome over the choir shows Christ giving blessing, surrounded by prophets and the Virgin. The mosaic dates from the 12th century. Parts of it were renewed after the fire in 1231; this is visible in the gold ground, where the old parts appear different from the new parts. The apse mosaic with the Pantocrator is from 1506.

Unfortunately, the mosaics in the right aisle of the choir are very difficult to decipher. They provide a lively description of the **legend of St Mark** and are among the oldest mosaics in the church.

and tritons, the northern one Neptune, to whom a satyr offers the fruits of the earth – a demonstration of Venice's rule on water and land.

The former Porta da Mar, the entrance from the sea which was used for ceremonial purposes, was removed in 1503 in favour of the Cappella Zeno (inside the church the portal, which is decorated with mosaics of the legend of St Mark, is still visible). The traceried gate to its right leads into the narthex of the baptistery. Next to it are the smooth, marble-clad outer wall of the Tesoro (treasury). For the second storey, the scheme of the west façade was used, but with more window openings and marble-clad tympana. Note the two griffins on the first arch, which may originally have been integrated into the portal, and the Byzantine Madonna mosaic (13th century) before which two lamps are lit every evening.

South façade

The Tetrarchs, four embracing porphyry men

The marble columns before the south façade, the so-called **Pilastri Acritani**, were probably made in Constantinople in the 6th century. At the south-west corner of the Tesoro, towards the Doge's Palace, the **tetrarchs**, four embracing men of porphyry, are built into the wall. These are also spoils from Constantinople, made in the 4th century in the Eastern Roman Empire. They may represent the jointly ruling emperors Diocletian, Maximian, Valerius and Constantius. Legend regards them as four thieves who were turned to stone during an attempt to rob the treasures of San Marco.

The structure and design of the north façade are similar to the west façade. A Romanesque relief above the Porta dei Fiori (4th arcade) tells of the birth of Christ.

◄ **North façade**

The vestibules (narthexes) of St Mark's Basilica originated in different phases of construction: the west wing with the main portal was part of Contarini's church, while the north wing was not added until the 13th century. Main items of interest include the polychrome marble floors (from the Contarini period in the west section and from the 13th century in the north section) and the 13th-century vault mosaics. The themes come mainly from the Old Testament (while the mosaics inside the basilica are from the New Testament)

★ ★
Vestibules

◄ **Mosaics**

ST. MARK'S BASILICA

✷✷ Private chapel of the doges, state church, and monumental shrine for the state saints – St Mark's Basilica, covered by a huge dome, is one of the most impressive architectural monuments of the city on the lagoon.

🕐 Opening Hours:
Mon - Sat 9.30am - 5.00pm, Sun from 2.00pm
One can also make an appointment for a tour - under tel. 0415 45 9611 or at www.alata.it (at least two days in advance). For photographers: Lighting in the church is usually best before noon.

① Portals
The portals with round arches on the western façade of St Mark's Basilica are deeply recessed. Their adornments: Columns of precious multi-coloured marble and mosaics as well as the work of stonemasons from the 13th century on the central main entrance.

② Façade mosaics
Hidden under a load of pork, merchants transported the body of St Mark's from Alexandria to Venice. The story of this »abduction« is depicted in the mosaics above the portals on the western façade.

③ Baptistery
Mosaics and reliefs on the baptismal font tell about the life of John the Baptist.

The magnificent retable, the so-called Pala d'Oro consists of 250 individual components.

④ Tetrarchs
Mysterious group of figures from the 4th century: Four porphyry men in a heartfelt embrace.

⑤ Tesoro
The booty carried off by Venetians from the vanquished Constantinople in 1204 is now the foundation of the church treasury.

⑥ Legend of St Marcus
The bones of St Mark's were missing since a fire in the church in 976. The mosaic describes the miracle of their rediscovery.

⑦ High altar
The canopy that rests on four columns is the pride of the high altar constructed out of ancient pieces.

⑧ Domes
The domes, which were extended after the conquest of Byzantium in 1204 and have since been visible from St. Mak's Plaza, imbue the structure with an oriental flair.

Section of the floor mosaic

The Dome of St John in the north transept is decorated with scenes from the life of St John (12th century), while the southern Dome of St Leonard depicts St Leonard, St Clement, St Blasius and St Nicholas. On the west wall below the south dome, the rediscovery of the relics of the St Mark is described. According to legend, they had been missing since the church fire in 976. Only long prayers by the doge and the Venetian population brought about the miracle: they appeared out of the opposite wall.

Transept domes

◀ Column miracle

The floor, laid from the 11th and 12th centuries by artists from the east, is of special interest. The mosaics, 2,098 sq m/22,583 sq ft in size and made of polychrome marble, porphyry, serpentine, chalcedony, lapis lazuli and malachite, represent perspective patterns, ornamentation and animal motifs, and are mostly fitted into a square frame – an inexhaustible source of inspiration for all later stone floors.

✶ ✶
Floor

The Zeno chapel (access through the baptistery) was not built until the early 16th century. The free-standing tomb of Cardinal Giambattista Zeno is here. Note the *Madonna della Scarpa*, the Madonna with the shoe: between St Mark and John the Baptist is the seated mother

Tour of Cappella Zeno

Interior of St Marcus Basilica: choir screen and mosaic decorations

of Christ, bronzes cast to designs of Antonio Lombardo (early 16th century). Legend states that a poor person gave the Madonna his left shoe, which was turned into gold as a sign of divine gratitude. The two lions of red marble which bear columns (12th century) may once have been part of the south portal.

Battistero

The mosaics of the baptistery are mid-14th century works. They show scenes from the life of St John the Baptist (on the walls) and the childhood of Christ. The dancing Salome is eerily beautiful, balancing the head of St John in a bowl on her head. The reliefs of the font also refer to St John the Baptist and alternate with depictions of the evangelists. It is likely that Jacopo Sansovino (1486–1570; he is buried before the altar) designed the font.

The baptistery contains the tombs of two doges: the vestibule that of Giovanni Soranzo, while the more detailed tomb of Andrea Dandolo is opposite the entrance; he donated the mosaics and in 1354 was the last doge to be buried in San Marco.

✳
Tesoro

The precious **church treasure** (access to the left beside the passage to the Doge's Palace) primarily consists of spoils brought by Venetians after the conquest of Constantinople in 1204: reliquary shrines of gold and silver, covered in gems and richly decorated, chalices, glasses, liturgical objects, ivory work, icons and tapestries. The most significant items include the throne of St Mark, a marble relic in the form of a seat, which, according to legend, was given to the patriarch of Grado in 630 by the emperor of Byzantium, and a censer of gilded silver in the form of a Byzantine church.

> ! **Baedeker TIP**
>
> **A better view**
> The distance and the dim lighting make it difficult to get a good look at the mosaics, especially the details. Binoculars are very helpful. Climb up to the galleries (to the left of the main entrance) to get closer to the wonderful mosaics.

✳
Canopy and high altar

The high altar, which was newly made from old pieces, houses the bones of St Mark, which were formerly kept in the crypt and could be seen through a window in the altar. The four columns of the canopy with reliefs are noteworthy. They show scenes from the lives of Jesus and the Virgin Mary. It is not certain whether the reliefs are 6th-century Byzantine or 13th-century Venetian work.

✳✳
Pala d'Oro

The famous 2.50m/8ft-high and 3.50m/11-ft wide altarpiece is behind the high altar today (there is an entrance fee). Its front, a masterpiece of the goldsmith's art, is covered in precious stones, pearls and about 250 small enamel medallions. The first version of the Pala d'Oro was created in the late 10th century in Constantinople. It was enlarged in the 12th and 13th centuries, and received its final appearance in 1345 under Andrea Dandolo, who had the individual parts newly arranged and mounted by the goldsmith Gian Paolo Boninsegna.

The small, round medallions which were placed within the frames are among the oldest works. The rectangular panels, labelled in Latin and showing scenes from the lives of St Mark and Christ, were probably made in Venice in the early 12th century. The mount with the archangel Michael at the centre and six scenes from the New Testament are Byzantine and reached Venice in 1204 after the plundering of Constantinople. At the centre of the lower section, the enthroned Christ is surrounded by the evangelists and apostles. Below them stand the mother of Christ, the sainted Byzantine empress Irene (left) and Doge Ordelaffo Falier (right), who ordered the first enlargement of the Pala in 1105. These medallions were created in Venice in 1345, when the many individual parts were combined to make the heterogeneous items into a single piece.

Christ as Pantocrator at the centre of the Pala d'Oro

In a niche of the apse stands a tabernacle with a bronze door by **Jacopo Sansovino**: its reliefs depict the resurrected Christ, surrounded by angels who present the instruments of martyrdom. The vestry door in the curve of the apse is one of the major works of Jacopo Sansovino. The door frame is of marble, and the slightly rounded door itself of bronze. Its two large rectangular reliefs represent the entombment of Christ below and the resurrection above. Prophets and saints stand in the frame panels. According to legend, the small portrait busts represent his artist's colleagues Aretino, Palladio, Francesco Sansovino (a 16th-century chronicler), himself, Titian and Veronese. He worked on the door between 1546 and 1570; his model was the paradise door by Ghiberti in the baptistery of Florence.

✷
◄ Vestry door

The iconostasis which separates the nave and the choir is by Jacobello and Pierpaolo dalle Masegne (1394). A row of eight squat columns supports the horizontal structure above. The triumphal cross stands at its centre, surrounded by the marble figures of the Virgin, St Mark and the twelve apostles. On both sides of the iconostasis stand col-

✷
Iconostasis

The horses of San Marco

umned pulpits which were assembled from old columns and marble panels in the 14th century: to the left, the gospel pulpit and to the right, the pulpit where the newly elected doge presented himself to the people.

The votive image of **Madonna Nicopeia** (the securer of victories) on the east wall of the northern transept was made in Byzantium in the 10th century. The icon, which is covered in jewels, pearls and gemstones, was once carried by the Byzantine army and reached Venice as war booty in 1204.

The chapel of St Isidore (**Cappella Sant'Isidoro**) houses the relics of the saint, which were obtained in 1125 in Chios and rest in a sarcophagus in a niche in the front wall. The recumbent figure on the sarcophagus represents the saint. The 14th-century mosaics relate various episodes from his life, partly in a highly dramatic manner.

Cappella dei Mascoli
The barrel-vaulted room was built in the early 15th century and has an altar with important sculptures of the Virgin between St Mark and St John, marking the transition from the late Gothic period to the early Renaissance. Note the mosaics from the first half of the 15th century and the holy water basin on the column shaft (12th century). The chapel received its name in the 17th century when it was the chapel of the mascoli (bachelors).

Altar of the Annunciation
The name of the Altar of the Annunciation refers to its canopy-like structure: a polygonal marble pyramid roof is borne by columns which enclose a mensa. The crucifix is booty from Byzantium which was brought to Venice in 1205. The statues for the annunciation were made in the 14th century.

★
Galleria and Museo Marciano
The steep steps to the Museo Marciano are to the right of the main portal. The rooms above the narthex were the workshops of the mosaic artists who worked in the church. Tapestries, sculptures and liturgical robes are exhibited in the museum. Mosaic fragments can be seen close up. The most prominent exhibits include the former drape for the Pala d'Oro, which covered the top section of the altar. In 1345, Paolo Veneziano and his sons made the polyptych with images of Christ, the Virgin, saints and the life of St Mark.

The main items of interest are the famous, originally fire-gilded **bronze horses of St Mark**. They surely served as a model for Donatello's equestrian monument Gattamelata in Padua and for Verrocchio's Colleoni in Venice. Their precise origins are unclear. The horses were probably made in the 4th century BC in Greece. From here, they went to Rome, where they decorated the triumphal arch of Emperor Trajan. They were taken to Constantinople in the 4th century. After it was plundered in 1204, they reached Venice, where they were set up a short time later on the gallery of St Mark's Basilica. In 1797, Napoleon removed them to Paris. After his fall, the horses were brought back in 1815. The tour ends with a visit to the gallery, where the copies of the horses stand.

✷ Burano

L/M 1/2

Population: 3,130

Quay: Burano (LN from Fondamenta Nuove)

Burano, the loveliest island of the lagoon, lies nearly 9km/5.5mi north-east of the main island of Venice. The boat trip takes about 40 minutes. The lively little fishing village has colourfully painted houses, generally with one or two storeys. According to legend, the façades are painted brightly so that the fishermen could find their way home even in dense fog. The fishing boats in the narrow canals are also brightly coloured and combine with a backdrop of houses mirrored in the water to form a magical sight. It is no surprise that the island also attracted painters. Some works can be seen in the renowned restaurant Da Romano (Via Galuppi 468). The most famous resident was the composer Baldassare Galuppi (1706–1785), after whom a street and Burano's largest piazza are named.

Lace island

Art lovers find little of interest on the island except for a crucifixion by **Tiepolo** (1725) in the 16th-century San Martino church. Burano is or was once famous throughout Europe for its lace. The museum of the **Scuola di Merletti**, which was founded in 1872, has an informative exhibition about the various techniques and some beautiful examples of lace (►Baedeker Special p.172). And those who finish with a visit to one of the excellent fish restaurants along Via Galuppi should try a Burano ring (bussola): it tastes best when dipped in sweet wine.

What to see

A wooden bridge leads to the small neighbouring island of (population 350), where the cultivation of vines and agriculture dominate the landscape. **San Francesco** del Deserto (► p.212; the name goes back to a period in the 15th century when the island was deserted because of the unhealthy living conditions in the lagoon) can also be reached from Burano.

◄ Mazzorbo

ALL ABOUT LACE

According to legend, a sea captain in love left his beloved behind on the Island of Burano and soon thereafter sailed past the Island of the Sirens. While the crew, overcome by the magical song, jumped overboard, he resisted temptation in favour of his true love. Thereupon the ruler of the sirens made a whitecap rise from the ocean, which turned into the finest lace in the hands of the sailor - the bridal veil for his beloved waiting on Burano.

In fact Burano lace does have a special relationship with the sea, since it is said that its pattern was derived from the techniques used to manufacture fishing nets.

Lace was produced in Venice and on the small islands as early as the 15th century; the Punto in aria, the complicated airy pattern that is the trademark of Burano, was not invented until the 16th century. Soon the fine products were in demand all over Europe and adorned nobles and rich citizens with precious accessories. In France, the lace was in such high demand in the middle of the 17th century that Minister Colbert even hired knitters from Burano in order to launch domestic lace production. The dissolution of the republic in 1797 also sealed the demise of lace production.

At the end of the 19th century the traditional craft was already all but forgotten when the Countess Marcello opened a new school of lace on Burano in 1872, where Francesca Memo, the last of the knitters who still knew the Punto in aria, passed on her skills. At the beginning of the 20th century the island had seven large lace production facilities where almost 5,000 knitters were employed. Today there are only a few masters of this art, and genuine Burano lace has long become a luxury item. Thus most of the articles in the stores along the Via Galuppi now come from low-wage countries or are machine-made locally.

A small museum in the Galleria del Merletto Antico (Via Galuppi 215; open during business hours) displays lace art from the last two centuries, including precious fans, veils, and dresses. The Scuola dei Merletti (Piazza Galuppi; opening hours: Apr to Oct Mon, Wed-Sun 10.00am to 5.00pm, otherwise only until 4.00pm) also provides information about the art of the Punto in aria technique.

★ Canal Grande (Grand Canal)

»Yes, I do believe that this is the most beautiful waterway in the world«, the ambassador Philippe de Commynes enthused nearly 500 years ago. He was speaking of the Grand Canal, Venice's main traffic artery, which extends like an inverted »S« from Santa Lucia railway station to the San Marco basin, dividing the city into two halves. The canal, actually the last segment of the river Brenta before it joins the sea, is nearly 4km/2.5mi long, 30–70m/35–80yd wide, and has a maximum depth of 5m/16ft. Only three bridges span this waterway. A fourth is planned between Piazzale Roma and the railway station. Venetians also refer to the waterway, which is constantly busy with gondolas, vaporetti, motorboats and rowing boats, as the Canalazzo, a combination of canal and palazzo.

The world's most beautiful waterway

 Baedeker TIP

A boat trip

All the sights in Venice can be seen on foot – the Grand Canal is the exception. Here, only a trip in a boat or gondola gives the full picture. The vaporetti on line 1 stop at every quay (journey time for the round trip: about 80 min.); line 82 stops only at the most important quays, such as the station, Rialto and San Marco (information on tickets, ►p.133).

More than 200 magnificent palazzi, 15 churches and other noble residences line its banks. They mirror Venetian architectural history from the 12th century on and provide a detailed illustration of the former richness and glory of the maritime republic.

From the Railway Station to the Rialto Bridge
L = left bank, R = right bank

Venice's railway station lies directly on the Grand Canal. Ponte della Libertà, the link between the mainland and the city, was built between 1841 and 1846; the first railway station began operations in 1860. Today's complex dates from 1954.

Railway station Ferrovia S. Lucia L

The domed building with the green patina is, for many visitors, the first church they see when arriving in Venice. It was built between 1718 and 1738. Its architect Giovanni Scalfurotto took the Pantheon in Rome and Palladio as his models: a wide outside stairway leads up to the columned portico adjoining the church itself.

San Simeone Piccolo R

The church of the »barefoot Carmelites« (actually S. Maria di Nazareth) was begun in 1670 as a monastery church to plans by Baldassare Longhena and was not consecrated until 1705. The two-storey marble façade in high Baroque style is by Giuseppe Sardi (1683–1689). The interior contains the tomb of Ludovico Manin, the last doge; there are only remnants of Tiepolo's paintings (second chapel to the right, third chapel to the left).

Chiesa degli Scalzi L

Ponte Scalzi	The bridge, which was built from Istrian stone, replaced an older iron construction in 1934. Every year, the boats of the regata storica start here – the finishing line is at Ca' Foscari (►p.181).
Palazzo Giovanelli R	The Gothic palace with beautiful pointed-arch windows was purchased in 1755 by the Giovanelli family. They had been admitted into the class of nobles after paying 100,000 ducats.
Palazzo Flangini L	The palazzo with its rusticated ground floor, designed by G. Sardi in the 17th century, remained unfinished; one side section is missing.
Santa Geremia L	Shortly before the mouth of the Canale di Cannaregio, on the left bank, lies the church **Santa Geremia**, recognizable by its great central dome. Carlo Corbelli was the architect who, in 1753, converted the traditional layout of the church with a dome over the crossing into a modern form. In the domed area to the right of the choir hangs a painting by Palma the Younger: *Venetia Crowned by Saints*.

Santa Geremia

Slightly behind it stands the four-storey **Labia palace**, which was begun at the end of the 17th century and completed in the second quarter of the 18th century. The Labia family, merchants from Catalonia, purchased their nomination to the patrician class in 1646 for the proud sum of 300,000 ducats. Today, RAI (Italian radio and television station) has its seat here. The main focus is on the fine frescoes in the ballroom, which were done by **Tiepolo** in the mid-18th century. The two murals show *Queen Cleopatra's Banquet in Honour of Mark Antony* (Tiepolo is said to have portrayed himself in the figure dressed in blue, second from left) and *Cleopatra Embarking for Rome*. The ceiling painting symbolizes *Time Rejecting Beauty* (viewing by appointment Mon–Fri 3–4pm; tel. 0 41 78 12 77).

Palazzo Correr Contarini L	Two water gates lead into the 17th-century palace, which is also called the »House of Hearts« due to the heart-shaped family coat of arms.
San Marcuola L	Also on the left side: the uncompleted brick façade of the church S. Marcuola, built 1728–1736 by Giorgio Massari. The *Last Supper* on the left side wall of the presbytery is by Tintoretto (1547). An old copy of his *Footwashing* hangs opposite. The altars of the church are richly decorated with sculptures.

Opposite S. Marcuola lies the ▶Fondaco dei Turchi.

Fondaco dei Turchi

In the crenellated structure from the 15th century (also known as the Deposito del Megio), the Venetian republic stored grain and flour for times of need. On the upper floor of the compact brick building, a relief shows the lion of St Mark (copy of an original destroyed in 1797).

Antico Granaio R

Palazzo Vendramin Calergion on the left bank is one of the the most beautiful early Renaissance palaces of Venice. It was built by Mauro Coducci around 1500 for the Loredan family. After the death of Coducci, Tullio Lombardo took over its completion. In the early 17th century, it came into the possession of the Calergi family, and in 1783 became the property of the Vendramins. The backset Grimani wing was the residence of **Richard Wagner** and his family from 1882 till his death on 13 February 1883 (viewing Saturday morning by appointment, tel. 04 12 76 04 07 or 04 15 23 25 44). Today, it houses the **casino** of Venice (daily 11am–2.30am; www.casino venezia.it).

Palazzo Vendramin Calergi L

A bird's eye view of the Canal Grande with the Rialto Bridge

Palazzo Belloni Battagia
R
✴ The beautiful adjacent Baroque palace with its conspicuous pointed towers was designed in 1647 by Baldassare Longhena for Bartolomeo Belloni, whose family had shortly before been admitted into the Venetian patrician class.

San Staè
R
✴ The Baroque church a little further on, known as S. Staè and S. Eustachio, was built in 1678 by Giovanni Grassi with the layout of a Greek cross. Its façade towards the Grand Canal was designed thirty years later by Domenico Rossi. The costs were met by the doge who held office from 1700 to 1709, Alvise Mocenigo II, whose tomb is here. It contains some works of the early 18th century, including works by Giovanni Battista Piazzetta, Sebastiano Ricci, Tiepolo and Pellegrini (open: daily 10am–5pm, Sun from 1pm).

▶ Ca' Pesaro, a Baroque masterpiece, houses two museums.

The large Baroque **palace Corner della Retina** was built almost beside Ca' Pesaro and only a short time later (1724). The architect was Domenico Rossi. The preceding building was the birthplace of **Caterina Corner** (1454–1510), later queen of the Mediterranean island of Cyprus, which held strategic significance for Venice. The Corner family, old Venetian patricians, had become so rich and powerful through sugar-cane plantations on Cyprus that the island king Giacomo II di Lusignano married the eighteen-year-old Caterina in 1472. Eight months later, the king was poisoned, and one year later, their son died. At the urging of Venice, Caterina finally ceded her kingdom to the republic. As a reward, she was allowed to live in keeping with her status in Castle Asolo and later in her palace on the Grand Canal. Today, the palace is the municipal pawnshop.

Palazzo Vendramin Calergi

Ca' d'Oro
L
Diagonally opposite to the left is the most famous Gothic building on the Grand Canal, the ▶Ca' d'Oro.
Shortly beyond it and on the same side lies **Palazzo Pesaro** (mid-15th century; the top floor was added in the 19th century) and **Palazzo Sagredo**, a 14th-century structure.

This palazzo takes its name from the unusually high and slender columns of the arcades of its lower floor.

Palazzo Michiel delle Colonne
L

The palace became known primarily as the residence of the English consul Joseph Smith, who made a name for himself as an art collector and patron. The English court and the British Museum owe many of their Venetian paintings to him, particularly masterpieces by Canaletto. Smith had the palace rebuilt in the mid-18th century by Antonio Visentini in the classical style, and the inner rooms redecorated at great cost by Antonio Selva.

Palazzo Mangili Valmarana
L

The **Pescheria**, a two-floor open hall on the opposite bank, was built by Domenico Rupolo and Cesare Laurenti in 1907 in the neo-Gothic style. The fish market has been held here for more than 600 years (▶Ponte di Rialto).

The long, three-storey **Fabbriche Nuove** was built 1554–1556 with loggias to a design by Sansovino. It provided storage and offices space.

Pescheria, Venice's fish market

Opposite the Fabbriche Nuove lies **Ca' da Mosto**. The palace with its fine marble arches on slender columns was built in the 13th century in the Venetian-Byzantine style. Alvise da Mosto, who in 1465 was the first European to sail around the Canary Islands and the Cape Verde islands, was born here in 1432.

A little further along on the right bank is the Fabbriche Vecchie, a structure with 37 window bays (1522, Scarpagnino).

Fabbriche Vecchie
R

The white marble palace on a corner directly before the Rialto bridge was once the seat of the highest Venetian financial authority. The imposing »palace of the finance secretaries« was built between 1525 and 1528 by Guglielmo Grigi from Bergamo. It is ornamented with semi-reliefs, a fine late flowering of Lombard Renaissance ornamentation.

★
Palazzo dei Camerlenghi
R

The building opposite was the seat of the German merchants (▶ p.191) and today houses the **main post office**.

Fondaco dei Tedeschi ? L

▶p.243

Ponte di Rialto

SINISTER SECRETS

As quaint and colourful as Venice appears to visitors – the city also has some obscure secrets. Thus Venetians avoid passing between the two columns in front of the doge's palace, which since 1172 depict a winged lion and St Theodore in a battle with a dragon. Murderers, thieves or swindlers used to be put to death here, and their bodies were often displayed for days as a deterrent. According to legend, anyone who passes between the columns will experience misfortune in the near future.

The Scuola della Misericordia on the Campo dell'Abbazzia is another magical place – an abbey from the 10th century, with all sorts of stories that revolve around its padres. It is said that a member of the order poisoned the abbot using bewitched coins; other tales tell of supernatural forces that possessed the brothers. One day God decided to send the plague as a punishment, which did in fact wipe out the entire community in one fell swoop during the Middle Ages. On the cemetery island of San Michele in the northern lagoon, witches are said to have assembled in order to fly to ceremonies or gatherings on the remote islands in gondolas that floated above the water.

The terrible secret of Ca' Dario

Although many spooky stories and haunting ghosts are ascribed to the Palazzo Contarini del Zaffo on the Fondamente Gasparo Contarini, the story surrounding the Palazzo Dario (also known as Ca' Dario) constructed in 1490 on the Canal Grande according to plans by Pietro Lombardo is enough to baffle even enlightened minds. It all began with the death of Marietta Dario at the end of the 15th century. The daughter of the builder Giovanni Dario died of a broken heart when her fiancé Vincenzo Barbaro was entrapped in political intrigues in order to first banish him from the city and finally murder him. Other, sometimes mys-

But it looks so harmless: The Palazzo Dario on the Canal Grande, which has tilted slightly over time

terious strokes of fate resulted in the family being eliminated by the middle of the 17th century.

The neighbours and new owners, the Barbara family, sold the Palazzo to an Armenian jeweller at the end of the 18th century but his business collapsed only a few months after he moved in. The next buyer, the Englishman Rawdon Lubbock Brown, overextended himself financially during renovations – and shot himself in the palace ballroom. He was followed by the poet Henri de Regnier, who was afflicted by a rare infection shortly after he made his purchase and died in 1936; the American Charles Briggs was exiled from Venice because he converted the Palazzo into a permissive gay bar; and a count from Turin, who was found slain in the palace in July 1970.

The building also proved unlucky for the next buyer Kit Lambert – manager of the well-known rock group The Who. He died of a brain aneurism at the age of only 45 after excessive consumption of alcohol and drugs. But even that is not all. Shortly after moving in during the mid-1970s, the new owner Fabrizio Ferrari also suffered a mysterious string of bad luck. Not only did his fortune seem to disappear into thin air - several family members also passed away in quick succession. And so the palace changed hands one final time: In 1985, it was purchased by the industrialist Raul Gardini. However, he became involved in numerous cases of corruption and then also failed economically; he took his own life in July of 1993 – not in the Palazzo Dario, but in Milan. Since then – no surprise here – the building has been vacant. Maybe one of the owners should have fallen into the Canal Grande – according to Venetian custom, that is supposed to bring luck.

From the Ponte di Rialto to Piazza San Marco
L = left, R = right bank

Palazzo Dolfin Manin **L**

On the left is Palazzo Dolfin Manin, one of the first works in Venice of Sansovino, a native of Florence (built 1532–1560). Two storeys rise above an open ground-floor hall; the arrangement of the columns follows the classic ideal of the Renaissance. The 120th and last doge, Ludovico Manin, lived here during his time in office 1789–1797 (today this is the seat of the Banca d'Italia). Next to it is the late Gothic Palazzo Bembo (15th century).

Palazzo Loredan **L**

The next two palaces, **Loredan** and **Ca' Farsetti**, have arcades open to the canal. They are beautiful and well-preserved examples of the Romanesque-Byzantine building style of the 12th century. The upper floors were later redesigned. Since the 19th century, the city administration (**Municipio**) has been based here.

Palazzo Grimani **L**

»The noblest of all houses in Venice is the house of Grimani«, wrote John Ruskin (1819–1900) in his treatise on art history, *The Stones of Venice*, of the three-storey palace at the place where Rio di San Luca flows into the Grand Canal. It was begun around 1540 by Michele

One of the most important symbols of Venice: the Rialto Bridge

Sanmicheli. The monumental façade was completed by Giangiacomo Grigi in 1559. Today, the palace houses the appeals court of Venice.

Slightly farther on, Palazzo Pisani Moretta stands out on the right bank with its apricot-coloured, perfectly symmetrical façade. It was built in the second half of the 15th century. Particularly beautiful aspects are the two gate arches which open towards the water on the ground floor, as well as the six-part loggias on the first and second piano nobile (upper floors), which are decorated with rich tracery. Tiepolo and Piazzetta were employed in 1742 for the palace interiors. Until 1857, the salon contained Veronese's work *The Family of Darius before Alexander*, which can be seen today in the London National-al Gallery. The palace is one of the few that are still in private ownership.

✱ Palazzo Pisani Moretta R

Palazzo Mocenigo shortly before the great curve of the canal actually combines three palaces of the Mocenigo family. Seven members of this family guided the fate of Venice between 1414 and 1778 as doges. In 1818/19 the first Palazzo Mocenigo Nero, a long double palace (17th and 18th century), was the residence of Lord Byron, who wrote *Don Juan* and his vision of Judgment Day here. The oldest Mocenigo palace is the adjacent Casa Vecchia, built in 1579 in the style of the late Venetian Renaissance.

Palazzi Mocenigo L

In the curve, referred to as the volta, the mouth of Rio Foscari, Palazzo Balbi catches the eye of those who pass. It was built between 1582 and 1590 to designs by Alessandro Vittorio. The façade has some attributes of Mannerism, the transitional style between late Renaissance and early Baroque, such as double columns between the windows on the first floor, broken pediments above the windows and oval window openings. A plaque reminds us that Napoleon watched the finish of a regatta from here in 1807 (ill. p.43). Since 1973 the palace has housed the central government of Veneto.

Palazzo Balbi R

On the other side of Rio Foscari stands the palace of the same name, one of the most magnificent examples of late Venetian Gothic, which accommodates the **university** today. The site was purchased in 1452 by Francesco Foscari, who had the two Gustiniani towers which stood here remodelled into a magnificent palace. In 1574, the young king of France, Henri III, stayed here on his way from Poland to Paris, where he was to receive the French crown. The adjacent **Palazzo Giustiniani** was probably built at the same time; together, they form the largest Gothic palace complex in Venice.

✱ Ca' Foscari R

The three-storey building on the other bank, whose relatively simple façade decoration lies between Baroque and classical, was built in the mid-18th century from plans by the architect Giorgio Massari. He was also responsible for ►Ca' Rezzonico. His patron was the mighty

✱ Palazzo Grassi L

Palazzo Grassi

Grassi family, which, for the sum of 60,000 gold ducats, was permitted to join the Venetian patrician class in 1718, and owned the palace until the mid-19th century, when the dukes of Tornielli acquired it. Later, it was the residence of the opera tenor Poggi, and in the late 19th century, the building housed the illustrious bathhouse Degli Antoni. Extensive restorations were made in the 1980s to plans by Gae Aulenti and in 2005 under the direction of Japanese architect Tadao Ando. François Pinault, who purchased the palace in 2004 from the Fiat group of companies, shows some of his contemporary art collection here. Temporary exhibitions also take place. The wall opposite the magnificent stairway is decorated with frescoes by Alessandro Longhi. The rooms on the upper floor still contain wall paintings by Jacopo Guarana and Fabio Canal in the Rococo style (open: daily 9am–6pm; www.palaz zograssi.it).

Ca' Rezzonico – R At the right is the Baroque ►Ca' Rezzonico (museum).

Gallerie dell' Accademia R Shortly before the wooden bridge Ponte dell'Accademia is the campo in front of the former church, followed by the Scuola della Carità, in which the art gallery of the Accademia is housed today (► Gallerie dell'Accademia).

Palazzo Cavalli Franchetti – L Immediately behind the bridge to the left lies the beautifully restored, late Gothic Palazzo Cavalli Franchetti with its fine tracery ornamentations. Temporary exhibitions are held here (www.istitutoveneto.it).

✳ **Palazzo Barbaro L** The adjacent Palazzo Barbaro is also from the Gothic period; it has a glorious six-arched window on the first floor. The four-arched window on the second floor already shows late Gothic style with high elongated arches. On the right is a Baroque extension by Antonio Gaspari. In 1815, the Curtis family from Boston took over the building and had the residential rooms magnificently refurbished. The palace rapidly became a favourite meeting place of artists and literary figures. Among the artists who wrote, composed and painted here were Robert Browning (1812–1889), Henry James (1843–1916), Cole Porter (1891–1964), Monet (1840–1926) and Whistler (1834–1903).

Today, a Renaissance palace which is worth seeing in itself (San Vio 1050) houses the private collection of mediaeval and Renaissance art of the industrialist Vittorio Cini. The following are especially worthy of note: the *Double Portrait of Two Friends* by Jacopo Pontormo, Sandro Botticelli's *Judgment of Paris*, Piero della Francesca's *Madonna with Child* as well as ivory carvings (open: March–June, Sept–Nov Tue–Sun 10am–1pm, 2–6pm; www.cini.it).

Palazzo Cini R

◄ Accademia quay

🕑

Peggy Guggenheim once lived in the palace on the right-hand bank, which remained unfinished (►Collezione Peggy Guggenheim).

Palazzo Venier dei Leoni – R

On the opposite side, in spring, the eye is drawn to the red flowers of the pomegranate tree in the garden in front of the house, where sculptor Antonio Canova (1757–1821) had his first studio. From 1915 to 1919, Gabriele d'Annunzio (1863–1938) lived in the palace. In his autobiographical Venice novel *Il Fuoco* (The Fire), he described his stormy affair with the celebrated actress Eleonore Duse.

Casina delle Rose – L

For the price of 22,000 gold ducats, Giorgio Corner, brother of the Queen of Cyprus, purchased the magnificent building in the early 16th century. In 1532, it fell victim to a major fire. His son Jacopo Corner thereupon commissioned the Florentine architect and sculptor Jacopo Sansovino to build a new, magnificent three-storey palace according to Renaissance ideas. He harmoniously composed the Venetian-style arcade with the Tuscan lower zone. In the early 19th century, the giant palace building became the property of Austria as the residence of the imperial viceroy. Today, the **Prefecture** has its seat here.

✹ Palazzo Corner Ca' Grande L

As the façades facing Rio delle Torreselle and the garden prove, **Palazzo Dario** was also originally Gothic until Pietro Lombardo began to redesign it in the Renaissance style in 1479 for Giovanni Dario. The palace has a reputation for bringing its owners bad luck and is presently unoccupied (► Baedeker Special p.178).

Bauer – Il Palazzo e Bauer Hotel

Dogana da Mar

Palazzo Gritti with its beautiful terrace was built in 1525 for Doge Andrea Gritti. Today, it is a well-known hotel in which such illustrious guests as John Ruskin, William Somerset Maugham and Ernest Hemingway stayed.

The adjacent narrow **Palazzo Contarini Fasan** with its late Gothic flamboyant windows, which was built around 1480, is said to owe its name to its owner's enjoyment of hunting. According to legend this was the home of the beautiful Desdemona, the innocent victim of Othello's jealousy in Shakespeare's tragedy.

On the right-hand bank the familiar silhouette of the church ▶ Santa Maria della Salute can be seen. The adjacent building (around 1669, B. Longhena) houses the **Pinacoteca Manfrediniana**. The exhibits include busts by A. Vittoria (1525 to 1608) as well as paintings and other pieces by A. Vivarini (15th century), Cima da Conegliano and F. Lippi (viewing by appointment only, tel. 04 15 22 55 58).

Dogana da Mar
R

At the point, a bronze goddess of fortune offers greetings to travellers from the tower of the old customs office Dogana da Mar (17th century). She balances on a globe which is supported by two atlases and functions as a weather vane. Behind the building, which is currently not in use, a panorama of the two islands ▶ Giudecca and ▶ San Giorgio Maggiore comes into view.

Capitaneria del
Porto
L

The Fontegheto della Farina on the left bank, a former grain store from the 15th century, today houses the port office Capitaneria del Porto.

Next door, a must for all those who enjoy famous cocktails, is **Harry's Bar**, once the favourite drinking haunt of Ernest Hemingway.

Giardini Reali
L

The royal gardens west of the Piazzetta were laid out in the early 19th century on the site of the former grain stores; at the west end of the park area stands a classical pavilion (1817) with a ▶tourist office.

Piazza
San Marco – L

▶p.237

★ Ca' d'Oro

Location: Grand Canal   **Quay:** Ca' d'Oro

Ca' d'Oro is Venice's most famous private building. Rarely is a name as fitting as that of the »golden house«. It is truly a jewel and one of the loveliest Gothic palaces in Venice. It was commissioned by the rich noble and high state official Marino Contarini, who employed no less than two renowned architects: Bartolomeo Bon and Mateo Raverti. The palace was built to their plans between 1421 and 1440. The façade, which was once generously gilded with gold leaf, is particularly famous; hence the name »golden house«. Even though the gold has paled by now, Ca' d'Oro is the climax of late Gothic decoration with its multi-coloured marble, balconies and pointed windows, and the gloriously playful tracery ornamentation. The first signs of the early Renaissance are found in the open columned hall with its central round arch on the ground floor and the side wing (there is only one torresello) which is divided into clearly structured rectangular fields.

Opening hours:
Mon 8.15am–2pm,
Thu–Sun
8.15am–7.15pm

Ca' d'Oro with its balconies and ogive windows

After a long series of owners, Baron Giorgio Franchetti (died 1922), an art lover, acquired the palace in 1894 and had it carefully restored. Today, Ca' d'Oro houses his art collection **Galleria Franchetti**.

Beautiful example of Venetian residential culture

In the small inner courtyard of the palazzo stands a well in the form of a capital, built from red Veronese marble by B. Bon. The floor of the portego (water hall) on the ground floor is also delightful. The owner of the house, impressed by the mosaics of San Marco, created it himself in 1896 from fine polychrome marble.

The interior, with the wooden ceilings of its main halls, gives an impression of the residential culture of Venetian patricians in the late Middle Ages. Among the works of art, sculptures, tapestries and numerous paintings, particularly from the 15th and 16th centuries, *St Sebastian*, a late work by Andrea Mantegna, as well as two paintings by Vittore Carpaccio, *Annunciation* and *Death of the Virgin*, are noteworthy on the first floor. The fragments of frescoes by Giorgione and his colleague Titian from 1508 on the second floor once decorated the façade of the ▶Fondaco dei Tedeschi. Do not miss the view from the loggia across the Grand Canal to the neo-Gothic Pescheria on the opposite bank.

> ! **Baedeker TIP**
>
> **Ca' d'Oro or Alla Vedova,**
>
> The Widow is the name of an osteria with genuine atmosphere where Venetians like to order a few cicheti and a glass of wine at the counter. If you prefer to sit down while eating, it is best to make a reservation (Ramo Ca' d'Oro, Cannaregio 3912, tel. 04 15 .28 53 .24; closed Thu and Sun midday).

★ Ca' Pesaro

Location: Fondamenta Mocenigo/Grand Canal

Quay: San Staè

🕐 Opening hours: Daily except Mon Apr–Oct 10am–6pm, Nov–March to 5pm

Baroque adorns modern – under this motto, after a long closure, the re-opening of Ca' Pesaro was celebrated in 2003. The imposing Baroque palace on the Grand Canal was built between 1676 and 1710 for the Pesaro family to plans by Baldassare Longhena, a master of late Baroque. His student Antonio Gaspari completed it after Longhena's death. Finally, the building was sensitively restored by the Viennese architect Boris Podrecca. Today, the palace is entered through a small inner courtyard at the back with a well by Sansovino, beyond which the magnificent andron (water hall) was once open to the canal.

★ **Galleria d'Arte Moderna**

The extensive holdings of the Galleria Nazionale d'Arte Moderna, which was founded in 1897, include paintings, graphics and sculp-

Said to be the largest palace on the Canal Grande: Ca' Pesaro

tures of the 19th and early 20th centuries. Main works include Gustav Klimt's erotic *Judith II* (Salome), the *Bather* by Max Klinger, Marc Chagall's *Rabbi of Vitebsk* and Rodin's *Citizen of Calais*.

★
Museo d'Arte Orientale

The third floor houses the museum of oriental art. This unique collection came into being »on a genuine journey around the world« by Duke Bardi 1887–1889 and mainly includes Japanese pieces of the so-called Edo epoch (1614–1868), as well as smaller Chinese and Indochinese sections. More than 30,000 (!) objects are said to be exhibited here, ranging from seals, weapons and armour to porcelain, enamel work and silk paintings.

Palazzo Mocenigo
🕐

The nearby Renaissance palace with original furnishings houses a **costume museum** with displays of exquisite fabrics (Centro Studi di Storia del Tessuto e del Costume; Salizzada San Staè; open: daily except Mon, Apr–Oct 10am–5pm, 4pm in winter).

★★ Ca' Rezzonico (Museo del Settecento Veneziano)

E 12

Location: Rio di Santa Barnabà/Grand Canal

Quay: Ca' Rezzonico

🕐
Opening hours:
Apr–Oct
daily except Tue
10am–6pm,
Nov–March
until 5pm

One of the most impressive palaces of the settecento (17th century) was begun in 1667–1682 by Venice's most important Baroque builder, Baldassare Longhena, for the Bon family. A century later Giorgio Massari completed the family residence for the Rezzonico family. In the mid-19th century, the palace came into the ownership of the English poet Robert Browning, who lived there until his death in 1889. The Baroque palace has been a museum since the 1930s. Matching the grounds and the magnificent decorations, the collection provides an overview of life in Venice at the time of the Rococo, the »settecento veneziano«. The approximately 40 rooms show salon art at its peak with silk wall coverings, tapestries from Flanders, playful armoires and dressers such as the precious Baroque furniture of **Andrea Brustolon** (1662–1732), who had a taste for negroes carved from ebony and the chinoiseries and varnished furniture which were so popular in this period, as well as Venetian porcelain, ceramics and bronzes.

Upper floor

An elegant outside stairway leads to the upper floor and into a gigantic ballroom; the ceiling paintings are by Crosato (1755). The main treasures include the wedding allegory in the adjacent hall by Giambattista Tiepolo, who immortalized the extravagant wedding of Ludovico Rezzonico to Faustina Savorgnan in 1758, and the humorous genre sketches of **Pietro Longhi** (1702–1785; second floor) about everyday life in Venice, such as *Breakfast Chocolate*, *Cruller Bakery* and *Rhinoceros*.

★ Chioggia

Excursion

Location: 40km/25mi south at the end of the lagoon

Population: 54,000

Little Venice

Chioggia (pronounced »kee-o-jah«), one of the most important fishing ports in the Adriatic, is reminiscent of Venice. Of course, it cannot compete with its »big sister« in terms of artistic treasures, but on the other hand, everything is a little smaller and more intimate here. And it is a good place to go swimming. From the Lido, bus stop S. Maria Elisabetta, take the bus to Pellestrina and the ferry through the southern lagoon to Piazzetta Vigo (about 1.5 hours total). The bus from Piazzale Roma is quicker but the trip is not nearly as scenic.

Getting there ►

What to See in Chioggia

The massive brick structure of the former Franciscan monastery San Francesco before the southern town gate houses the **tourist information office** and the **Museo della Laguna Sud**, which is devoted to the history of the lagoon (open: Mon–Sat 9am–1pm, Tue–Sat 3.30 to 7.30pm, in summer until 11.30pm).

The two main axes of Chioggia are the 830m/900yd-long and 24m/26yd-wide **Corso del Popolo**, Chioggia's »board walk« with pretty old palazzi and many cafés, and the main canal with several bridges, the **Canale Vena** with the bragozzi, the colourful fishing boats typical for Chioggia.

Little Venice: Chioggia

The cathedral S. Maria Assunta with its 64m/210ft-high campanile (14th century) was changed into a simple Baroque structure by Baldassare Longhena. The Gothic Oratorio San Martino beside the cathedral houses an altar by Paolo Veneziano from 1349. Along the Corso, the Baroque church **San Giacomo** appears on the right. In the house on the opposite side, the painter Rosalba Carriera was born in 1675 (died 1757), and **Carlo Goldoni** resided here during his time in Chioggia. In his comedy *Le Baruffe Chiozzotte* (Much Ado in Chiozza), Venice's celebrated poet describes the peculiarities of the locals. A few steps farther, at the Canale Vena, the old grain store, the **Grannaio**, is now home to the fish market, which takes place daily except on Mondays. The north end of the Corso is Piazzetta Vigo, where the excursion boats from and to Venice dock. Cross Ponte Vigo to Isola San Domenico and the church of San Domenico, which is graced by Carpaccio's altar painting of St Paul (1520). The atmosphere of this city quarter is of greater interest, for San Domenico lies on the canal of the same name in Chioggia, the backbone of this small town where fishermen repair their nets, unload boats or meet in a bar in the afternoon for coffee. To see the everyday life of Chioggia, take a walk along the canal and through one of the many narrow alleys back to the Corso del Popolo.

Isola San Domenico

A bridge 800m/0.5mi long links the old town to the popular seaside resort of Sottomarina. Behind the wide sandy beach with its endless rows of small bathing huts runs a four-lane shore road. Most hotels are in rows behind the Lungomare with a view of the beach. There are camping sites at the south and north ends of the beach.

Sottomarina

★★ Collezione Peggy Guggenheim

Location: Grand Canal/ Fondamenta Venier

Quays: Salute, Accademia

Opening hours:
Daily except Tue
10am–6pm,
Apr–Oct
Sat to 10pm
www.guggenheim-
venice.it

By comparison with the other palaces on the Grand Canal, Palazzo Venier dei Leoni almost seems like a modern building. Construction began in 1749 to plans by Lorenzo Boschetti. It is unknown why only the lower floor was carried out. The name goes back to the stone lion heads which embellish the façade at the level of the water. The American art patron Peggy Guggenheim (►Famous People), lovingly and respectfully called »Venice's last doge«, lived here from 1949 to her death in 1979. It is true that Peggy Guggenheim bequeathed the palace and the collection to the Solomon Guggenheim foundation in New York, but on condition that the works of art would remain in Venice and accessible to the public. The high-quality works in the collection represents all important movements in the art of the first half of the 20th century. The entrance is through an iron gate by Claire Falkenstein (1961) into a small garden. Here, aside from sculptures by – among others – Arp, Max Ernst and Henry Moore, are her grave and those of her dearly beloved dogs.

! *Baedeker* TIP

Guided tour

The audio tour of the exhibition provides a lot of interesting details on the works of art. The walls of the museum café are decorated with excellent photos from the life of Peggy Guggenheim, an extraordinary collector and patron.

The exhibits include works by Braque, Dalí, Chagall, Duchamp, Ernst, Kandinsky, Mondrian, Picabia, Picasso, Pollock, Arp, Brancusi, Calder and Moore. Max Ernst, to whom Peggy Guggenheim was married, and Jackson Pollock, whom she discovered and supported, are particularly well represented. One of the most beautiful sculptures is Constantin Brancusi's *Maiastra*, one of the most provocative Marino Marini's sculpture of a naked rider *Angel of the City* on the terrace to the Grand Canal.

Fondaco dei Tedeschi

Location: Ponte di Rialto

Quay: Rialto

Directly ahead of the Rialto bridge lies the Fondaco dei Tedeschi, the trading house of the German merchants (Arabic funduk means storage house, accommodation), first mentioned in 1228. Today it is the

main post office. The present structure was built in 1505 after its medieval predecessor burned down. Following Venetian tradition, the main façade to the Grand Canal has three parts. Five large gates on the canal side gave easy access to the building. The dining halls were above them in the corners. A battlement-like decorative moulding tops the façade. The architecture of the building corresponds to its purpose: four floors with 160 rooms, of which 80 are bedrooms, surround an inner courtyard. The outer rooms of the ground floor were used as sales rooms; the other rooms were stores. The upper rooms were used as living space and for administration. The customs office was on the canal. The outer façade was decorated by Giorgione and Titian, but unfortunately only fragments of the frescoes are still in existence (►Ca' d'Oro).

Both the prominent location on the Rialto and the fact that the city bore costs for rebuilding the Fondaco bespeak the economic benefit which Venice drew from the German trade: with every completed transaction, a percentage had to be given to the Venetian state. It was not for nothing that the Fondaco was referred to as the »golden ark of the senate« in the 16th and 17th centuries. German merchants were allowed to live, store and sell their wares only here. They ate and lived together (only men were permitted) and were subject to Venetian supervision. Outside the Fondaco, they were not allowed to trade or make dealings individually, but only as a brotherhood (which had its own church, ►San Bartolomeo). In this manner, Venice kept its foreign guests firmly under control.

The Fondaco dei Tedeschi (left) on an anonymous painting from the 18th century; the Rialto Bridge is in the background, the Palazzo dei Camerlenghi and the Fabbriche Vecchie on the right.

✳ Fondaco dei Turchi
Museo di Storia Naturale

E 10

Location: Fondamenta del Megio/
Rio Fortego dei Turchi

Quay: San Staè

🕐 Opening hours:
Sat–Sun
10am–4pm

Museo di Storia Naturale

The Fondaco dei Turchi is one of the oldest palaces in Venice. It was built in the mid-13th century in the Venetian-Byzantine style for the Pesaro merchant family. Towards the canal, it has an open columned hall. On the right and left are two tower-like three-storey wings. The central section has two storeys and two arcades. The entire building is crenellated. From the end of the 14th century, the palace served as a residence for state visitors. From 1621 to 1838, Turkish merchants used it as their trading base. In the 19th century, it was rebuilt in the style of the 13th century and today houses the **Museum of Natural History**. The main attractions are a 7m/23ft-long and nearly 4m/13ft-high dinosaur skeleton discovered in the southern Sahara in 1973, and a brand-new aquarium. The exhibition about the animal and plant world of the lagoon is also well worth seeing.

✳ Fondazione
Querini-Stampalia

H 12

Location: Campiello Querini-Stampalia

Quay: San Zaccaria

🕐 Opening hours:
Tue–Sun
10am–5pm,
Fri–Sat to 10pm
www.querini
stampalia.it

The beautiful 16th-century Renaissance palace near the church Santa Maria Formosa was owned by an old Venetian family. In 1886, the structure and its furnishings came into the possession of the city. A visit provides a beautiful impression of a patrician palace of the early 19th century. The ground floor and the gardens were carefully redesigned in the 1970s by the Venetian architect Carlo Scarpa (1906 to 1978); in 2003, extensions were made by Mario Botta. The building houses a café-restaurant as well as an interesting bookstore. The first floor houses the richly endowed **library** (open: Mon 4pm–midnight, Tue–Sat 10am–midnight, Sun to 7pm).

Pinacoteca

The collection, with paintings by Venetian artists of the 14th to 18th centuries, was largely assembled by Giovanni Querini-Stampalia. The cycle of paintings in room 1 by **Gabriele Bella** is especially noteworthy. It includes the famous *Women's Regatta on the Grand Canal* and *Carnival Celebration on Maundy Thursday on the Piazzetta* (mid-18th century), descriptions of everyday life in Venice. Donato Veneziano's *Coronation of the Virgin* (1372) is also well worth seeing. The most important room is room 8 with two works by **Giovanni Bellini** (*Madonna and Child* and *Christ in the Temple*), portraits of Francuerini and his wife Paola by Palma the Elder, as well as Lorenzo di Credi's *Virgin with Child and the Infant St John*. The genre scenes by **Pietro Longhi** (rooms 12 and 13) provide pleasurable viewing.

Scarpa turned the inner courtyard into a green space with Arabic and Japanese influences. The so-called Water Hall with its exit to the canal is also very lovely.

Inner courtyard

✶ Gallerie dell'Accademia

E 13

Location: Grand Canal/ Porta dell'Accademia

Quay: Accademia

The gallery of paintings at the art academy, called Accademia for short, has the most significant collection of Venetian paintings worldwide from the Gothic period to Rococo. The museum is housed in three buildings: the convent of the Lateran Canons, which was designed by Palladio in 1561, was built 1441–1452 by B. Bon, and the Scuola della Carità. The buildings were secularized around 1800. Shortly thereafter, art lovers turned it into a »collection site« for works of art which had become »homeless« after the dissolution of monasteries and churches as well as the clearance of nobles' palaces. This very soon resulted in a unique collection which today, housed in 24 rooms and more or less chronologically organized, offers a fascinating overview of more than 500 years of Venetian painting.

🕐 Opening hours: Mon 8.15am–2pm, Tue–Sun 8.15am–7.15pm

✔ **DON'T MISS**

- Room 1: polyptych, Paolo Veneziano
- Room 2: *Virgin Enthroned with Six Saints*, Giovanni Bellini
- Room 5: *The Tempest*, Giorgione
- Room 10: *Miracle of St Mark*, Tintoretto, and *Pietà*, Titian
- Room 17: vedute by Canaletto and genre paintings by Pietro Longhi
- Room 20: *Miracle of the Holy Cross Relic*, Gentile Bellini, Carpaccio and others
- Room 21: *St Ursula Cycle*, Carpaccio
- Room 24: *Mary in the Temple*, Titian

The tour begins on the top floor, in the former meeting room of the Scuola, which has a beautiful coffered ceiling. Altarpieces by Gothic masters of the 14th and early 15th centuries are displayed here. **Paolo Veneziano** (who worked from 1333 to 1358), Venice's first important painter, painted the altarpiece (polyptych, around 1350) from the church S. Chiara, with the coronation of the Virgin on the central panel and four scenes from the life of Christ on each of the two side panels. Delicate colours and icon-like rigidity of the figures, particularly in the central panel, stand out in Paolo's painting, which is

✶ **Room 1**

influenced by Byzantine forms, but becomes closer to life in the scenes of Christ.

Room 2 Room 2 exhibits altar panels from the 15th and early 16th centuries. The so-called **Pala di San Giobbe** (before 1490), one of the major works of Venetian painting in the early Renaissance by **Giovanni Bellini** (1430–1516) exemplifies the change from the small and multi-section panels of the late Gothic period to the large-format altar panel of the Renaissance. Bellini composed the space within the painting as a church, with the gold mosaic of the apse arch and the marble wall coverings as a reference to the Basilica di San Marco. By showing individual saints around the enthroned Virgin (Sacra Conversazione), Giovanni Bellini created the Venetian prototype of a Renaissance altarpiece, which was frequently imitated, e.g. by Giambattista Cima da Conegliano (c. 1459 to 1517) with his enthroned *Virgin with Child* or by Vittore Carpaccio (c. 1465–1526) with his *Presentation of Jesus in the Temple*. Masterpieces by Giambattista Cima da Conegliano, Piero della Francesca (1416/1417–1492), Bellini's brother-in-law Andrea Mantegna (1431–1506) as well as Jacopo (1424–1470/71) and Giovanni Bellini are exhibited in the following rooms.

Room 5 contains numerous Madonna images, mostly half-length figures, by **Giovanni Bellini**, which prove the wide range of expression of this important Venetian Renaissance painter, including the *Madonna of the Trees* (1487) with great atmospheric effect and human dignity, as well as the *Virgin and Child between St John the Baptist and a Saint* (c.1505) before the backdrop of a charming mountain landscape. Bellini's *Pietà* (c.1505) shows his interest in the man-made environment and late Gothic piety. The grieving Virgin with Christ's body in her lap appears before a wide landscape background, a combination of views of Vicenza (cathedral, basilica of the council) and Cividale (Nasone bridge).

Giovanni Bellini: Pala di San Giobbe

Aside from Titian, **Giorgione** (1476/1477–1510) was the most important pupil of Giovanni Bellini. His famous painting *The Tempest* (La Tempesta; ► p.51) was done shortly after 1505 and shows the mood just before a thunderstorm breaks. Using layers of colour which flow into each other, Giorgione produces a new synthesis of colours and space. On the other hand, stark realism marks Giorgione's portrait of a woman with the inscription »This is what time made of me.«

Mannerist works include the legendary *Handing of the Ring to the Doge* (1545–1550) by a fisherman at the prompting of the evangelist Mark, which **Paris Bordone** (1500–1571) from Treviso set at the centre of a fantastic architectural prospect in exquisitely cool colours. Similar narrative qualities are found in the *Rich Man's Banquet* (1543–1545) by **Bonifacio de' Pitati**, an allegory comparing the rich waster with musicians in joyous company under the portico of his villa with the ragged Lazarus who waits for alms in vain. The falcon hunt and the lovers in the garden refer to the pleasures of life, while the burning buildings in the background probably represent the fires of hell. **Titian's** Mannerist depiction of the powerful figure of St John the Baptist, on the other hand, porbably alludes to the sculpture of Michelangelo.

Room 6

Lorenzo Lotto's portrait of a young man

The portrait of a young noble in his study by **Lorenzo Lotto** (1480–1556) in room 7 is a masterpiece of Mannerist portraiture.

Room 7

Among the impressive works of the 16th century are Bonifacio de' Pitati's *Massacre of the Innocents*, *Holy Family with Saint Catherine and St John the Baptist*, a late work in an extended triangular composition with diffuse light and perfect colour harmony by Palma Vecchio (1480–1528; also known as Palma the Elder), as well as *Christ Mourned with Saints* (1510), the first known work of the Lombard artist Girolamo Romani (Romanino).

Room 8

A comparison between Paolo Caliari (1528–1588), known as Veronese, and Jacopo Robusti (1514–1594), known as Tintoretto, illuminates various currents of painting during the Counter-Reformation. On the end wall of the room hangs a giant painting by **Veronese**,

✶ ✶
Room 10

Galleria dell'Accademia *Plan*

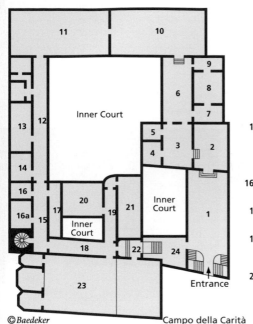

1 Early masters
2,3 Great 15th-century altar panels and Giovanni Bellini
4,5 Mantegna, Piero della Francesca, Cosmé Tura and Giorgione
6 Titian (Tiziano), Jacopo Tintoretto and Paolo Veronese
7,8 Lorenzo Lotto, Romanino and Jacopo Palma the Elder
9 Book shop
10 Titian, Jacopo Tintoretto and Paolo Ver
11 Bonifacio Veronese, Jacopo Tintoretto, Bernado Strozzi and Giambattista Tiep
12,13 Marco Ricci, Francesco Zuccarelli, Giuseppe Zais, Jacopo Bassano and portraits by Jacopo Tintoretto
14 17th-century works
15 Giovanni Antonio Pellegrini, Tiepolo an Giannantonio Guardi
16,16a Works of the young Tiepolo, Alessandro Longhi, Giambattista Piazz and Fra'Galgario
17,18 Canaletto, Francesco Guardi, Tiepolo, Pietro Longhi, Rosalba Carriera and works of academicians
19,20 Bartolomeo Montagna, Giovanni Agost da Lodi, Boccacio Boccaccino and the »Miracle of the Relic of the Cross«, Vittore Carpaccio
21,22 »Miracle of St Ursula«, Vittore Carpacc and room in classical style
23 Former church Santa Maria della Carità Works of 15th-century Venetian school murals of Scuola di San Marco
24 Sala dell'Albergo; Titian, Antonio Vivarir and Giovanni d'Alemagna

© Baedeker Campo della Carità

Banquet in the House of Levi, a commission for the refectory of the Dominican church Santi Giovanni e Paolo completed in April 1573. Barely three months later, Veronese was ordered to the Holy Office of the Inquisition under suspicion of heresy, since his depiction of the Last Supper with figures such as a jester with a parrot, German lansquenets and dogs had been too free. Despite Veronese's defence on the grounds of artistic licence, he was ordered to alter the painting within three months at his own expense. His only correction was to change the title, probably in agreement with the Dominicans who commissioned him, making reference to the fifth chapter of the gospel of St Luke: »And Levi prepared a feast for him in his house.« So the Last Supper became a feast for guests, a theme which Veronese often depicted as a magnificent celebration.

By contrast, drama and unreality are the hallmarks of the art of **Tintoretto**. The work that he painted for the chapter house of the Scuola Grande di San Marco in 1548, **Saint Mark Frees a Slave** shows one of the miracles of St Mark, according to which the evangelist protected a pious slave, who had defied the orders of his master by going away to worship the relics of St Mark, from the punishment of being blinded and having his legs shattered. No less spectacular are the unusual suites of rooms in Tintoretto's depiction of the *Abduction of the Body of Saint Mark from Alexandria* (1562). His *Saint Mark Saves a Pious Saracen at Sea* was probably done in the same year – another example of his lively powers of expression with intense red, blue and yellow colouring.

The harrowing **Pietà**, the last, uncompleted work by **Titian** (1488/90–1576), uses muted colours to show the fall from life into death, the group of mourners with the body of Christ before an architecture of niches with the statues of Moses and a sibyl. By comparison to the infectious joy of life in his early works, e.g. in the Assunta in the Frari church, the work of Titian's old age shows the relentlessness of death.

Titian's incomplete »Pietà«

The ***Mystic Marriage of Saint Catherine*** (1575) at the front of the room is a late work by **Veronese** with an almost Baroque pathos. Further works by Veronese, usually former ceiling paintings which were meant to be viewed from below, include *Ceres and Hercules Pay Homage to Venezia* (1575–1577) and the *Arrival of Saint Nicholas as Bishop of Myra*. Veronese's enthroned Virgin with Christ and the infant St John as well as Joseph, St Jerome, St Francis and St Justina is a groundbreaking Baroque altarpiece. **Tintoretto**'s early works (c. 1550) include the two paintings *Adam and Eve* and *Cain and Abel*, each of whom is shown naked from the front and rear, the former resting in harmony, the latter engaged in conflict, within a landscape. Venetian painting reached new heights with the light world of colour and joyous compositions of the Rococo painter Giovanni Battista **Tiepolo** (1696–1770), who rendered the large ceiling painting of *Saint Helena Finds the True Cross*.

Room 11

Significant works in the following rooms include the portrait of the procurator Jacopo Soranzo by **Tintoretto**, *St Jerome in Meditation* by Jacopo da Ponte, also known as **Bassano** (1517–1592), both in **room 13**, as well as the four mythological scenes *The Rape of Europa, Diana and Actaeon, Diana Discovers Calypso* and *Apollo and Marsyas*, early works (1720–1722) by Giambattista **Tiepolo** in **room 16**.

Room 17 Fantasy architecture, capricci of ruins and vedute with strong contrasts of light and shade are characteristics of Antonio Canal, also known as **Canaletto** (1697–1768), who combined observation of life with imagination in an entertaining manner. **Rosalba Carriera** (1675–1758) gained great fame with her pastel portraits. Few artists proved to be such keen-eyed chroniclers of Venetian everyday life in the 18th century as **Pietro Longhi** (1702–1785).

✶ ✶
Room 20 The cycle of paintings on the **miracles of the relic of the True Cross** is unique. Renowned Venetian artists painted it between 1494 and 1502 for the Sala dell'Albergo of the Scuola di San Giovanni Evangelista, in which a relic of the cross of Christ was kept from 1369. **Gentile Bellini** (1429–1507) painted the procession on Piazza San Marco with a detailed reproduction of the piazza from the time around 1500. The 13th-century medieval mosaics, which were later replaced, can still be seen above the five portals of St Mark's Basilica. The exhi-

Carpaccio has his »Healing of a possessed man by the relic of the True Cross« take place at the Rialto Bridge; this is probably how it appeared at the end of the 15th century.

bition continues with **Gentile's** depiction of the miracle of the True Cross relic at the Ponte San Lorenzo, where the relic had fallen into the water during the annual procession. It reappeared in the hand of the searching grand master of the Scuola and pulled him ashore. Witnesses to this event shown on the left of the painting include Catarina Cornaro, Queen of Cyprus, with her court and members of the Scuola to the right. Gentile sets the miraculous healing of Pietro de Ludovici in the interior of a church, most likely San Giovanni Evangelista. Vittore **Carpaccio** (1465–1526) has the miracle of the healing take place at the Rialto bridge and draws a precise picture of the buildings in the busy merchant quarter.

The **cycle on the life of Saint Ursula** in room 21, which was painted for the Scuola di Sant'Orsola, is the work of Vittore **Carpaccio** (c. 1465 to 1526). According to legend, Ursula, a Christian princess from Brittany, consented to marry Aetherius, the son of a heathen English ruler, on condition that he would be baptized and make a pilgrimage to Rome with her. On the return journey, Ursula and her companions suffered martyrdom, as had been predicted to her in a dream, before the gates of Cologne, which was besieged by the Huns.

✷ ✷
Room 21

The former church contains works of the early Venetian Renaissance, including altarpieces from the 1460s by Giovanni **Bellini** and his assistants. The last room, the guest house of the Carità brotherhood, houses **Titian's** *Mary in the Temple* (1534–1538). The only painting which he created for the brotherhood still hangs in its original place.

Room 23

Room 24

For centuries, the Ponte di Rialto was the only bridge across the Grand Canal. It was only in 1854 that the Austrian occupying power – Venice was part of the Habsburg kingdom of Lombardo-Venetia from 1815 – decided to build a second pedestrian crossing. This resulted in the iron academy bridge, which was replaced with a higher wooden bridge in 1932.

Ponte dell'Accademia

✶ I Gesuiti

G/H 9/10

Location: Campo Gesuiti   **Quay:** Ca' d'Oro

The Jesuits were not allowed into Venice until 1657, due to tensions between the republic and the pope. In 1715, the order decided to build a large monastery. In 1729, the church was completed to plans by Domenico Rossi. Its richly decorated protruding façade in the Baroque style, following the pattern of the mother church Il Gesù in Rome, impressively reflects the self-confidence of the order.
The barrel-vaulted hall with its side chapels, transept and choir is impressively furnished: wall coverings of green and white marble,

🕐
Opening hours:
Mon–Sat
10am–5pm,
Sun from 1pm

mighty columns, pilasters, gilding and a high altar with an altar canopy and sculptural decoration. The main item of interest, one of the paintings in the first chapel on the left, is Titian's *Martyrdom of Saint Lawrence* (1558–1560): beside the tortured saint, a light shimmering in the dark night announces the heavenly message, the soul's hope of eternal life. The *Assumption of the Virgin* by Tintoretto in the left transept, and the wall and ceiling paintings by Palma the Elder in the sacristy are also worthy of note.

★ ★
Titian's
*Martyrdom of
St Lawrence* ▶

**Oratorio dei
Crociferi**

In the adjacent Oratorio, an cycle by Palma the Elder (1583–1591) relates the story of the order of the Templars (open: Apr–Oct Fri 10am–12.30pm, Sat 3.30–7.30pm).

★ Ghetto

E 9/10

Location: Ghetto Vecchio and Ghetto Nuovo

Quays: S. Marcuola, Ponte Guglie

**Oldest ghetto of
the world**

In Cannaregio, not far from S. Lucia railway station, lies the world's oldest ghetto. Today, only a few of the approximately 500 Venetian Jews live in this city quarter, including pensioners in the old people's home Casa Israelitica de Riposo, and in other ways, too, the ghetto scarcely differs from the rest of the city. Nevertheless, a special atmosphere has remained here. It is revealed during a stroll through the quarter, when visiting the little museum and in a tour of a synagogue.

The Venetian republic was always home to people of varied nationalities and religions, who were all subject to strict control. This particularly applied to the Jews (▶Baedeker Special p.202), who only had limited residence rights. When anti-Semitic feeling intensified in the early 16th century, the Serenissima thought of a solution which was later adopted by nearly all cities: in 1516, the approximately 700 Jews were resettled to a city quarter in Cannaregio which had once been part of a cannon works, was surrounded by water and was called the »ghetto« in the Venetian dialect. This expression soon came into use for the Jewish quarters in all Italy. The Jews were allowed to move about freely in the daytime, but at dusk, they had to return to the ghetto. The entrances were closed at night and guarded by armed men. The Jews lived their own life in the ghetto. There were three communities of differing origins: Alemagni (Jews from Germany, Poland and other parts of eastern Europe), Levantines and Spanish Jews. The Jewish population increased greatly. In 1541, the ghetto was expanded to include the Ghetto Vecchio (old ghetto), and in 1633, the Ghetto Nuovissimo (newest ghetto). At times in the 17th century 5,000 people lived here, and the shortage of space forced the residents to build upwards. In this way, up to five-storey »skyscrapers« were constructed. Behind simple house façades, the ghetto contains the five best-preserved synagogues of the Middle Ages, a unique documentation of Jewish customs.

Viewing

The so-called schools and synagogues in the ghetto can only be viewed with guides (in Italian and English); the meeting and information point is at the Jewish museum, beginning hourly from 10.30 am.

The best way to reach the ghetto is from Fondamenta di Cannaregio and through a narrow access passage (Sottoportego, next to the kosher restaurant Gam-Gam, ►above), which was once closed at night. Only a few steps away, above on the left in the wall, is a stone tablet from 1704 with the catalogue of punishments for Jews who secretly adhered to their religious customs despite converting to Christianity. The narrow alley leads to Campiello delle Scuole, on which there are two synagogues. The **Scuola Spagnola** from the second half of the 16th century was redesigned in 1635 by the Baroque architect Baldassare Longhena. Brass chandeliers, gilded wood, multi-coloured marble and an elaborately ornamented balustrade decorate the interior. The **Scuola Levantina**, probably Venice's most magnificent synagogue, impresses with a richly carved lectern (teva) on spiral columns by Andrea Brustolon from Belluno.

 Baedeker TIP

Mouth-watering

Volpe, a bakery in the Old Ghetto, makes traditional Jewish delicacies including empade (almond pastries) and unleavened bread (pane azzimo; Paneficio Volpe, Calle del Ghetto Vecchio, tel. 0 41 71 51 78.
Gam-Gam, the only kosher restaurant in Venice, is situated at the entrance to the ghetto and has a wide range of traditional dishes (Sottoportego del Ghetto Vecchio, Cannaregio 1122; closed Fri evening and Sat, tel. 0 41 71 52 84.

Campo di Ghetto Nuovo

A narrow bridge leads to Campo di Ghetto Nuovo. Narrow, high buildings line the piazza. A memorial by sculptor Arbit Blatas tells of Rabbi Ottolenghi and 200 Venetian Jews who were deported with him between 1943 and 1944. At the house number 2912, a faded inscription marks the site of the »banco rosso«, one of the Jewish pawn houses, which were called »verde«, »negro« or »rosso« depending on the colour of their receipts, and lent money to all classes of Venetian society.

★ ★ ◄ Synagogues

Behind high, inconspicuous façades, three synagogues are concealed on the upper storeys. Five windows, a Baroque dome and a cartouche with the inscription »Santa Communità Italiana« identify the **Scuola Italiana**, the most modest of the Venetian synagogues, which was built in 1575. The adjacent **Scuola Ganton** – the name may go

Scuola Tedesca, the oldest synagogue in the ghetto

OLDEST GHETTO IN THE WORLD

The most famous Jew in Venice, Shylock, may be an invention by William Shakespeare (»The Merchant of Venice«, 1596/1597), but the city's ghetto actually exists. It is actually the oldest ghetto in the world.

There were probably small Jewish communities in Venice around the year 1000, when it was one of the most important reloading points between Europe and the Levant, the orient. In 1152, 100 Jews are mentioned in a census. As successful businessmen, they maintained trade relationships across all oceans. This was beneficial to the republic, since – using Jewish intermediaries – it was even able to sell goods to those countries with which it was feuding. This was one of the reasons that Jews settled in northern Italy and especially in Venice during a period when their fellow believers were being persecuted in Europe. However, their freedom was restricted. They were not permitted to own real estate, nor could they pursue a trade other than becoming a doctor (they were barred from the Christian guilds); they also had to pay taxes »for their protection«. However,

they were very successful in the business of loaning money (in which Christians could not engage since the New Testament forbade charging interest).

Fear of Foreign Infiltration

When ever more Jews streamed to the city after the infamous decree by Ferdinand the Catholic in 1492, which banished all Jews from Spain and Portugal, even the Venetians began to have misgivings. To make it easier to monitor them, the republic assigned the Jews a specific residential area in March of 1516: »All Jews must live together in the complex of houses located in the ghetto near San Girolamo; to ensure that they are not out and about all night, two gates shall be erected on the side of the Ghetto Vecchio where there is a small bridge, and also on the other side of the bridge; that is, one gate for each of the

Garb of a Levantine Jew in Venice

מוזיאון
עברי
MUSEO
EBRAICO

der of the city). Due to the lack of space, the houses grew upwards; some of them had up to eight storeys.

Three Nations

Three communities, called nations, existed side by side: Ashkenazim, Jews from Germany, Poland and other parts of eastern Europe; Levantines from the orient; and Sephardim, fugitives of the inquisition in Spain and Portugal. They had their own synagogues, called Scole – which now provide a unique point of reference regarding Jewish customs and culture during the renaissance – as well as their own teachers and judges, rabbis and social institutions. The group that represented their interests, Università, which was a panel with twelve and later six members with far-reaching social, religious and economic authority, was the negotiation partner for the Venetian government and regulated the distribution of the financial burdens that were imposed on them by the community in the form of taxes and forced loans. In short, the ghetto was a city within the city. This multicultural Jewish community pro-

locations mentioned. Each gate must be opened in the morning at the sound of the Marangona bell and must be locked in the evening at 12.00 midnight by four Christian guards, who are hired and paid for their services by their Jews at a price our council deems appropriate.« The name of the site where a foundry used to be located, Getto in Venetian, soon became the accepted term for the Jewish quarters in Italy and then all over the world. In 1516 the population of the ghetto was 700; by 1536 the number had more than doubled, and by 1630 it peaked at 5,000 residents. Thus Jews represented between 2.5 and 3.3 % of the total population of Venice in the 17th century. Soon the ghetto was overcrowded. At times, 897 persons per hectare lived here (236 in the remain-

Scuola Levantina, synagogue of the oriental Jews

duced eminent rabbis, scholars and poets, including Leone da Modena (1571-1648), Simone Lazzatto (1583-1663), Simone Calimani (1699-1784), and Sara Coppia Sullam (1590-1641), whose correspondence with the Genoese clergyman Ansaldo Céba represents an important contribution to the understanding between Christians and Jews. Hebrew printing, for which Venice was the most important centre, was essential in order to spread all of these ideas.

The end of the ghetto

Although the Jewish community in Venice was frequently subjected to hostilities, the Jews lived in relative safety by and large. When the situation of the republic continued to worsen during the 18th century, even Jewish capital was unable to stem the decline of Venice. Since the forced loans continued to increase in the face of the Turkish wars – the Jewish community paid the enormous sum of 800,000 gold ducats between 1669 and 1700 – the financial means of the Jewish lenders were finally exhausted; by 1737, the banks actually went bankrupt. The population shrank. Towards the end of the 18th century, only 1,620 Jews lived in the ghetto; approximately one third of them was well off, while the rest lived on the edge of poverty. In the end, outside forces were required to change their fate. On July 7, 1797, French soldiers tore down the ghetto gates; the residents became free citizens. The Jewish population gradually settled in other parts of the city. The ghetto degenerated. This did not change until Italy capitulated and the country was occupied in September 1943. 200 Jews were deported in August 1944. There are two monuments in their memory. Only a few Jews live in the ghetto today. There are only about 200 in the entire city, since young Jews are also moving to the mainland. And so the oldest ghetto in the world is kept alive by tourism alone.

The synagogues are scarcely recognizable from the outside, since they were actually built right into the residences. They can only be viewed as part of a guided tour (meeting place and information in the Jewish Museum, page 205).

back to the donor family or the location on a corner – was founded in 1531. The building is not recognizable from the outside, except for a small wooden cupola. In the interior, it is similar to a church, with a prayer pulpit (bima) in a small domed apse. The **Scuola Tedesca** is in the same building as the museum. The oldest synagogue in Venice can be recognized by its five large arched windows in the façade (three have been bricked up). It was built into the existing houses in 1528, which produced its slightly asymmetric layout. In the 18th century, it acquired a worldly character, and was rebuilt in the manner of a theatre. At that time it received its oval, gilded women's gallery.

Museo Ebraico
⏱
Opening hours:
Daily except Sat
Oct–May
10am–6pm,
June–Sept
10am–7pm

The little museum of the Jewish community exhibits liturgical items, manuscripts and documents about the history of the Venetian Jews, including oil lamps, crowns and cases for the law scrolls as well as a protective covering for the Esther scroll, which has been dated to the 5th century BC. This scroll tells of the rescue of the Persian Jews by Queen Esther. The museum has a bookstore and a café. Further information: www.jewishvenice.org.

There are tours of the Jewish cemetery on the ►Lido (information in the museum; in winter: Sun 2.30pm, in summer: Wed, Sun 2.30pm, Fri 10.30am and by appointment, tel. 0 41 71 53 59; meeting point Lido, Riviera S. Nicolò, opposite the quay).

Campo di Ghetto Nuovo, centre of the former Jewish ghetto

Giardini Pubblici

L/M 14

Location: Riva dei Sette Martiri   **Quay:** Giardini

The public gardens at the south end of the Venetian peninsula were built in 1807 at the command of Napoleon I. Since the founding of the **Biennale**, the exhibition pavilions of the various nations have stood here, including high-class examples of modern architecture. Nonetheless, there is enough space for Rococo and 19th-century statues and for a stroll under palm trees, acacias and plane trees. The most impressive buildings – which, however, are accessible only during the Biennale – include, to the right of the main entrance (by Antonio Selva, 1810) the Venetian pavilion (1954–1956) by Carlo Scarpa and beside it, the Russian pavilion (1914). The broad avenue leads straight ahead to the Italian pavilion in the classical style. Other renowned architects represented here are Josef Hoffmann (Austrian pavilion, 1934), Gerrit Thomas Rietveld (pavilion of the Netherlands, 1954) and Alvar Aalto (Finnish pavilion, 1956). The book pavilion, built of glass, was designed by the Glaswegian James Stirling (with Michael Wilford, 1991), the Australian pavilion (1988) by Peter Cox.

Sant' Elena   Sant' Elena, the outermost residential quarter in Castello, was not reclaimed from the lagoon until the 19th century. In addition to a naval school, the football stadium of the city is situated here.

The US Pavilion in the Giardini Pubblici on Biennial 2006

BIENNIAL

The oldest international forum for contemporary culture, the biennial of Venice, goes back to the initiative of the Venetian mayor, man of letters and artist Riccardo Selvatico in the year 1895.

When the gates opened for the first biennial on 30 April 1895 on the site of the Giardini in the Castello district, 516 works by 285 artists were on display in a single pavilion, which attracted almost 225,000 visitors. Success with the public was sustained during subsequent biennials; in 1909, a full 457,960 art connoisseurs came to Venice, a record that was not broken until 1976.

Initially, the art show was organized by topics instead of nationalities, and the works were selected through consultation with domestic and foreign art associations.

The 1907 biennial was the first to feature national pavilions. Today, the biennial site is home to approximately 30 pavilions administered by national commissioners, including some architecturally very interesting buildings.

Critics of the art show allege that little new material is being displayed and that the biennial is serving the art market and tourism. However, the art show has defended its place in the international art scene.

It takes place in odd-numbered years and runs for almost six months (June to October). It has also claimed additional exhibition spaces all over the city in addition to the Giardini, including the arsenal which is not accessible except during the art show. There is a varied music, dance and film supporting program parallel to the biennial. The next art biennials will take place in 2007 and 2009. In even-numbered years, the architecture biennial which is also very prestigious provides information on current trends. More information is available at www.labiennale.com.

View across the Canale della Giudecca on the Pallachio's Il Redentore

La Giudecca

Population: 4,640

Quays: Zitelle, Redentore, Palanca, Sant'Eufemia (Vaporetto 82, 41, 42)

Largest island of the lagoon

From the Zattere quay the Isola della Giudecca, to the south of the Canale della Giudecca, looks like a 2km/1.25-mi-long stage set. Three buildings dominate it: at the two ends, the church Le Zitelle and the massive former pasta factory Stucky, and at its centre, Palladio's Il Redentore church. La Giudecca actually consists of eight islands separated by canals (rii) and linked by bridges. Its original name was **Spina Lunga** (long fishbone); it probably owes its present name to the Giudicati, people who were banished here from Venice in the 9th century. Then well-off patricians discovered the island as a summer retreat. From the 14th century to the early 19th century, they built beautiful villas with extensive parks on the side towards the city centre, tucked away behind walls. The side towards the lagoon was occupied by seven monasteries and small palazzi of the literary academy, whose most brilliant member was Carlo Goldoni. In the 19th and 20th centuries, several industrial operations moved here, and the island became a workers' quarter. Aside from housing and a women's prison, there are still some workshops here, as well as the legendary Hotel Cipriani, the youth hostel and a few artists' studios. In 1924, the composer Luigi Nono (died 1990) was born on Giudecca. He was an uncompromising modernist and the son-in-law of the composer Arnold Schönberg.

> **! Baedeker TIP**
>
> ### Cheap sleep and Harry's Dolci
>
> For budget accommodation in a wonderful location: Ostello Venezia, the **youth hostel on the island of Giudecca**. It is necessary to book well in advance (Zitelle quay, bed and breakfast €17,50, vehostel@tin.it, www.ostellionline.org). For a break from sightseeing, go to **Harry's Dolci** at Fondamenta S. Biagio 773. Harry's Dolci is cheaper than its famous »big brother« Harry's Bar and has a magnificent view of Dorsoduro and San Marco from the terrace (wide selection of sweet delights as well as main courses; closed Tue and mid-Nov to mid-March, tel. 04 15 22 48 44.

✳ I Redentore

The white Franciscan church is regarded as one of the main works of Andrea Palladio (► Famous People). He was guided by models from antiquity, particularly the ten books of architecture by Vitruvius from the time of the Emperor Augustus. Consequently, Palladio composed the front of I Redentore from three temple façades placed one inside the other. Palladio adopted the double pediment and attic storeys from the Pantheon in Rome, while the dominant dome between the nave and the monks' choir forms the centre of the aisle-less hall church.

◄ Quay: Redentore
🕐
Opening hours: daily 10am–5pm, Sun from 1pm

The **Festival of the Redeemer** (Festa del Redentore) and the church have their origins in a plague epidemic of 1576, which claimed the lives of 50,000 people, one third of the population of the city. At that time, the senate vowed to build the church and hold a celebration for the Redeemer (Redentore). The Franciscan order took responsibility for holding services. Construction began in July 1577. After Palladio's death, the building was completed by Antonio da Ponte, the architect of the Rialto bridge, in 1592. Three oval chapels lie on each side of the nave, whose design is reminiscent of a hall in Roman baths. Their altarpieces depict scenes from the life of Christ. The *Baptism of Christ* originates from the workshop of Veronese, while the two altarpieces *Flagellation* and *Transfiguration of Jesus* are from the school of Tintoretto. While the late Baroque main altar was built only in 1680, the bronze crucifixion group dates from the late 16th century. Like the high altar, it is by Girolamo Campagna (1550–1623).

Il Redentore Plan

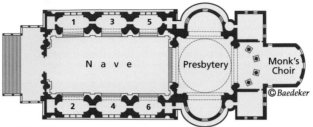

© Baedeker

Altar Paintings

1 »Ascension of Christ«,
   school of Tintoretto
2 »Nativity« by Francesco Bassano
3 »Resurrection« by Francesco Bassano

4 »Baptism of Christ«, school of Veronese
5 »Entombment of Christ«
   by Palma il Giovane
6 »Flagellation of Christ«, school of Tintoretto

Festa del Redentore

After the church was consecrated, the doge made a procession here over a floating bridge of boats every year with the leading persons of the state to attend the mass of thanksgiving. This **Festival of the Redeemer** is still held. On the third Sunday in June, the Venetians take part in a procession, now across a pontoon bridge, from Zattere across the Canale della Giudecca to the Redentore church. The festival ends in the evening with magnificent fireworks and a parade of illuminated boats.

Le Zitelle

500m/550yd east, the church Le Zitelle, whose official name is Santa Maria della Presentazione, derives from Andrea Palladio. However, it was only built after his death, from 1582–1586, by Jacopo Bozzetto. The church itself is largely a structure of the 18th century. The monastery that was once associated with it was a foundation for girls from poor families (Le Zitelle = virgins), who produced famous lace here.

Sant'Eufemia

The church dedicated to the Roman martyr Euphemia, about 600m/650yd to the west, was founded in the 9th century. It received its classical colonnade from Tommaso Temanza, who rebuilt it in the 18th century. At that time, its interior was also painted by Giambattista Canal, following the example of ►Il Gesuiti. Bartolomeo Vivarini painted the triptych *San Rocco and the Angel* as well as the scene in the lunette above it, *Virgin with Child* (1480; first altar in the right aisle).

Mulino Stucky

The giant brick complex Mulino Stucky occupies the end of the island. Despite vigorous protests, the well-off pasta manufacturer Giovanni Stucky had it built in 1895, with a mill, grain silos and warehouses, by the architect Ernst Wullekopf in the neo-Gothic style. It was in operation until 1954 and was then left to decay. It is currently being converted. In addition to a luxury hotel, the complex will house a conference centre, offices and apartments.

On the plot Giudecca 484, where the company Junghans once manufactured clocks, student apartments, apartments, stores and a cultural centre are being built to plans by Cino Zucchi between sections of the Junghans building.

Other points of interest

Islands in the Lagoon

Excursion

Small islands lie like enchanted oases in the shallow waters of the Venetian lagoon. Emilio Casteler described them as »floating gardens«, and Lord Byron saw the islands »rising from the waters as if invoked by fairies«. Except for ► Burano, ► Murano and ► Torcello, few islands are inhabited today. And those who see the lonely, partly overgrown islands can scarcely imagine that Venice's history began here 1500 years ago (►p.31). In the past, the islands served a variety of purposes. Some had monasteries, accommodation for pilgrims on their way to the Holy Land, or hospitals and quarantine stations. Others were made into octagonal forts, semicircular batteries or powder stores for Venice's defence system. Nearly all these structures have been abandoned. The buildings fell into ruin, though the building material often found new uses, and nature took over. In recent years, the city authorities have leased or sold some islands to private investors or environmental organizations. Other islands were rediscovered by Venetians as places for excursions – especially in summer, when Venice is »flooded« by tourists. The larger islands are served by the vaporetti network. Out-of-the-way islands can be explored individually or on guided tours.

The archipelago of Venice

Northern Lagoon

The cypress-covered cemetery island, halfway between Fondamenta Nuove and ► Murano, was used in the 13th century by Camaldolese monks. It has been the cemetery island of Venice since 1870. Among others, the Russian ballet impresario Sergei Diaghilev (1872–1929), his countryman and composer Igor Stravinsky (1882–1971) and the American poet Ezra Pound (1885–1972) rest here. Of the monastery, the 15th-century Gothic cloister and the lovely Renaissance church San Michele by Mauro Coducci (1469–1478) remain. A connecting door gives access to the hexagonal Cappella Emiliana, which is decorated with red and green marble and was added in 1530 by Guglielmo Bergamasco. There are plans to have the cemetery island expanded by the architect David Chipperfield.

✷
San Michele
◄ Vaporetto 41, 42 from Fondamenta Nuove

Harvesting cauliflower on Sant'Erasmo

Sant'Erasmo and Le Vignole

Vaporetto 13 from Fondamenta Nuove
▶

For centuries, Le Vignole and particularly Sant'Erasmo have been Venice's vegetable gardens and popular places for excursions: miles of wet, fertile land with extensive fields on which asparagus, artichokes (castraure), onions, potatoes and grapevines grow – all of which are sold in the Rialto market. Both islands were fortified in the 19th century. Reminders of this include the Forte di Sant' Andrea on Le Vignole and the Torre Massimiliana on Sant'Erasmo.

The ferry first stops at **Le Vignole**. The island used to be named Isola delle Sette Vigne, island of the seven vineyards. Wine is still grown here, and is known for its slightly salty taste (wine festival, Festa del Mosto on the first Sunday in October). **Sant'Erasmo** is the largest island in the lagoon and suitable for a long hike. About 800 people still live here, mainly engaged in agriculture (there are three quays as well as private automobile traffic). It is best to disembark at the first stop (Capannone) and walk in the direction of Torre Massimiliana. There is a small beach at the fortification tower in the south-east of the island, where Ai Tedeschi has simple, tasty dishes (open daily). From here, the road leads through fields and meadows around the island. At its centre, there is a second bar, Ca' Vignotto (usually only open in the evenings).

★
San Francesco del Deserto

Legend tells that St Francis stopped on this tiny island between Burano and Sant'Erasmo on his way home from the Holy Land in 1220. Franciscan monks lived on the island from the 13th to the 15th century. From that time, it remained abandoned until the 19th century. Today, nothing reminds visitors of the times of decay. The seven monks who live here offer guided tours for a small donation. The monastery buildings are built of grey brick and grouped at the centre of the island. The small church dating from 1228 is situated amongst cypress trees and has an enchanting atmosphere. There are also options for overnight stays (register in advance; guided tours daily except Mon 9–11am, 3–5pm; **get there** by vaporetto to Burano, continuing by water taxi).

The first residents of this island south-west of Sant'Erasmo were hermits. From 1846, a quarantine station for people and goods was located here. In 1576, during the plague epidemic, up to 10,000 are said to have been housed here. Today, nature has largely reclaimed the island. Visits by appointment (tel. 04 12 44 40 11).

Lazzaretto Nuovo

South Lagoon

The ferry to San Lazzaro (►below) first stops on San Servolo, once a monastery, then a psychiatric institution. Today, the island houses the Venice European Restoration Centre for conservation crafts, where stonemasons, carpenters, painters, stucco plasterers and others from various countries learn and work. It is also home to the Venice International University, a joint project of various universities for students and lecturers (information tel. 04 12 71 95 11 and www.uni-viu.org).

San Servolo

San Lazzaro, the island before the Lido, is only 3 hectares (7 acres) in size – space enough for a monastery, a garden and a little cemetery. Today, eight Mechitharist monks live here. In 1717 Mechithar, the Armenian founder of the order (born 1676 in Sivas, Anatolia; Armenian: Sebaste) fled to Venice from Ottoman forces with 19 brothers of the order. The doge granted them the use of the little island. The monastery museum exhibits documents on Armenian history and a 3,000-year-old Egyptian mummy, below a ceiling painting by Tiepolo. Its most precious treasure is the Armenian library with about 150,000 books and writings from the years 862 to 1700, among them the Armenian translation of a lost Greek biography of Alexander the Great as well as a medical book from 1281. In the monastery's own publishing house, the monks published the main works of Armenian literature, translations of important works of Italian literature, and a series of dictionaries. One exhibition room displays mementoes of Lord Byron. The romantic poet and traveller lived on the island in 1816 to learn the language of the monks. The monastery can be viewed daily on a guided tour by the monks between 3.30pm and 5.30pm.
About 300,000 of the eight million Armenians belong to the Armenian Catholic church. It recognizes the pope, but celebrates its mass with old Armenian liturgy. The patriarch is based in Lebanon.

★ ★
San Lazzaro degli Armeni

◄ Vaporetto 20 from S. Zaccharia, departure at 3.10pm

◄ Viewing

The many pilgrims who sailed from Venice to the Holy Land in the Middle Ages had their own accommodation on the islands La Grazia

La Grazia and Lazzaretto Vecchio

San Lazzaro degli Armeni: Mechithar monastery in the lagoon of Venice

and Lazzaretto Vecchio. Later, epidemics and infectious diseases were treated here. Lazzaretto Vecchio has recently found use as an animal home.

Lido di Venezia

Population: 16,000   **Quay:** Santa Maria Elisabetta

Vaporetto 1, 51, 52, 61,62; car ferry from Tronchetto ▶

In the 19th century, writers such as Lord Byron, Shelley and Musset »discovered« the Lido, then an uninhabited flat strip of sand separating the lagoon of Venice from the sea. The island, which is 12km/ 7.5mi long and no more than 4km/2.5mi wide, with its flat sandy beaches was an inviting place for a stroll, swimming or riding – a seaside holiday. In the early 20th century, the Lido was the most elegant seaside resort in all of Europe. Today, it is a suburb of Venice, and mostly draws Venetians and vacationers to its beaches in the summer. However, with the exception of one small strip, the beaches in front of the large hotels are mainly private. There are also numerous facilities for sport, including a golf course on the Lido (in Alberoni).

Venice has always been a favourite backdrop for cinematic history. **The Golden Lion**
The first Venetian **film festival** took place in 1932 in the Hotel Excelsior, with great success. Three years
later, the Palazzo del Cinema, designed by Luigi Quagliata, was
opened on the Lido. Every year at
the end of August and in early September, the famous Premio Leone
d'Oro di San Marco, the Italian
variant of the American Oscar, is
awarded to the best films and actors here. Films are shown in the
Palazzo del Cinema and in some
smaller cinemas (information:
www.labiennale.org). Major directors such as John Ford, Louis
Malle, John Cassavetes, De Sica,
Fellini and Visconti enjoyed major triumphs here. And even today,
the Golden Lion is one of the most coveted awards in the art of film.

> ! **Baedeker** TIP

Hire a bike

The best way to explore the Lido is by bicycle.
Hire one at Barbieri (Via Zara 5, tel.
04 15 26 14 90), Gardin (Piazzale Santa Maria
Elisabetta 2/A, tel. 04 12 76 00 05) or Lazzari
(Gran Viale Santa Maria Elisabetta 21/B, tel.
04 15 26 80 19). But remember: after a few days
in car-free Venice, on the Lido you will have to
get used to traffic again.

Today, only a few 19th-century buildings, villas in the Liberty style **What to see**
(the Italian variant of Art Nouveau) and hotel complexes serve as re- **on the Lido**
minders of the imposing past, particularly the neo-Moorish Grand
Hotel Excelsior and the exclusive »Des Bains«, the illustrious setting
of Thomas Mann's *Death in Venice*, which was filmed by Luchino
Visconti. To reach it, start at S. Maria Elisabetta quay and follow the
Gran Viale to the beach on the other side of the island.

Until 1797, the church of San Nicolò at the north end of the Lido **San Nicolò**
was the goal of the **Sposalizio col Mare** (the marriage of the doge ◄ San Nicolò quay
with the sea). According to a custom first documented in 998, the
doge went out onto the sea once a year and tossed a ring into the
waves as a symbolic marriage of Venezia to the sea. In the 17th century, the church was remodelled in the Baroque style. This was the
resting place of the bones of St Nicholas, which Venetian sailors had
stolen from the cathedral of Myra on the south coast of Asia Minor
– or so it was thought. However, the Venetians then discovered that
the residents of Bari (Apulia) had got there first. The choir stalls
(1635) by Giovanni da Crema tell the legend.
From S. Nicolò there is a lovely view across the lagoon to the fortifications of Sant'Andrea, which were built in 1543 by Michele Sanmi-
chele and expanded after the battle of Lepanto in 1571.

Jews have been buried in the cemetery at San Nicolò since the 14th **Cimitero**
century. The old section is especially picturesque. Here, a simple **Israelitico**
stone slab over a mass grave is a reminder of the plague epidemic of
1630 to 1631, which claimed the lives of nearly 2,000 Jews. The Jewish museum offers guided tours (►Ghetto).

Upscale address on the Lido: Grand Hotel Excelsior

Malamocco, Alberoni

Pellestrina ►

The quiet villages of Malamocco and Alberoni lie in the south of the island. From here, a car ferry operates across the busiest opening in the lagoon to Pellestrina, a narrow sliver of land protected since the mid-18th century by the **murazzi**, embankments of Istrian stone. At the outermost end of Pellestrina, the ferry crosses to ►Chioggia.

Littorale del Cavallino

Excursion

Punta Sabbioni, Litorale del Cavallino

The sandy beaches and pine forests of the 15km/9mi-long, very narrow spit of land to the east of Venice, Littorale del Cavallino, make it an excellent camping and bathing area. From Punta Sabbioni, the peninsula across from Venice (where there is car parking for a fee), boats make regular crossings (quays in Fondamenta Nuove and Paglia near S. Marco).

✱

Lido di Jesolo

Lido di Jesolo (population: 23,000) is a **superlative beach resort**: a row of deck chairs about 15km/9mi long on a fine sandy beach, more than 400 hotels, several camping sites, innumerable restaurants, cafés, bars and discos as well as a large variety of sports. The popular place in the evenings is the main shopping street Via Andrea

Bafile, which runs parallel to the beach. During the main season, it is closed to traffic from 8pm, turning it into a promenade about 10km/ 6mi long. Buses go to Venice from here (Piazzale Roma; 1 hour 10 min) as well as via Cavallino to Treporti, from where a boat goes to S. Zaccaria. The little country town from which it takes its name, Jesolo, lies a few kilometres inland. Three monasteries and 40 churches serve as reminders that this town was once a centre of Christian culture.

◄ Jesolo

★ Madonna dell'Orto
Santa Maria dell'Orto

F/G 8/9

Location: Fondamenta della Madonna dell'Orto

Quay: Madonna dell'Orto

The fact that the church was originally dedicated to St Christopher is commemorated in a statue by Bartolomeo Bon above the entrance. According to legend, its present-day name derives from the discovery of a Madonna statue in a nearby vegetable garden (»orto« in Italian).

🕐 Opening hours: Mon–Sat 10am–5pm, Sun from 1pm

The conspicuous brick façade of the church, which was completed in 1462, combines the Gothic and Renaissance styles. It is adorned by figures of the twelve apostles which are ascribed to Jacobello dalle Masegne and his workshop.

The interior contains the tomb of Jacopo Rubusti, also known as **Tintoretto**, who was buried in the chapel to the right of the presbytery. His son Domenico rests at his side. The artist, who lived nearby, created several works for this church, among them *The Last Judgment* (on the right in the choir), *Worship of the Golden Calf* (on the left in the choir), *St Agnes Revives Licinius* (fourth chapel to the left) and *Presentation of Mary in the Temple* (about 1552) above the entrance to St Mark's chapel in the right aisle. Other items of interest include a Madonna (1480) by Giovanni Bellini (last chapel in the left aisle) and a panel depicting

Tintoretto's »private church« Madonna dell'Orto

St John the Baptist with Saints (1493) by Cima da Conegliano (first altar to the right).

Campo dei Mori

On the other side of the canal lies Campo dei Mori. Its name probably comes from the Mastelli merchant dynasty, who had the palace of the same name built here in the 12th century and originally came from the Morea (the Venetian name for the Peloponnese). The merchants are immortalized in strange statues, identifiable by their turbans, in the façade of a corner house.

Casa del Tintoretto ►

The painter Tintoretto died on 31 May 1594 in the house next to the fourth negro figure (Cannaregio 3399).

Sant'Alvise
⏱
Opening hours:
Mon–Sat
10am–5pm,
Sun from 1pm

The church with the impressive brick façade to the north-west of Madonna dell'Orto was built in the late 14th century. It is dedicated to St Louis of Toulouse (Alvise is the Venetian form of Louis). In the interior, the column-borne nuns' choir above the entrance as well as the *Ascent to Calvary* on the right wall of the choir, by **Tiepolo**, are of interest. He also painted the *Flagellation* and the *Crowning with Thorns* (1740).

✴ Mercerie

G/H 11/12

Location: Between the Rialto bridge and Piazza S. Marco

Quays: Rialto, Vallaresso S. Marco

The classic shopping street

The Mercerie, a chain of several streets, is the oldest and most important link between the political-religious and economic centres of the Serenissima: San Marco and Rialto. Merchants have always offered their wares here (»mercerie« means dry goods). Today, it is *the* shopping quarter of Venice. Anything can be found here – unusual jewellery stores, shops with an assortment of kitsch, elegant fashions, artistic carnival masks and costumes. However, bargain-hunters will quickly be disappointed: Venice is expensive.

Campo San Bartolomeo

Keep right from the Ponte di Rialto to reach the small Campo S. Bartolomeo. This piazza – where a monument to Carlo Goldoni stands – is the meeting place of Venetian youth in the evenings. Past the church S. Bartolomeo and across Via 2 Aprile is Merceria San Salvador, named after the church (► below). In its further course, the Mercerie changes its name and joins the large Piazza San Marco below the clock tower (Torre dell'Orologio) as Merceria dell'Orologio.

✴ San Salvador
⏱
Opening hours:
Mon–Fri 9am–12
noon, 3–6pm

The church at the centre of the Mercerie was built between 1507 and 1534 by Tullio Lombardo and Sansovino in the Renaissance style. In the 17th century, Giuseppe Sardi designed its Baroque façade. The interior, which is covered by three domes, contains some precious

Shopping paradise Via Larga XXII Marzo

art treasures, among them the magnificent tomb of Doge Francesco Venier (1556 by Sansovino; after the second altar on the left), as well as the wall tombs of the Corner family on the end walls of the transept arms, including the tomb of Caterina Corner (1454–1510), Queen of Cyprus. Titian painted the *Annunciation* (last altar to the right before the crossing; the marble frame is by Sansovino) and the *Transfiguration of Christ* (above the high altar). Further items of note are the *Martyrdom of St Theodore* by Paris Bordone (to the right of the choir) and *Christ in Emmaus* by Vittore Carpaccio (in the Cappella del Santissimo to the left of the high altar).

✷ Other shopping streets

Even more exclusive (and expensive) shopping is found below the arcades of Piazza San Marco, **Calle Vallaresso** to the west and its extension, **Calle Larga XXII Marzo**, which is unusually wide for Venice. Top designers, high-class leather shops, jewellers and exquisite antique shops have settled here. For a pleasant break after a long shopping tour, there is a wide selection of small bakeries and restaurants with irresistible delicacies and local specialities.

San Moisè

Even though the Baroque façade, done in 1668 by Alessandro Remignon, seems excessive to some connoisseurs, Venetians love their church of San Moisè, which was dedicated to Moses in the 9th century and lies on Campo San Moisè. The interior houses a *Washing of Feet* by Tintoretto and a *Last Supper* by Palma the Younger. The stone-sculpted altar by Heinrich Meyring shows Moses receiving the Ten Commandments on Mount Sinai. The concrete-grey façade next to S. Moisè is part of the luxury hotel **Bauer Grünwald**.

Santa Maria del Giglio

⊙
Opening hours:
Mon–Sat
10am–5pm,
Sun from 1pm

The donor of the church with its unusual Baroque façade (1680, Giuseppe Sardi; at the west end of Calle Larga XXII Marzo) was Antonio Barbaro. In return, the successful capitano da mar had himself immortalized on the façade: he stands carved in stone above the main portal, with some of his ancestors below him. The lower zones are decorated with reliefs showing panoramas of the cities which played a role in his career: Padua, Chania (Crete), Zadar (left), Rome, Corfu and Split (right). The interior contains the following notable paintings: two early works by Tintoretto (about 1550) and one by Peter Paul Rubens (17th century) in the Molin chapel.

✶✶ **Murano**

J–M 4–7

Population: 4,930   **Quay:** Murano

Vaporetto
41, 42 from Fondamenta Nuove ►

The »**island of glass blowers**« (►Baedeker Special p.222) is reminiscent of Venice itself, with its main canal and numerous small side canals.

From the Colonna quay, follow the two main streets Fondamenta dei Vetrai and Fondamenta Cavour past workshops where the glassblowers can be watched at work and stores are filled with glass souvenirs. The island makes its living from glass production even today. Murano was one of the first islands to be settled. Until 1291, the residents lived from fishing and the salt trade. The decision to move glass production from Venice to Murano brought prosperity to the island. In the 16th century, when Murano had about 30,000 residents, the island became a popular summer residence for rich Venetian patricians, who had palaces and pleasure gardens here – and finally, Italy's first botanical gardens were laid out here. Even today, the island is one of the main attractions during a visit to Venice and easy to reach.

> **!** *Baedeker* TIP
>
> **Glass art**
> The following ateliers are recommended:
> Cenedese, Fondamenta Venier 48,
> Mazzega, Fondamenta da Mula 147,
> Venini, Fondamenta Vetrai 47–50
> Ferro & Lazzarini, Fondamenta Navagero 75.
> The ateliers and shops are mostly closed at weekends.

The church, which was rebuilt in 1511 after a fire, has valuable art treasures: the *Enthroned Madonna* (1488) in the right aisle is by Giovanni Bellini, likewise the *Assumption of the Virgin* (1505–1513). The left aisle contains Veronese's paintings *St Jerome in the Desert* and *St Agatha in the Dungeon*. There is also the beautiful Palazzo Da Mula, a Renaissance villa.

San Pietro Martire

The glass museum in Palazzo Giustinian (17th century; Fondamenta Giustinian 8) has one of the largest collections of Venetian glass. Exhibits from Roman times as well as from Bohemian and Moorish glass-blowers are also on display. One of the most famed exhibits is the **Coppa Barovier**, a unique wedding chalice from the 15th century. It is made of dark blue glass decorated with enamelled medallions showing pictures of the couple and allegorical scenes. This work is probably by the daughter of Angelo Barovier, from Murano's most famous family of glass-blowers.

✱
Museo del Vetro
🕐
Opening hours:
Daily except Wed
10am–5pm,
Nov–March
to 4pm

Murano's most beautiful church was initially dedicated only to the Virgin. From the 12th century, it was also dedicated to St Donatus. It was built between the 7th and 12th centuries and is one of the oldest places of worship in the lagoon. The apse is especially beautiful – an

✱
Santi Maria e Donato

Arches, alcoves, columns and marble incrustations: Santa Maria e Donato

In a glassworks on Murano

BLOWN JEWEL

Glass manufacturing was known in Venice as early as the end of the 10th century. It received a significant boost after the fourth crusade in 1204 when oriental techniques were adopted. From then on, the glass industry was guarded like a state secret. Venice had a glass monopoly for centuries.

At the time, the workshops were still located at the centre of the city on the lagoon. After repeated catastrophic fires, the last one of which took place in 1291, the senate ordered them to be moved to Murano – the official reason was to reduce the risk of fires, but the unofficial reason that probably comes closer to the truth was to prevent espionage. The first known guild rules also come from this period; the »Mariegola« from 1441, framed with velvet and silver, can be admired in the Museo Correr. Murano glass was a coveted luxury item as early as the middle of the 14th century; pearls, lenses for glasses, chandeliers and filigree drinking glasses were exported all the way to China. Starting in the 15th century, the list of products also included magnificently framed mirrors after Muzio da Murano discovered that applying a solution of tin and quicksilver creates a lasting reflective surface.

Discoveries

In the middle of the 15th century, Angelo Barovier invented Cristallo, a glass reminiscent of rock crystal that is free of bubbles and tints. Around the same time another master created Calcedonio, a multi-coloured glass similar to agate. Rubino, tinted pink by the addition of a gold solution, was an invention from the 16th century; Aventurin, sprinkled with copper particles and exuding a mysterious shimmer, was invented by Briani in the 17th century. The most sophisticated techniques include the filigree net and Reticella glass known since the 16th century, with fine white and coloured threads applied to the surface of the blown glass. In the old

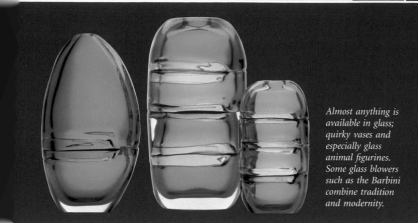

Almost anything is available in glass; quirky vases and especially glass animal figurines. Some glass blowers such as the Barbini combine tradition and modernity.

technique known as Murrine or Millefiori, coloured rods are incorporated in transparent glass. Lattimo is a milky white glass, which was usually decorated with lacquer in the 15th century and then looked like porcelain. The most important raw materials – quartz sand (mostly pebbles from the Tessin river up until the 17th century), limestone and soda – are brought to the melting point in an oven at 1,400°C. After cooling to between 1,000 and 500° C the glass is formed; afterwards, the item is allowed to fully cool slowly. Various colours are created by adding metal oxides.

Privileges and Threats

Glass production was the best-kept secret until the 17th century. The guild of the Vetrai, the glass blowers, was held in high esteem and enjoyed numerous privileges. Murano had its own government and a Libro d'Oro that listed the long-established families. However, they were prohibited from leaving the lagoon under pain of death since this meant a betrayal of secrets. An edict from 1454 said: »A glass blower who brings a skill to another country to the detriment of the republic shall be asked to return home; if he refuses, his nearest relatives shall be thrown into prison… if he persists in his disobedience, clandestine measures are to be taken in order to eliminate him wherever he may be.« In spite of these threats, some fled to northern Europe in the 16th century. In the 17th and 18th centuries, flourishing manufactures were set up with glass blowers lured away from the city on the lagoon, mainly in France and Bohemia. Foreign competition and the end of the republic in 1797 ultimately led to the demise of glass manufacturing on Murano; it was finally revived in the middle of the 19th century through the engagement of traditional glass blower families such as the Barovier, Seguso, Salviati and Teso. Today there are almost 100 glassworks employing around 6,000 people on the island, with most of the products destined for the export market. But now it is no longer a secret; instead, one can watch the glassmakers ply their trade in many of the facilities.

ensemble of arches and columns with detailed designs, combining Venetian-Byzantine and early Romanesque elements and forming a contrast to the simple brick façade. In the interior, columns of Greek marble with Venetian-Byzantine capitals separate the two aisles from the nave. The lovely 12th-century mosaic floor with its lively animal figures and fine ornamentation is like an oriental carpet. The painted relief icon of St Donatus above the first altar to the left dates from 1310 and is one of the earliest works of Venetian painting. Other items of interest include a Byzantine mosaic *Madonna at Prayer* (c. 1450), the altarpiece *Death of the Virgin* (late 14th century) on the wall of the left aisle, *Madonna with Saints* at the entrance to the baptistery (1484) by Lazzaro Bastiani, and within the baptistery, a sarcophagus from Altinum, which was formerly used as a baptismal font.

★ Palazzo Contarini del Bovolo

F 12

Location: Calle della Vida/Rio dei Barcaroli   **Quay:** Rialto

⊕
Opening hours:
Apr–Oct
daily 10am–6pm,
Nov–March Sat–Sun
to 4pm

Palazzo Contarini del Bovolo is probably the only palace in Venice whose inner courtyard is more interesting than the canal façade, which faces Rio dei Barcaroli (to get there, start at Campo Manin; beside the monument for the freedom fighter of 1848, Calle della Vida leads to the palace). The inner courtyard contains the wonderful spiral staircase, the »bovolo«, which was built onto the palazzo in 1500 by the Lombard architect Giovanni Candi (bovolo is the Venetian word for chiocciola, snail). The stair tower links the five loggias of the palace, and its round-arch arcades are reminiscent of the Leaning Tower of Pisa. The spiral staircase is accessible and offers a beautiful view.

★★ Palazzo Ducale

H 12

Location: Piazza San Marco   **Quay:** Vallaresso S. Marco, San Zaccaria

⊕
Opening hours:
Apr–Oct
daily 9am–7pm,
Nov–March to 5pm,
last admission 1
hour earlier

The Doge's Palace, Palazzo Ducale, was the seat of power of the republic for more than 1000 years – both the residence of the doge and the state prison. Today, it is one of the most important secular buildings in the world.

The first Doge's Palace on this site was built in 814. It was a dark wooden structure with massive fortified towers, protected by canals on three sides and by the lagoon to the south. In the 12th century, it was replaced by a new structure in the Byzantine style with loggias

Palazzo Ducale, symbol of the republic, seen from the wharf

and arcades. Around the mid-14th century, the membership of the Grand Council had risen to more than 1,000. Since a new, more spacious meeting hall was needed, it was decided to build today's Doge's Palace.

Outside view

The palace is 71x75m/233x246ft in size and consists of three wings around an inner courtyard that is roughly trapezium-shaped. From 1340 to 1400, the south wing facing the Molo was built. Between 1424 and 1438, the west wing on the Piazzetta followed, and finally, in 1483, the east wing, which took until the 17th century to build. The ▶ Basilica di San Marco forms the northern boundary. Fires in the palace repeatedly caused great damage, but mainly affected the interior furnishings.

The façade of the Doge's Palace is derived from those of Venetian nobles' palaces of the 12th and 13th centuries: on the ground floor, open arcades rest on low columns without bases, which are sunk nearly 40cm/16in into the pavement (the level of the piazza has been raised several times). Above this is a loggia with slender and more closely spaced columned arches. The pointed arches and quatrefoil openings in the gaps served as a model for Venetian ornamentation of the entire late Gothic period. The upper part of the façade is clad in white and red marble, with pointed-arch windows as openings in the wall surface. Pierced crenellations crown the building.

Ponte dei Sospiri The east façade toward Rio di Palazzo was designed by Mauro Coducci. Here, the elegant »Bridge of Sighs« catches the eye (►photo p.16). It links the Doge's Palace to the **Prigioni Nuove** (the new prisons, 1589–1614) on the other side of the canal. They were built of Istrian stone to plans by Antonio Contin, and already herald the Baroque style in Venice.

★★ South façade The south façade – the main view from the lagoon – is one of the oldest parts of the exterior. Only the balcony of the central window breaks through the uniform surface of the upper structure. According to an inscription, Doge Michele Steno was the donor in 1404. The Gothic window framing was produced in the workshop of Pierpaolo dalle Masegne. The crowning balcony was renewed after the fire in 1577. The statue of Justice is by Alessandro Vittoria, the statue of St George by Giovanni Battista Pellegrini (18th century).

 DON'T MISS

- Scala dei Giganti
- Collegio and Anticollegio
- Sala del Maggior Consiglio with the world's largest painting on canvas
- Itinerari Segreti, a guided tour to the inner workings of the Doge's Palace
- Hieronymus Bosch in the Sala del Magistrato

The sculptural decoration on the corners of the building dates from the 14th century; the statues on the side to the Ponte della Paglia show the archangel Raphael and Tobias (top) and the drunken Noah. In the direction of the Piazzetta, they show the archangel Michael as well as Adam and Eve. Both here and on the façade towards the Piazzetta, there are 14th-century **capitals** (many have been replaced by copies; the originals are exhibited in the Museo dell'Opera). Various motifs – leaf capitals, busts of emperors, mythical beasts, animals, allegories of virtues and vices, seasons and the ages of man – are freely combined here.

★★ West façade The façade towards the Piazzetta, which was carried out between 1424 and 1438, is a mirror image of the older south wing. The balcony followed in the 16th century. A lion of St Mark is enthroned above it, and above the lion, Justice. It was from here, between the two pink columns, that the doge observed the executions that were carried out on the Piazzetta. The sculptures at the corner towards the Porta della Carta – the archangel Gabriel with the judgement of Solomon below – are ascribed to Bartolomeo Bon.

Porta della Carta The Porta della Carta forms the architectural link between St Mark's Basilica and the Doge's Palace. Aside from Ca' d'Oro, it is regarded as the most important work of the Gothic period in Venice. Giovanni and Bartolomeo Bon worked on the design from 1438 to 1442. Two large supporting pillars frame the entrance and the window above it. Above the gate, Doge Francesco Foscari kneels before the lion of St Mark, demonstrating the subordination of the individual to state power (photo p.38). Above the window, St Mark is shown, and above him, the allegory of Justice, accompanied by two lions. The name, »Gate of Paper«, comes from the supplicants who were not allowed to enter the palace. At this gate, the council and government officials received written requests and petitions. Due to the gilding, which has faded today, the door was also called the »porta aurea«. The laws of the republic were announced at this gate.

Inner Courtyard

Today, the palace is entered through the Porta del Frumento on the lagoon side. In the inner courtyard, two bronze wells (mid-16th century) and the Scala dei Giganti are visible before the east wing. The »giants' stairway«, designed by Antonio Rizzo from 1483, was the scene for major events. Newly elected doges swore loyalty on the top

✷
Scala dei Giganti

Arco Foscari in the courtyard of the Palazzo Ducale

step. After the vow, the embroidered "corno ducale", in the form of a stylized Phrygian fisherman's cap, which was embroidered by the nuns of Zaccaria, was placed on the doge's head. The name of the stairway comes from the two colossal statues of Mars and Neptune (1550) by Jacopo Sansovino, representing the rule of Venice on water and on land. The fine relief decoration of the stair balustrade and the pedestal of floral Renaissance ornamentation are noteworthy.

Arco Foscari ✸ The richly decorated triumphal arch, Arco Foscari, lies opposite the stairway. The niches of the lower floor contain the figures of Adam and Eve by Antonio Rizzo (replicas stand here today; the originals are in the Andito del Maggior Consiglio). On the second floor above the door, allegories of virtues and vices stand on turrets and pedestals. Above the gate, St Mark gives blessing. The arch was completed under Cristoforo Moro between 1462 and 1471. The side towards the courtyard was covered in the early 17th century.

! *Baedeker* TIP

Secrets of the Doge's Palace

The tour reveals the historic centre of power of the Serenissima: the headquarters of the secret police was in the middle of the Palazzo Ducale, invisible to the world outside. The tour (several times daily in English, lasting about 75 min.) has to be booked at least two days in advance (tel. 04 12 71 59 11 and 04 15 20 90 70).

Cortile dei Senatori To the left of the main courtyard lies the Cortile dei Senatori with a late Renaissance front: arcades on the ground floor, windows crowned with pediments on the upper floor, and the crowning balustrade, behind which there was originally a small roof terrace. The senators gathered in this small courtyard before receptions. The small adjacent chapel was the private chapel of the doge.

On secret pathways More can be learned about the workings of the lagoon republic on the guided tour **Itinerari Segreti** (»secret pathways«). The tour concentrates on the hidden part of the Palazzo Ducale, including the offices of the secret police, the torture chamber and the (old) prison below the roof. It was from one of these cells that **Casanova** succeeded in making his spectacular escape in 1755 with the aid of a monk. The tour ends on the top floor above the Sala del Maggior Consiglio. Here, the system of the Venetian **soffitto** (flat ceiling with paintings) is presented. It is found in all palazzi, but can normally be seen only from the painted – that is, the lower – side.

Palazzo Ducale, 2nd Floor *Plan*

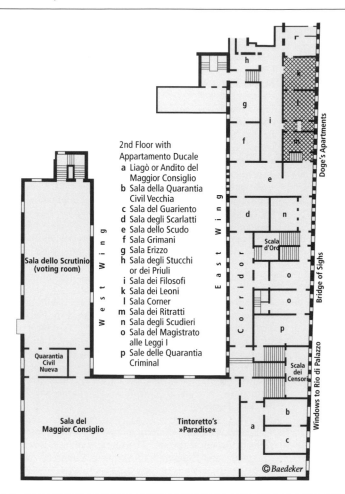

2nd Floor with
Appartamento Ducale
a Liagò or Andito del
  Maggior Consiglio
b Sala della Quarantia
  Civil Vecchia
c Sala del Guariento
d Sala degli Scarlatti
e Sala dello Scudo
f Sala Grimani
g Sala Erizzo
h Sala degli Stucchi
  or dei Priuli
i Sala dei Filosofi
k Sala dei Leoni
l Sala Corner
m Sala dei Ritratti
n Sala degli Scudieri
o Sala del Magistrato
  alle Leggi I
p Sale delle Quarantia
  Criminal

Doge's Apartments

Bridge of Sighs

Windows to Rio di Palazzo

East Wing

West Wing

Corridor

Sala dello Scrutinio
(voting room)

Quarantia
Civil
Nueva

Sala del
Maggior Consiglio

Tintoretto's
»Paradise«

Scala
d'Oro

Scala
dei
Censori

© Baedeker

Halls of the Doge's Palace

As the official seat of government and the highest judges, as well as the election and meeting place of the representatives of the people, the Doge's Palace contained, in addition to the doge's residence, meeting halls, courts, torture chambers and prison cells. Today's decoration was newly carried out after several fires in the 16th century. Leading artists participated in the work, particularly Tintoretto, Titian and Paolo Veronese. The paintings describe the most important events in the city's history, from the myths of the founding period to the greatest military successes.

From the inner courtyard, the route first leads via the Scala dei Censori (censors' stairway) up to the loggia (first floor). The **bocca di leone**, the so-called lion's mouth (▶p.228) set into the wall, was a letterbox for secret (not anonymous!) reports.

✳ Scala d'Oro From the loggia, the »**golden stairway**« leads up to the former apartments of the doge (second floor) and then to the rooms of office on the third floor. The staircase was designed by Sansovino (1538), but only completed after 1577. It is named after the gilded stucco ornamentations of its coffered ceiling (Alessandro Vittoria). The frescoes (Battista Franco) describe the defence of Cyprus and Crete and the *Virtues of Good Government*. The beautiful floor is noteworthy (it creates a three-dimensional impression to those looking back).

Atrio Quadrato The Scala d'Oro ends in the square anteroom. As is the custom in Venice, the ceiling (soffito) is divided into fields in magnificent frames. The main painting by Jacopo Tintoretto (1561–1564) shows the sword of justice being handed to Doge Girolamo Priuli.

Sala delle Quattro Porte The four doors, which are framed by marble columns, give the large waiting hall, which may have been designed by Palladio, its name. The ceiling paintings are by Tintoretto (1578–1581): at the centre, Jupiter symbolically gives Venice rule over the Adriatic; the eight oval paintings represent the Venetian cities and regions on the mainland. The most important wall painting, a votive image of Doge Antonio Grimani on the north wall, was begun by Titian and completed by his nephew. The painting *Neptune Offers Venice the Treasures of the Sea* is by Tiepolo.

✳ Sala dell' Anticollegio The paintings in the »waiting room« for foreign representatives deal with mythological themes. The central ceiling fresco *Venice Awards Recognition and Honours* is by Veronese. Tintoretto painted the four works on the sides of the doors: *Minerva separates War and Peace*, *Vulcan's Forge*, *Mercury and the Three Graces* and *Venus Marries Bacchus to Ariadne* (1577/1578). On the wall opposite the windows hangs Paolo Veronese's *Rape of Europa* (1580) and the *Return of Jacob from Canaan* by Jacopo Bassano (1574).

✳ Sala del Collegio The highest-ranking visitors were received in the conference hall of the state council. The ceiling paintings by Veronese celebrate the power and glory of Venice, showing *Mars and Neptune*, *Faith as the Strength of the Republic* and *Venetia Enthroned with Justice and Peace*. The fields around the edges show the virtues: the dog stands for loyalty, the cornucopia for growth and success, the crane for alertness,

Sala delle Quattro Porte: Tiepolo, »Nepune offers the treasures of the sea to Venice«

the spider's web for industry, the eagle for moderation, the sceptre for generosity, the dove for peace and the lamb for gentleness. On the wall painting above the doge's throne, Veronese immortalized Doge Sebastiano Venier, the supreme commander in the battle of Lepanto (1571). On the wide-format painting opposite, Doge Andrea Gritti kneels before the Virgin. Both this composition and the three votive images on the side opposite the windows are ascribed to Tintoretto and his workshop.

The senate hall was the meeting place of the senate, which met twice weekly and had 40, then 60 and later 100 members. The doge and his committee used the seats at the end, while the senators in red robes sat at the sides.

★ **Sala del Senato**

The ceiling paintings by Tintoretto and his workshop again serve to represent Venice. At the centre, Venetia is made the ruler of the seas by the Olympian gods. Other scenes are devoted to the right of coinage, the veneration of the eucharist, while military power and the protection of thought and literature are depicted in the smaller paintings. On the wall above the tribunal hangs another painting by Tintoretto, *The Dead Christ Supported by Angels*. On the opposite wall, Doge Pietro Lando and Doge Marcantonio Trevisan pray to the body of Christ which is borne by angels (Palma the Younger). The allegory of the League of Cambrai above the door to the Sala del Collegio is also by him: Venetia attacks a bull, the symbol of the powers which were allied against Venice (the pope, the Holy Roman Emperor, France and Spain). The wall clock is intended to serve as a reminder of human mortality.

The Council of Ten, a body shrouded in secrecy, met in this hall. It held power over the security services and over public and private life. The seating for the council has a rounded apsidal form. The ceiling was unaffected by the fires and still has its original wooden ceiling. The central scene in which Jupiter sends his arrows against the vices,

Sala del Consiglio dei Dieci

DOGE'S PALACE

✱✱ **At the beginning of the 9th century, the government of the City of Venice was relocated to the Canal Grande and the first doge's residence was constructed. The Pala Ducale still stands at the site today. It was the residence of the incumbent doge and seat of government of the Serenissima. The assembly hall of the Grand Council, the off of the public authorities, the court, the jail, and the arsenal were all located here.**

🕐 Opening Hours:
Apr - Oct daily 9.00am - 7.00pm, otherwise only until 5.00pm, the cash closes 1 hour earlier.

① Balcony to the Piazzetta
The balcony on the western façade was supplemented in the 15th century. From here, the doge attended executions which took place on the Piazzetta between the two columns.

② Southern façade
The southern façade is the oldest part and the representative side of the doge's palace. Groups of figures from the 14th century stand at both corners of the building.

③ Cortile
In the past one entered the doge's palace through the Porta della Carta, and today through the Porta del Frumento. It is located on the side facing the lagoon. One first enters the courtyard. Here there are two beautiful bronze fountains.

④ Arco Foscari
The Arco Foscari, a richly decorated triumphal arch, opens across from the Scala dei Giganti where the crowning ceremonies for the doge took place. The domes of St Mark's Basilica tower above it.

⑤ Sala del Maggior Consiglio
The assemblies of the Grand Council took place in the most impressive room of the palace; here the doges were elected and the members of government and high civil servants were sworn into office. It was painted after a fire in 1577. Directly below the ceiling is a frieze with (mostly imaginary) portraits of the first 76 do A black curtain covers the spot where the image o doge Marino Falier was supposed to hang. He wa executed as a traitor in 1335. The throne wall is decorated by Tintoretto's »Paradise«.

⑥ Appartamento Ducale
The doges' quarters were located in the east wing. are unfurnished, since the doges had to bring their furniture when they moved in and also had to hav removed after their death.

⑦ Sala dello Scrutinio
The elections to fill various state offices took place this room.

⑧ Museo dell'Opera
The museum displays some capitals from the 14th century that originally decorated the exterior façade the palace (and here were replaced by copies).

⑨ Ponte della Paglia
The »Straw Bridge« across the Rio di Palazzo, one of oldest bridges in Venice (mid-14th century) offers a vi of the »Bridge of Sighs«, Ponte dei Sospiri. Inmates crossed it from the palace to the cells in the »new jai either in the Piombi (lead chambers) in the attic or the Pozzi (wells), the cells in the basement.

⑩ »Drunken Noah«
The relief on the south-east corner of the palace depic the »Drunken Noah«. The sculpture from the 14th century may be a symbol for human weaknesses. The statues of Adam and Eve can be seen on the corner facing the Piazzetta (page 234).

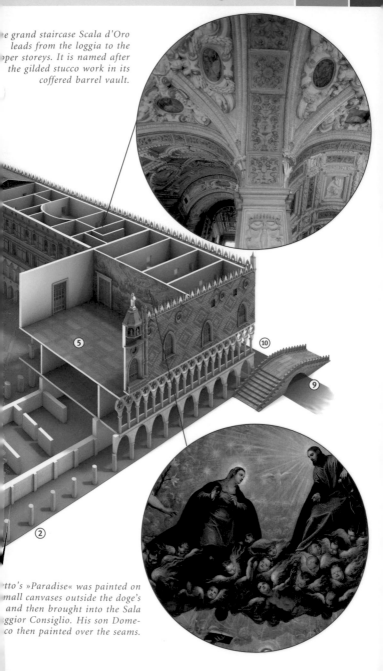

The grand staircase Scala d'Oro leads from the loggia to the upper storeys. It is named after the gilded stucco work in its coffered barrel vault.

⑤

⑩

⑨

②

Tintoretto's »Paradise« was painted on small canvases outside the doge's palace and then brought into the Sala Maggior Consiglio. His son Domenico then painted over the seams.

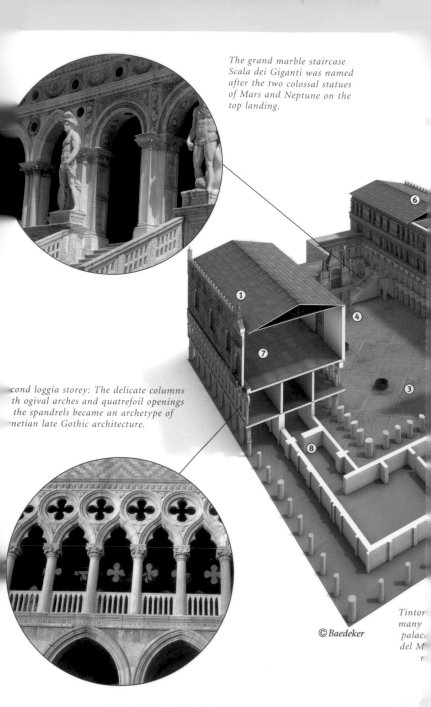

The grand marble staircase Scala dei Giganti was named after the two colossal statues of Mars and Neptune on the top landing.

...cond loggia storey: The delicate columns ...th ogival arches and quatrefoil openings ...the spandrels became an archetype of ...netian late Gothic architecture.

© Baedeker

Tintor...
many
palac...
del M...
r...

Juno Showers Jewels on Venetia, and *The Old Oriental and the Young Woman* are by Veronese. The latter symbolizes the threat to Venice from the Turks. The three murals above the seats represent the *Adoration of the Magi* (Aliense). To the left, the arrival of Venetian representatives before Pope Clement VII and Emperor Charles V in Bologna can be seen, to the right, Pope Alexander III blessing Doge Sebastiano Ziani after he overcame Barbarossa.

Sala della Bussola The waiting room (bussola = compass) before court sessions takes its name from the wooden structure in the right rear corner. It gave access to the secret wing of the palace.

Armeria The following rooms exhibit a part of the weapons arsenal (more than 2,200 exhibits). A well-ordered display of innumerable suits of armour, swords, lances, halberds, fire-arms, coats of mail and trophies provides an idea of Venetian weapons technology and an insight into its military organization. The armour of Henry IV of France is a notable exhibit.

Andito del Maggior Consiglio From the Sale d'Armi, the tour reaches the second floor with the Andito del Maggior Consiglio, a hallway which served as a waiting room for the members of the Grand Council before sessions or during breaks. Note the gilded beam ceiling which is decorated with ornamental paintings. At the rear of the L-shaped hall, the so-called Liago, stand the originals of the bronze figures of Adam and Eve (c. 1470) by Antonio Rizzo.

Sala della Quarantia Civil Vecchia The Sala della Quarantia Civil Vecchia is the first room to the left from the Andito. This is where the 40-member (quaranta) civil court authority met. The painting framed in an aedicula is a fresco from the late 15th century, while the remaining furnishings date from the 17th century.

Sala del Guariento In the second side room of the Andito, remnants of the *Coronation of the Virgin* painted by the Paduan Guariento for the Sala del Maggior Consiglio in the 14th century can be seen. After the fire in 1577, the painting was covered by Tintoretto's *Paradise*.

Sala del Maggior Consiglio The largest hall in the palace is the impressive Sala del Maggior Consiglio (54 x 25 m / 177 x 82 ft). Here, the up to 1,800 members of the Grand Council elected the members of government and high state officials, debated and made all important decisions of the republic, including that of its dissolution in 1797.

The eye is drawn to the mural ***Paradise*** behind the doge's throne, the largest painting in the world at the time of its unveiling at 7x22m/23x72ft. It was begun by Veronese. After his death in 1588, the commission passed to Tintoretto, who was nearly 70 years of age at the time. He worked on *Paradise* for four years. Christ is enthroned at the centre. Before him kneels Mary, surrounded by seven stars as reminders of her seven joys and pains, as well as more than 500 other figures, of which only the heads are visible in most cases.

The ceiling paintings celebrate the Serenissima. Veronese's *Triumph of Venice* is above the dais, while the work at the centre, *Venetia gives Doge da Ponte an Olive Branch* is by Tintoretto. At the end of the hall *The Provinces Pay Tribute to Venezia* is by Palma the Younger. The two side ceiling paintings represent heroic deeds by individual army commanders, while the large murals show events from the history of the city. Directly below the ceiling is a frieze with 76 portraits of doges by Domenico Tintoretto. One painting is covered by a black cloth. The inscription refers to Doge Marino Falier, who was beheaded for high treason (and therefore not shown).

The small **Sala della Quarantia Civil Nuova**, where a court was responsible for affairs of provinces that were subject to Venice (decorations relating to the legal system in the 17th century), leads to the Sala dello Scrutinio. Public election procedures were carried out here. The murals and ceiling paintings show sea and land battles, among them Tintoretto's *Victory of the Venetians over the Hungarians before the gates of Zara in 1346*. The *Last Judgment* is by Palma the Younger, while the marble triumphal arch (1694) honours the army commander and Doge Francesco Morosini.

Sala dello Scrutinio

The seating of the **Sala del Magistrato alle Leggi** in the **Sala della Quarantia Criminal** dates from the 17th century. The walls are ornamented with paintings by Flemish artists; the altarpieces by Hieronymus Bosch are particularly impressive.

✱ **Hieronymus Bosch**

The private chambers of the doge are on the second floor. They are empty, since every newly elected doge had to bring his own furniture when he entered office and arrange for it to be removed after his death. The **Sala degli Scarlatti**, a kind of anteroom for the doge's advisors, has a beautiful wood ceiling and ornamented fireplace (1507) by Antonio and Tullio Lombardo. The hall of maps, **Sala dello Scudo**, documents the regions ruled by Venice. The **Sala Grimani**, named after Doge Marino Grimani, has a lovely ceiling (15th century) and a fireplace by Lombardo. The **Sala Erizzo**, named after Doge Francesco Erizzo, is graced by a frieze of cherubs and symbols of war. The stucco decorations in the **Sala degli Stucchi** were newly created in the 18th century. The *Portrait of Henri III* is ascribed to Tintoretto. The **Sala dei Filosofi** was a room giving access to the doge's chambers. The twelve paintings of philosophers are from the 18th century.

Appartamento Ducale

The **Chiesetta** (chapel, currently not accessible) was designed in 1593 by Scamozzi. On the altar stands a Madonna statue by Sansovino. Today, two paintings by D. Tintoretto hang in the **Sala degli Scudieri**, a passageway.

Detail of Tintoretto's »Paradise« in the Sala del Maggior Consiglio

Prigioni Nuove Cross the Bridge of Sighs, built in 1603 (►p.16), to the »new prison«. The place of imprisonment was originally in the Doge's Palace. In the 16th century, a new structure was built on the other side of Rio di Palazzo. The so-called pozzi (wells), the rooms of the lower prison floors, were regarded as cold and humid. The piombi (lead chambers) on the higher floors were feared due to the unbearable heat of summer. These rooms were probably partly responsible for the fearful reputation of the Venetian state prison.

Sala Censori Back in the palazzo, enter the Sala Censori. Civil cases were heard here; a frieze shows the portraits of several judges (17th century).

Avogaria The exit is reached via the Avogaria, once the seat of the state attorneys in the republic. The Avogaria – three patricians with an office term of one year – monitored compliance with the laws. On the wall at the entrance is a *Resurrection with Three Avogadri* (D. Tintoretto); opposite the windows hang three more paintings by Tintoretto. The tour ends via the Sala dello Scrigno, where the Golden Book (list of noble families) was kept, and the Sala della Milizia da Mar.

✳ Palazzo Pesaro degli Orfei Museo Fortuny

Location: San Benedetto **Quays:** S. Zaccaria, Vallaresso San Marco

At the pretty campo of the Benedictine church, which houses a depiction of St Francis by Tiepolo, the eye falls on the Gothic palace with a seven-arched window. From 1899 to his death in 1950, the Granada-born painter, sculptor, theatre-set maker and designer Mariano Fortuny y Madrazo, known as Fortuny, lived here. He became famous for his precious pleated fabrics and filigree silk lamps. Inspired by Greek tunics, Fortuny designed a dress in tiny pleats of silk satin in 1907. This design brought him world fame. The fabric was hand pleated and dyed in various steps, so that it shone in different shades depending on the light. The cut itself was simple, flattered the figure, and transformed its wearer into a cross between an ancient goddess and an oriental princess. His clothes struck a chord in the early 20th century; his clients included stage stars like Sarah Bernhardt, Isadora Duncan and Eleonore Duse. In 1919, Fortuny even patented his process for permanently fixing pleats. On the island of Giudecca, fabrics are still manufactured to his designs today (information: www.fortuny.com).

⊙ Opening hours: Currently open for viewing only during exhibitions

 Baedeker TIP

Fortuny

The legendary Fortuny fabrics are on sale at Trois (San Marco, Campo San Maurizio 2666, tel. 04 15 55 29 05).
Venetia Studium sells fabrics inspired by Fortuny as well as hand-painted lamps to Fortuny designs and other items (Calle Larga XXII Marzo 2403, tel. 04 15 22 92 81, Mercerie S. Zulian 723, tel. 04 15 22 98 59 and at Marco Polo Airport; www.venetiastudium.it).

The piano nobile of his palazzo houses a small museum, which tells of his life and accomplishments, and shows unusual designs by this all-round genius.

✶ ✶ Piazza San Marco

Quays: San Zaccaria, Vallaresso San Marco

The centre of Venetian life is Piazza San Marco, which Napoleon called »the finest drawing-room in Europe«, and is also known as la piazza (since all other squares are called Campo, there is no danger of confusion). It is unlikely that any other city in the world can greet visitors with a comparable entrée. This is the site of the most famous

Heart of the lagoon city

buildings, proof of a glorious past, and the very first look leaves an unforgettable impression. To the east, the ▶ Basilica di San Marco dominates the piazza. On its other three sides, it is bordered by the clock tower, the Procuratie Vecchie (in the north), the Ala Napoleonica and the Procuratie Nuove (in the south). The transition to the Piazzetta with the library is formed by the high Campanile and elegant Loggetta. The piazza narrows from Basilica di San Marco to the Ala Napoleonica, which gives it greater depth (on average it is 175m/190yd long, 82m/90yd at the church, and 56.6m/66yd wide at the Ala Napoleonica). There is nothing to distract from the closed architectural feeling of the piazza, which is paved in slabs of brown trachyte and white marble.

In the course of the centuries, Piazza San Marco has always been the religious, political and social heart of Venice and has lost nothing of its effect to the present day, when it is the preserve of onlookers and, of course, the famous pigeons.

The city's greatest treasures lie all around the Piazza San Marco.

The piazza has a long history. It was originally an island through which the canal flowed, and on which the nuns of the Zaccaria monastery grew fruit and vegetables. In 1174, the canal was filled in, and in 1267 paved with bricks. At that time, St Mark's Basilica and the Campanile were the only buildings which still exist today. The Procuratie Nuove were built in the 16th century. Shortly before this, the clock tower, the Procuratie Vecchie, the Biblioteca Marciana and the mint – Zecca – had been built. The piazza acquired its present paving in 1735, when the characteristic lines of white marble were set to show the position of the vendors' stands which occupied the piazza for various markets. Piazza San Marco was primarily a market place until the end of the republic – except when it served as the stage for celebratory parades and processions. The Ala Napoleonica was not added until the early 19th century.

History of the piazza

Today, Piazza San Marco is a place for strolling and a venue for open-air concerts and theatrical productions. Every visitor should enjoy the pleasure of sitting over a coffee in one of the surrounding concert cafés and listening to the waltzes and evergreen melodies. The pigeons of San Marco are also part of it all, regardless of whether they are descended from the doves which the Venetian founding fathers brought to the lagoon in the 5th century on their flight from the Huns, or from those released into freedom by the doges every year on Palm Sunday, or from those that brought to the lagoon the message of the conquest of Constantinople in 1204.

The two three-storey lengthwise wings with their arcades, the Procuratie Vecchie and Procuratie Nuove, bound Piazza San Marco to the north and south. The Procuratie Vecchie (from 1500, Bartolomeo Bon) were the seat of the procurators, the most important officials in the city after the doge. They managed St Mark's Basilica and the great fortune of the church, which derived from public and private donations as well as ongoing income. Later, when their tasks were extended to cover all communal government and their numbers increased, the new Procuratie Nuove building was erected on the other side (1583–1640, Vincenzo Scamozzi, Baldassare Longhena). Scamozzi used the library by his teacher Sansovino as a model, added a third floor and finished with a cornice instead of a balustrade (today, it houses the Archaeological Museum ► p.243). As well as exclusive stores, the arcades are home to Venice's most famous cafes.

★ Procuratie

The piazza is closed off at the west end by the Ala Napoleonica, a connecting building added by Giuseppe Soli in 1810 at Napoleon's wish. Soli simply continued the first two floors of the Procuratie Nuove, left out the third floor to avoid disturbing the Procuratie Vecchie, and added a wide band of stone relief at the top to maintain the height. Between 1805 and 1814, it formed the entrance to the residence of Napoleon, which he had installed for himself as »King of Italy« in the library and in the Procuratie Nuove.

Ala Napoleonica

High-end stores and the Caffè Florian enliven the arcades of the »New Procurates«

★
Museo Correr
⏱
Opening hours:
Apr–Oct.
daily 9am–7pm,
otherwise only to
5pm,
last admission 2hr
earlier

The core of the museum is the art and city history collection of Teodoro Correr (1750–1830). The first neo-classical halls are devoted to statues by Antonio Canova (1757–1822). In the other rooms, much local history is revealed by coins, weapons and official garments, and a city view by Jacopo de' Barberi dated to 1500 is also on display. Right at the very beginning, the highlights of the gallery of paintings on the second floor include the Venetian-Byzantine panels by Paolo and Lorenzo Veneziano (*Handing over the Key*, 1369) and a Gothic *Madonna with Child* by Jacobello del Fiore. The early Renaissance is represented in the expressive *Pietà* by Cosmé Tura and the *Portrait of a Young Man* by Baldassare Estense. A separate hall is devoted to the three Bellinis. Vittore Carpaccio's idiosyncratic painting *Two Venetian Patrician Ladies* is also noteworthy (around 1510).

The adjacent **Risorgimento Museum** provides information about the political development of Venice from the end of the republic (1797) to the time when it joined the kingdom of Italy (1866).

★
Torre dell'
Orologio

The great clock tower on the north side of the piazza, above the passage to the ► Mercerie, was built by Mauro Coducci in the Renaissance style in 1496–1499 to complete the Procuratie Vecchie. The top floor with the star-covered blue mosaic and the lion of St Mark were added by Giorgio Massari in 1755. On his platform, two bronze negroes with hammers strike the hour. The large decorated clock, a work of Ranieri and his son, show the months, zodiac signs and phases of the moon in addition to the time. In Ascension week as well as on the day of the Epiphany, the Three Magi, led by an angel, move around the Madonna and child at every full hour.

The three legendary cafés under the arcades of the Procuratie are the classic places to meet in Venice. In summer, each café has its own band, which adds to the atmosphere of Piazza San Marco with well-known melodies.

The first coffee house to open, in 1720, was Café **Florian**, which is now a protected monument. It was known as »Venezia Trionfante« before it took the name of its owner Floriano Francesconi. The thematically decorated interiors such as the Chinese, Turkish and Senate rooms have long been assured of their place in world literature. Among others, Ernest Hemingway, Mark Twain, Goethe, Honoré de Balzac, Marcel Proust and Thomas Mann drank their coffee here. The choice of café reflected political divisions in the 19th century, when the Venetian patriots Manin and Tommaseo preferred Florian while the Austrian officers went to **Quadri**. Quadri, which is only half a century younger and known for its irresistible pastries, is thus also a historic site. The coffee house owes its name to its former owner Giorgio Quadri, a Levantine from Corfu, who, in his day, made the best »coffee in the Turkish style«. Founded in 1750 and lovingly restored in 1990, Café **Lavena** with its nostalgic furnishings is reminiscent of the period of Austrian imperial rule, when it was still called »Ungheria«. Giuseppe Verdi was often a guest here, as was Richard Wagner with his wife Cosima and his father-in-law Franz Liszt.

►Basilica di San Marco

★
Campanile
◷ Opening hours:
Apr–Oct daily
9am–7pm,
Nov–March
9.30am–4.15pm,
last admission 1hr
earlier

The tall rectangular Campanile is the link between Piazza San Marco and the Piazzetta. It was begun in the 10th century. However, the work took until the 12th century; finally, in the 15th century, the pointed spire of the tower which greets approaching ships from afar was also added. The tower collapsed on 14 July 1902 without injuring anyone. It buried the small Baroque hall at its base, the **Loggetta**, which had been built in 1540 to plans by Sansovino. The careful rebuilding was completed after ten years. Today, an elevator ascends the almost 99m/325ft-high Campanile to the bell chamber, which presents a **wonderful panoramic view** over the city and lagoon.

The Piazzetta, the true reception room of Venice, is bordered towards the sea by two immense granite columns, the **Colonne di Marco e Teodoro**. Originally three columns were brought from Tyre (now in Lebanon) by Doge Michieli in 1125. However, one fell into the sea during unloading. One column is crowned with the lion of St Mark, the symbol of the evangelist Mark. On the top of the second column stands the statue of St Theodore. He was a Greek, later the head of a monastery in Constantinople, until he was banished to Venice. He was the first patron of the city until St Mark took his place. Public executions formerly took place between the columns and the bodies were left exposed. For this reason, superstitious persons do not walk between them.

View across the sea of houses of San Marco to the church of San Zanipolo, with the two islands of S. Michele and Murano in background

★
Libreria Sansoviniana

The venerable library opposite the ►Palazzo Ducale is the principal work of architect and sculptor Sansovino. After his death, Vincenzo Scamozzi completed the work (to 1588). The façade is regarded as one of the most perfect works of the Italian Renaissance. Palladio praised the structure, which is also referred to as the Biblioteca Marciana or the Libreria Vecchia, as the most magnificent building since ancient times.

Biblioteca Marciana

The Biblioteca Marciana (St Mark's Library) originated in Cardinal Bessarion's collection of manuscripts, donated in 1468. An appointment is required to use the library. However, the magnificent stairway (Alessandro Vittoria), the ceiling paintings (*Wisdom* in the vestibule by Titian, 1560) and the Great Hall are accessible (Sala Grande; open: Apr–Oct daily 9am–7pm, Nov–March to 5pm, last admission one hour earlier). The exhibition rooms contain astonishing treasures, cameos, manuscripts, calligraphy and book illustrations, including the Breviarium Grimani (1510–1520), 831 pages long with numerous Flemish miniatures. The actual Biblioteca Marciana with more than 750,000 volumes is housed in the adjacent **Zecca**, a structure with a façade towards the lagoon which was built in 1545 – also to plans by Sansovino – and housed the mint until 1870.

The entrance to the Museo Archeologico is approximately at the centre of the Libreria with Greek and Roman exhibits (open: Apr–Oct 9am–7pm, Nov–March until 5pm, last admission 90 minutes earlier).

Museo Archeologico

✳ Ponte di Rialto

G 11

Location: Grand Canal   **Quay:** Rialto

The Rialto bridge is one of the best-known symbols of Venice. For a long time, it was the only bridge across the Grand Canal – the Academy bridge was built in 1854, and the Ponte dei Scalzi near the railway station followed in the 20th century. The name is derived from Rivus Altus (high bank); the first Venetians settled on this island in the early 9th century. As early as 1180, the first wooden bridge was built across the canal on this site. It was replaced by a drawbridge which collapsed in 1444 under the weight of onlookers who were watching a procession of boats from the bridge. On the painting in the Accademia, *The Miracle of the Cross* by Vittore Carpaccio, a wooden bridge from this time is recorded (►p.198).

Where Venice began

Many renowned architects participated in the competition for today's bridge. In 1588, Antonio da Ponte was chosen for his single-arch solution. Three years later, the 28m/92ft-long bridge of Istrian marble was inaugurated. It rests on 6,000 oak piles at each end, which were driven into the muddy underground. Its span is 48m/157ft, and the clearance height beneath it is 7.50m/25ft. Three pathways lead across the great bridge arch; they are separated by two rows of stores selling leather, jewellery and souvenirs. From the upper bridge platform, there is a magnificent view of the life and activities on and around the Grand Canal.

Rialto was the business centre of Venice for many centuries; not only did the long-distance traders unload their wares at the docks (as the names still show today), but the largest banking and merchant houses also had their headquarters here. The central market of Venice still takes place here today. The range of products is enormous – fruits and vegetables from the surrounding islands, seafood and much more – and an atmosphere unlike any other (daily except Sundays; the fish market in the Pescheria Tue–Sat 5am–11pm).

Rialto market

The colourful market begins right inside the Rialto Bridge.

San Giovanni Elemosinario At the end of Ruga degli Orefici, where the goldsmiths traditionally had their workshops, the little church of S. Giovanni Elemosinario (1539, Scarpagnino; open: Mon–Sat 10am–5pm, Sun from 1pm) stands on the left surrounded by houses. Items of interest include an altar painting by Titian and in the right side chapel, a painting by Pordenone.

! *Baedeker* TIP

For gourmets

Dreams come true for keen cooks in Drogheria Mascari (Ruga dei Spezieri 381; closed on Sundays and Wednesdays). After shopping, there are inviting places to enjoy a drink around Rialto: for instance Bancogiro in the arcade of the Fabbriche Vecchie (Campo S. Giacometto 122, tel. 04 15 23 20 61). Small snacks are served on the ground floor, warm dishes on the first floor, and there are even a few tables with a view of the canal in front of the house.

The church **San Silvestro** (restored 19th century, founded 9th century), at the end of Fondamenta del Vin, where the boats of wine traders used to dock, contains a noteworthy work by Tintoretto, *The Baptism of Christ* (c. 1580; first side altar on the right). Unlike the depiction of the same theme in the ▶Scuola Grande di San Rocco, this painting is limited to a personal meeting between St John the Baptist and Christ, with the dove of the Holy Spirit radiating light above him.

San Francesco della Vigna

Location: Campo San Francesco della Vigna **Quays:** San Zaccaria, Celestia

As the name says, there were numerous vineyards (vigne) on this site before it passed to the Franciscans, who built their first monastery here, in 1253. Sansovino began the construction of the large church in 1543, but it was only completed 30 years later by Andrea Palladio. He designed the façade (1568–1572) in the style of an ancient temple, which also forms a central design element in his churches ►San Giorgio Maggiore and Il Redentore (►La Giudecca).
The hall-like interior has numerous side chapels with tombs of important Venetian families. The high-class works of art include the panel *Enthroned Madonna* in the right aisle (c. 1470) by Antonio da Negroponte. The Cappella Santa (access from the left aisle) is adorned by a *Madonna with Saints* (1507) by Giovanni Bellini. The sacristy contains a triptych by Antonio Vivarini (15th century). A *Madonna with Saints* (1551) by Paolo Veronese hangs in the fifth chapel. The cycle of sculptures (c. 1500) in the Cappella Giustiniani to the left of the high altar is ascribed to Pietro Lombardo.

San Giacomo dell'Orio

Location: Campo S. Giacomo dell'Orio **Quay:** San Staè

The name of the church is probably derived from lauro, meaning laurel. Its foundation stone was laid in the 9th or 10th century. The massive Veneto-Byzantine Campanile and the transept were built around 1225, the nave received its present form in the 15th century, and the three-section presbytery followed in the mid-16th century. In the interior, a richly carved wooden ceiling in the form of a ship's hull is noteworthy. Among the exhibits, the following are of particular interest: in the choir, a *Sacra Conversazione* by Lorenzo Lotto (1546); in the old sacristy (beside the left choir chapel) two works by Palma the Younger, in the new sacristy (beside the right choir chapel) – among other things – a lovely ceiling painting by Paolo Veronese. The pulpit in the unique chalice form dates from the 16th century; the column of green marble in the south transept is a spolia from the 6th century.

⊙
Opening hours:
Mon–Sat
10am–5pm,
Sun from 1pm

On the lovely Campo, the heart of San Croce, benches and cafés are a pleasant place to take a break. In the summer months, excellent pizza is available on the small Campiello dei Morti behind the church (tel. 04 15 24 00 16, closed Mon–Tue.)

**Campo
S. Giacomo
dell'Orio**

San Giacomo dell' Orio

★ San Giobbe

Location: Campo San Giobbe   **Quay:** Stazione S. Lucia

The church of San Giobbe, which is dedicated to Job, is an excellent example of Venetian religious architecture of the early Renaissance. Its builders from 1450 onward were Antonio Gambello, who began the church with the campanile in the late Gothic style, and Pietro Lombardo, who continued the beautiful portal, the choir dome and the Cappella Martini from 1471 in the Renaissance style.

Noteworthy features are the Cappella Martini (second side chapel) with its colourfully glazed terracotta tiles from the school of the Florentine Lucca della Robbia, the 16th-century *St Peter* by Paris Bordone in the fourth side chapel to the right, and the tombstone of the doge and church donor Cristoforo Moro (doge from 1462 to 1471) before the high altar. The sacristy contains a portrait of Moro and a triptych by Antonio Vivarini (c. 1445).

> ! **Baedeker** TIP
>
> ### Dalla Marisa
>
> The little trattoria at the Ponte dei Tre Archi cooks only according to traditional (mainland) recipes, e.g. sguazzetti alla bechera, stewed beef innards, or tasty venison ragout. When ordered in advance, there are extremely delicious menus, fish lasagna, stuffed clams or fish. Dalla Marisa, Cannaregio, Fondamenta S. Giobbe 652/b, tel. 041720211.

A few steps from here is the end of the canal, where there is a lovely ◄ Fondamenta di
view of the lagoon. The Ex-Macelli, the 19th-century former slaugh- S. Giobbe
terhouse, accommodates part of the University of Venice today.

★ San Giorgio Maggiore

H 14

Location: Canale di S. Marco   **Quay:** San Giorgio (Vaporetto 82)

The first church was built in the late 10th century, when a Benedictine monastery was founded. Today's structure goes back to a design
by Andrea Palladio from 1563. However, the great architect did not
witness its completion in 1610. San Giorgio Maggiore is an important landmark in the city, built to be seen from a distance in the lagoon, with a picturesque combination of campanile, dome, the nave
and façade that appears to particularly good effect from the Piazzetta
and the Doge's Palace. As in Palladio's other Venetian churches,
► San Francesco della Vigna and Il Redentore (► La Giudecca), the
façade is reminiscent of an ancient temple with colossal columns,
niches and pediments; however, it seems slightly disproportional
when viewed up close.

⏱
Opening hours:
Daily
9.30am–12.30pm,
2.30–6pm

With reference to Roman and ancient architectural ideas, Palladio
designed the white-grey interior like a relief, using columns, pillars,
pilasters and entablature, as a basilica with semicircular ends to the
transepts and a central dome over the crossing, leading east into a
square presbytery and an apsidal monks' choir. The gaze is drawn to
the high altar (1591–1593) in the presbytery, a masterpiece by Girolamo Compagna, a student of Sansovino. The side walls of the altar
space are adorned by two large-format works which Tintoretto completed late in life: *Rain of Manna* and *The Last Supper*, both done in
1594, the year of his death. The monks' choir has magnificent choir
stalls (1594–1598) of walnut wood decorated with scenes from the
life of St Benedict.

Interior

To the left of the monks' choir, a hallway leads to the elevator of the
campanile. The 60m/197ft-high tower was originally part of the previous buildings from 1470. It collapsed later and was rebuilt in 1791,
using the Campanile of San Marco as a model. The view from the
belfry across the lagoon is overwhelming.

★★
**Campanile
View**

The monastery was in an advanced state of decay when the banker
Vittorio Cini (1885–1977) purchased and renovated it in the 1950s.
Today, it is the seat of a cultural foundation, **Fondazione Cini**, (tours:
Sat–Sun 10am–5pm and by appointment, tel. 04 15 24 01 19). The
complex includes two cloisters: the rear cloister was built between
1520 and 1540, while the front cloister was begun in 1579 by Andrea

Monastery

San Giorgio Maggiore, also known as the Island of Cypresses by the Venetians

Palladio and completed by Baldassare Longhena, who also designed the early Baroque stairway and the library (1641). The 128m/420ft-long dormitory was built between 1488 and 1521. The modern Teatro Verde, an amphitheatre at the centre of the beautiful monastery park, occasionally stages shows and concerts (information at the tourist office and under www.cini.it).

San Giovanni in Bragora

Location: Campo Bandiera e Moro   **Quays:** Arsenale, San Zaccaria

⏱ Opening hours:
Mon–Sat
9am–11pm,
3.30–5.30pm

The church was built in late Gothic style between 1475 and 1494. The interior with wooden roof trusses has three highlights of early Renaissance Venetian: in the choir apse, the *Baptism of Christ* by Cima da Conegliano (1494), who chose an atmospheric Veneto landscape as his background; in the left choir chapel, a triptych with the Virgin, St John the Baptist and St Andrew (1748) by Bartolomeo Vivarini. In the first side chapel on the left beside the entrance, a *Resurrection* (1498) by Alvise Vivarini; above the entrance there is a notable work by Palma the Younger, *Christ before Caiaphas* (1600). The choir walls are decorated with *Washing of the Feet* and *The Last Supper* by Titian's pupil Paris Bordone (1500–1571). The composer Antonio Vivaldi was baptized in the font in the left aisle; a copy of his baptismal certificate is displayed.

To the south, on Campiello del Piovan, stand three of the typically Venetian well heads (vere da pozzo, ►S.113). **Campiello del Piovan**

San Giovanni Crisostomo

G 11

Location: Campo S. Giovanni Crisostomo   **Quay:** Rialto

The domed church in the Renaissance style, in a lively quarter near the Rialto, is dedicated to St John Chrysostom, one of the four Greek fathers of the church. It is a masterpiece by Mauro Coducci, who built it from 1497 to 1504 on the foundations of a previous church. Notable items include a late work of Giovanni Bellini, *St Jerome, St Christopher and St Augustine* (1513) in the first side chapel to the right as well as the painting for the high altar by Sebastiano del Piombo, *Madonna with Saints* (among them St John Chrysostom; 1509–1511). On the second altar to the left, the marble mount by Tullio Lombardo is noteworthy.

Right behind the church, there are two small inner courtyards, Corte Prima and Corte Seconda del Milion, whose names refer to **Marco Polo**. It is likely that his family lived here. In the Teatro Malibran, founded in 1678, concerts and opera performances take place. ◄ Teatro Malibran

San Nicolò da Tolentino

D 11

Location: Campo dei Tolentini   **Quay:** Piazzale Roma

The monastery church of the Theatine order was built between 1591 and 1601 by Vincenzo Scamozzi – probably using plans by Andrea Palladio. The open portico in front of the church building by A. Tirali dates from the 18th century. The paintings to the left of the entrance, *St Lawrence* by Bernardo Strozzi (1581–1644) and to the left of the choir arch *The Inspiration of St Jerome*, a significant late work by Johann Liss (1597–1630) are noteworthy.

! *Baedeker* TIP

For nautical fans

The bookstore Mare di Carta between the church and the Grand Canal has (nearly) everything about the sea and navigation: Italian and foreign-language ocean charts, books, magazines, CD ROMs etc. (Fondamenta dei Tolentini 222, www.maredicarta.it).

Today, the Theatine monastery houses part of the architectural faculty. One of the entrance portals is by Carlo Scarpa, who taught at this institution. It is also worth looking at the cloister (1600). Cross a bridge to reach **Papadopuli Park**, site of lavish festivals in the 19th century.

San Pietro di Castello

M 12/13

Location: Isola di San Pietro   **Quay:** Giardini

Opening hours:
Mon–Sat
10am–5pm,
Sun from 1pm

The island San Pietro di Castello, which is connected to Venice by two bridges on the eastern edge of the city, was home to one of the oldest settlements in the lagoon, by the name of **Olivolo**. According to legend, St Peter appeared to Bishop Magnus of Altinum here in the 7th century and commanded him to build a church "where he would find goats and sheep grazing«. San Pietro was the seat of the bishops of Venice from 775 to 1807 when this function was transferred to St Mark's Basilica (which, until that time, was »only« the palace chapel of the doges).

The present church was built in the 17th century; its façade is assumed to be the work of Andrea Palladio. The impressive campanile was created by Mauro Coducci from 1482 to 1488 in the style of the early Renaissance. Only the tower cap dates from the 17th century. Important features besides the Baroque high altar (1649) are the choir frescoes (1735) by Girolamo Pellegrini, the altarpiece, which is ascribed to Veronese and shows St John the Evangelist, St Peter and St Paul, and the so-called cattedra di San Pietro, the seat of St Peter. St Peter is said to have sat on this marble throne in Antioch; the backrest is an Arabic tomb stele inscribed with texts from the Koran. The Cappella Vendramin owes its rich sculptural ornamentation to Baldassare Longhena.

✱ San Polo

E/F 11

Location: Campo San Polo   **Quays:** S. Silvestro, S. Tomà

Mon–Sat
10am–5pm,
Sun only from
1pm ▶

The first church on this site dedicated to the apostle Paul, after whom this city quarter is named, was built in 837. Today's structure is largely from the 15th century; the campanile opposite the entrance (14th century) and its two lions at the base (12th century) are older. The church interior was altered in the 19th century. The beautiful 15th-century wooden ceiling, a feature surviving in Venice only in S. Stefano and San Giacomo dell'Orio, contrasts with the classical colonnades of bright marble.

Initially, **Tintoretto's** *Last Supper* (1568/69) to the left of the entrance draws the eye. This is his third version of this subject (the first, from 1547, is in the church San Marculoa; a second version is in San Trovaso; in his old age, he painted a further version for San Giorgio Maggiore.) The second altarpiece on the left, *Mary Appears to St John Nepomuk* (1751) by Giovanni Battista is a masterpiece of composition in light. **Tiepolo's** son **Giovanni Domenico**, who was only 22 years old at the time, painted the 14 stations of the cross in the Oratorio del Crocefisso (1749; the entrance is below the organ). It is a fine depiction of Venetian nobles in all their magnificence.

Until 1750, a canal led along the east side of the city's second largest plaza: **Campo San Paolo**. Its course can be traced by the winding line of the late Gothic Palazzo Soranzo. Palazzo Corner Mocenigo on the opposite side is a late work of Michele Sanmicheli (mid-16th century). The campo was also the site of the first carnival organized by local merchants in 1497 and the beginning of a lively trade in masks and costumes that continues until today. The piazza, where festivals and bull fights took place into the 19th century, is an open-air cinema from the end of July to the end of August (information from the tourist office or from daily newspapers).

Take Calle Saoneri to reach **Casa Goldoni**. The house in which the comic poet Carlo Goldoni (1707 to 1793) was born, a Gothic palace, exhibits items related to the famous author (Palazzo Centani, Campo S. Tomà; Mon–Sat 10am–5pm).

Tiepolo, »Appearance of Mary before St Nepomuk«

✷ San Sebastiano

C 13

Location: Campo San Sebastiano   **Quay:** Ca' Rezzonico

🕐 Opening hours:
Mon–Sat
10am–5pm,
Sun from 1pm

The Renaissance church was built from 1505 to 1546 according to designs by Scarpagnino. To the left in the choir is the tomb of the painter **Paolo Veronese**, who became famous here with a cycle of paintings begun in 1553, The most significant of his works in the sacristy include the ceiling paintings *Coronation of the Virgin* and *Four Evangelists* as well as – in the nave – the story of Esther, the Jewish wife of the Persian king Xerxes: *Esther is Led before Ahasuerus, Coronation of Esther* and *Triumph of Mordechai*. The wall paintings in the nave are by Veronese and his brother Benedetto. The organ case is also Veronese's work. His paintings *St Sebastian before Diocletian* and *Martyrdom of St Sebastian* in the nuns' choir date to around 1558. At the high altar, his late work *Virgin Enthroned with St Sebastian, St Peter, St Catherine and St Francis* can be seen. Today, the convent of S. Sebastiano houses a part of the university; the portal to the left of the church was designed by Carlo Scarpa in 1980.

Sant'Angelo Raffaele
The church a few steps to the north-west goes back to the 17th century. The organ gallery depicts the history of the blind prophet Tobias, a masterpiece by **Antonio Guardi** (18th century).

San Trovaso • Santi Gervasio e Protasio

E 13

Location: Campo San Trovaso   **Quays:** Accademia, Zattere

🕐 Opening hours:
Mon–Sat
3–6pm

The church, which was built in 1590, has two beautiful façades: according to legend, these were the entrances of two feuding families. The church is dedicated to saints Gervasius and Protasius, whose names were shortened into Trovaso. The church is plain, but has some paintings by well-known masters, including **Tintoretto:** in the left transept, a *Last Supper*, the second of four versions of this theme, and in the left choir chapel, the *Temptation of St Anthony* (around 1557) as well as **Michele Giambono's** altarpiece *St Chrysogonus* (c. 1440) in the right choir chapel. The altar reliefs in the right transept, marble works by an unknown master which were probably done around 1470, are also of interest.

Squero di San Trovaso
On Rio di San Trovaso is one of the last **gondola shipyards** in Venice, Squero di San Trovaso, where the gleaming black symbols of the city are built to this day according to the ancient tradition

(► Baedeker Special p.254). The low wooden houses with pretty flower balconies are a reminder that many shipbuilders originate from the Dolomite valleys near Cortina d'Ampezzo.

! *Baedeker* TIP

Ombra and cicheti

Not far from the Zattere vaporetto quay are several popular addresses which sell »liquid shadows« and small sandwiches (►p.86): Cantine del Vino Schiavi (next to the Ponte S. Trovaso), Cantinone (San Trovaso 992) and Al Bottegon (Fondamenta Nani 992).

The popular shore promenade **Zattere**, which was built in 1519, stretches along the Giudecca Canal from the Stazione Marittima to the ► Punta della Dogana. This is where the giant rafts (zattere) of tree trunks which were needed to build Venice arrived from the forests of the Alps or Dalmatia. They were processed in the nearby workshops.

The wooden ceiling of the Renaissance church (1494–1524) was painted with 58 portraits of prophets and saints in the 16th century by Umbrian artists. The façade of the adjacent former monastery includes a so-called **bocca di leone** (lion's mouth), a letterbox for letters containing anonymous denunciations from the time of the republic.

Santa Maria della Visitazione

The name of the church is a reminder of the Jesuit order, which had a monastery here until its dissolution at the end of the 17th century. The monastery was subsequently taken over by the Dominicans. The church is in voluptuous Baroque style and was built between 1726 and 1736 to designs by Giorgio Massari. The sculptural decorations are by Giovanni Maria Morlaiter (1699–1781). The ceiling frescoes by **Giambattista Tiepolo** show *The Life of St Dominic* (1738). Tiepolo also painted the *Virgin Enthroned with Saints* (1738). **Piazzetta** painted the panel representing *St Dominic* (c. 1743; second altar to the right) and the painting with the Dominican saints Vincenzo Ferrer, Ludovico Bertrando and Giacinto (third altar to the right). The altarpiece *The Three Saints* (c. 1733) is by **Sebastiano Ricci**, the *Crucifixion* by **Tintoretto** (c. 1560; first and third altars to the left).

★ Santa Maria del Rosario ai Gesuati

★ San Zaccaria

H 12

Location: Campo San Zaccaria   **Quay:** San Zaccaria

Today's church is in honour of St Zacharias, the father of St John the Baptist. It was built between 1460 and 1500 to plans by the two great architects Antonio Gambello and Mauro Coducci. The massive façade is an astonishing example of a fundamentally Gothic building altered in the forms of the early Renaissance. The campanile is still

QUEEN OF THE CANALS

According to legend, the gondola was created when the half moon fell from the heaves to give refuge to a pair of young lovers. A beautiful image – but the long, narrow watercraft which can navigate even the shallowest canals has been around for about 1,000 years.

The gondolas used to be magnificently decorated and some were even equipped with Felze, roofed cabins, until the doge Girolamo Priuli prohibited the display of wealth in 1562. Since then, all gondolas are black. Making them is a special art in which only very few are still proficient. One of the last and oldest workshops is the Squero di San Trovaso.

The gondola

Eight types of wood are required to build a gondola: The flat bottom is made of fir which expands in water and creates a tight seal; the rounded planks are made from hard oak. Basswood is used for the bow and stern, the cross members are made from flexible elm, lightweight birch is used for the interior floor, the curved parts of the superstructure are made from cherry, and the sheathing from

mahogany and larch. In about two months, a 10.87m/35.66ft long and 1.42m/4.66ft wide, 350kg/772lb boat impregnated with linseed oil and four layers of luscious black paint is created out of 280 components. The gondola owes its wilful form partly to its asymmetry: Around 1880, the ingenious designer Tramontin came up with the idea of shortening the boat by 24cm/9in on the right-hand side: The result of this slight curvature is that the gondola can travel straight and not just in circles, even though the gondolier always stands and rows only on one side (to the rear and on the left). The up to 80kg/176lb Forcola, the cradle for the oar installed astern on the starboard side, is a wood craft masterpiece. It is customized to the stature of the gondolier, permits eight different oar positions, and has become a popular collector's

Shapely Forcole have long since become popular collector's items.

item. Another typical element is the 20kg/44lb Ferro, which is attached to the rear of the bow and makes the gondola more stable. Its points represent the six quarters of Venice, the seventh the Island of Giudecca.

The trade of the gondoliers

When gondolas were for Venetians only, being a gondolier was a job for starvelings. Today, this Venetian tradition comes at a price. Such a black lacquered beauty costs around €20,000. Training takes a long time. Maintaining the boats is expensive, they usually require repairs after twelve years and their life expectancy is no more than 45 years. Moorings and licenses also have to be paid for – the latter are usually passed on from father to son, or else sold for €300,000 and more. And in spite of all efforts to make the boats more elaborate, they have no chance of survival against the motorized competition on the canals. Of the formerly more than ten thousand gondolas in Venice, less than four hundred remain today. This is in spite of the fact that they are the ecologically superior alternative since they cause little undertow and wash. Those who have retained a sense of romance should take a trip in the elegant watercraft, which is then carefully guided through the postcard backdrop by a (hopefully singing) gondolier. No need to mention that such a pleasure comes at a price: A gondola currently costs around €120 for 60 minutes. A cheaper (and shorter) alternative is a trip in a Traghetto. These boats, which are somewhat wider and longer than classic gondolas, offer standing room for 19 persons. Traghetti take locals and visitors across the Canal Grande at several locations (for a subsidized price). For those who want to know more about gondola construction: The Squero Canaletto offers one-week to two-semester workshops (Information: Squero Canaletto, Cannaregio, Rio dei Mendicanti 6301, phone and fax 04 12 41 39 63, www.squero.com).

San Zaccaria

Byzantine, the choir Gothic, and the nave embodies the style of the early Renaissance.

The altar painting in the left aisle is particularly noteworthy – an *Enthroned Madonna with Saints Peter, Catherine, Lucia and Jerome* (1505), a late work by **Giovanni Bellini** (the figures are outstanding examples of Venetian craftsmanship). Pass through the right-hand transept to reach the chapel of Athanasius – the choir stalls are by **Francesco** and **Marco Cozzi** (1455 to 1460) – and the Tarasius Chapel. The mosaic floor around the altar is from a previous church (12th century). Paintings by Antonio Vivarini and frescoes by Andrea del Castagno on the vault (1442) can be seen here. The crypt of the church is usually under water.

San Zaccaria was regarded as the most worldly monastery of hedonistic 18th-century Venice. The monastery balls and amours of the pious women were the gossip of the city. There was probably one main reason: it was San Zaccaria, in particular, which received the unfortunate daughters of patrician families who were put into a monastery for dynastic or financial reasons, and the ladies, whose lives had been stolen, avenged themselves in this way.

✴ Santa Maria Formosa

Location: Campo S. Maria Formosa   **Quay:** Rialto

Between 1492 and 1500, Mauro Coducci built the church on the foundations of a place of worship which must have dated from the 11th century. The façade on the Campo and the Baroque bell tower were added in the 17th century. The nearly free-standing Renaissance structure has small domes on slender columns and barrel vaults covered in outstanding Renaissance ornamentation. The main item of interest is the altar by Bartolomeo Vivarini with the panel of *Madonna of Mercy* (1473) as well as *St Barbara* (early 16th century) by Palma the Elder on the altar in the chapel to the right of the high altar. The name »formosa« (Venetian for »thick«) is attributed to the legend that Bishop Magnus had vision of the mother of Christ in the form of a rotund matron who told him to found the church.

Until the end of the republic, the doge visited the church every year at Candlemas. This tradition goes back to the following occurrence: in 944, a group of girls was abducted by Dalmatians as they were going to church. The guild of chest-makers, who had their scuola in the church, freed the girls. As thanks, they asked the doge to visit every year at Candlemas. »And what shall I do if it rains?« said the doge. »We will give you a hat.« »And what if I am thirsty?« »We will give you wine.« From then on, the doge was given a straw hat and a pitcher of wine in Santa Maria Formosa. One of the hats is in the ► Museo Civico Correr.

⏱ Opening hours: Mon–Sat 10am–5pm, Sun from 1pm

Beautiful palazzi line the broad piazza. South of the church, a visit to the ►Fondazione Querini-Stampalia is recommended.

Campo Santa Maria Formosa

✴ Santa Maria Gloriosa dei Frari – Frari

Location: Campo dei Frari   **Quay:** San Tomà

Since the San Marco and Rialto quarters offered little space to build large new churches, the doges provided the two main mendicant orders, the Franciscans and the Dominicans, with properties in the thinly populated west and north regions of the city in the mid-13th century. The Franciscans (frarti = monks) soon regarded their first church as inadequate, and began new construction in the choir and the transept around 1340. The nave did not follow until the 15th century, and with the consecration of the high altar in 1469, the simple Gothic brick structure, which reflects the Franciscans' ideal of

⏱ Opening hours: Mon–Sat 9am–6pm, Sun 1–6pm

Santa Maria Gloriosa dei Frari Plan

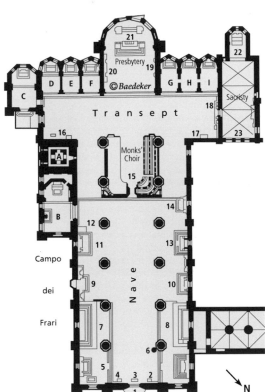

G. Campagna (1593)

7 Tomb of A. Canova († 1822)
8 Monument to Titian († 1576)
9 Tomb of Doge Giovanni Pesaro († 1659) at side door
10 Altar of Purification
11 »Madonna di Ca' Pesaro« (Titian)
12 Tomb of Bishop Jacopo Pesaro († 1547)
13 Altar of St Joseph of Copertino
14 Altar of St Catherine
15 Choir stalls (1468)
16 Monuments to Genero Orsini
17 Tomb of General I. Marcello († 1484)
18 Tomb of Admiral Benedetto Pesar († 1503)
19 Tomb of Doge Francesco Foscari († 1457)
20 Tomb of Doge Niccolò Tron († 1473)
21 High altar with Titian's »Assumpti of the Virgin« (»Assunta«, 1516–1
22 »Madonna Enthroned with Saints by G. Bellini (1488)
23 »Madonna and Child with St Fran and St Elizabeth, who accompany doge and his wife« by Paolo Veneziano
A Bell tower

CHAPELS

B Emiliani
C Corner: marble statue of John the Baptist (1554); altarpiece by Bart. Vivarini (1474)
D Milanesi: tomb of Claudio Montev († 1643); altarpiece by Al. Vivarini
E Trevisan (Melchiore Trevisan, † 150
F San Francesco
G Fiorentini: wooden statue of John the Baptist by Donatello (1451)
H Sacramento: wall tomb of the Florentine envoy Duccio degli Alberti († 1336)
I Bernardo: altarpiece by Bart. Vivari (1488)

1 Main entrance
2 Tomb of Alvise Pasqualino († 1528)
3 Tomb of Girolamo Garzoni († 1688)
4 Tomb of Pietro Bernado († 1538)
5 Crucifix, altar
6 Holy water basin with statuettes by

poverty, was completed. Today, the church is usually entered through a side entrance under the campanile (at 83m/272ft the second-highest building in Venice). The hall-like interior is divided into a rather dark nave with aisles, an aisle-less transept and a straight choir at the end with the well-lit wall of the main choir chapel, which is framed on both sides by three narrow, low chapels. The magnificent interior furnishings, particularly the tomb monuments and the altar painting with their donors, are like a pantheon of Venetian history and include the graves of four dogi and five high-ranking military officers.

Above the main portal on the inside of the façade is the wall tomb in black-and-white marble of Girolamo Garzoni, who fell in the Turkish war in 1688. The deceased, who is crowned by a genius, is flanked by the personifications of religion (left) and Venezia (right). The tomb to its right honours the procurator Pietro Bernardo († 1538), while to the left rests the procurator Alvise Pasqualino († 1528).

Nave

The second arch of the left aisle contains the tomb pyramid of **Antonio Canova** (1757–1822), in which the heart of the most important classical sculptor was entombed. His body rests in the mausoleum in his birthplace of Possagno. The design is by Canova himself (it was originally intended for **Titian**, who died of plague in 1576; the tomb of the latter on the opposite side was built by pupils of Canova more than 250 years after his death). The following tomb for Doge Giovanni Pesaro († 1659) derives from a design by Baldassare Longhena. The next altar shows a famous painting by Titian, the so-called **Pesaro Madonna** (1519/1526), a religious image and a secular group portrait rolled into one: framed by an ensign bearer and a captured Turk, the donor Jacopo Pesaro, who fought against the Turks in the pope's service, kneels to the left; his brother Francesco and younger members of his family appear on the opposite side.

A magnificent rood screen (1468–1475, Bartolomeo Bon and Pietro Lombardo) separates the nave from the monks' choir. The choir stalls were carved by Marco Cozzi in 1468; the marble reliefs of the outer sides are from the workshop of the Lombardo brothers.

◄ *Rood screen and choir stalls*

In the main choir chapel, red flames radiate from Titian's monumental altar painting of the *Assumption of the Virgin* (1518). At the centre of the image, the lovely mother of God floats heavenwards in a sun-like gloriole on an arc formed by numerous winged cherubs, and is received by God the Father.

★
Assumption of the Virgin

Among the doges' tombs in the main choir chapel, the late Gothic monument by Antonio and Paolo Bregno for Francesco Foscari († 1457) on the right wall is of particular interest. This doge extended Venice's rule to the mainland (terra ferma). Two knights with shields have drawn the curtain aside and give a view of the recumbent figure of the deceased, which is surrounded by the virtues of rulers. The tomb for Doge Nicolò Tron († 1473) on the left wall was done by Antonio Rizzo in the early Renaissance style with niche figures which hark back to antiquity.

The left transept contains the impressive altar painting of the enthroned Madonna with saints (first half of the 16th century), which was created by Bernardino Licinio under the influence of Titian, in the Capella San Francesco. The adjacent Capella Trevisan contains the tomb (early 16th century) of Melchiore Trevisan by Lorenzo Bregno. In the Cappella Milanesi, the tombstone commemorates the composer **Claudio Monteverdi** (1567–1634), the first director of mu-

Left transept

sic at San Marco and founder of Venetian opera with works such as *Orfeo* (1607) and *L'Incoronazione di Poppea* (1642). On the altar is a panel entitled *St Ambrose with Saints* and a *Coronation of the Virgin* (around 1503) by Alvise Vivarini. The Cappella Corner is ornamented by a holy water basin with the figure of St John the Baptist (c. 1554) by Jacopo Sansovino as well as the triptych *St Mark Amongst Saints* (c. 1474) by Bartolomeo Vivarini.

The right-hand transept, inside the Cappella Fiorentini, shows the expressive, coloured wooden statue of St John the Baptist (1451), the city patron of Florence, by **Donatello**, which depicts the ascetic saint in an urgent posture of preaching. The adjacent Cappella del Sacramento contains the wall tomb of the Florentine envoy Duccio degli Alberti († 1336), and in the adjacent Cappella Bernardo there is a surprising multiple-section altar panel (1488) with the Virgin and saints in a beautiful Renaissance frame by Bartolomeo Vivarini. Above the passage to the sacristy is the triumphal arch-like funerary monument for Admiral Benedetto Pesaro († 1503) and to its right, on the wall, the monuments to General Jacopo Marcello († 1484) in the early Renaissance style as well as the equestrian monument, the first in Venice, for General Paolo Savelli († 1405).

Right transept

! Baedeker TIP

Ice cream dream
Especially good ice cream is found in the Gelateria Millevoglie between the Frari church and the Scuola Grande di San Rocco. The selection is gigantic – and all the ice cream is homemade. Upon request, Tarcisio allows customers to sample first.

The apse of the sacristy contains a masterpiece by **Giovanni Bellini**. In 1488, the Pesaro family commissioned Bellini's triptych for its family burial vault. The central section shows the enthroned Virgin with the Christ child, while the wings represent St Nicholas and St Peter on the left as well as St Benedict and St Mark on the right, the name patrons for Pietro Pesaro, the father, and for his sons Nicolò, Marco and Benedetto. The harmony and tranquillity radiated by this altarpiece with its rich colours also fascinated Albrecht Dürer, who saw the panel in Venice in 1495 and later used it as a model for his famous *Four Apostles*. The *Madonna with Child, St Francis and St Elizabeth Accompanying the Doge and his Wife* (1339) is by Paolo Veneziano.

Sacristy

The Franciscan monastery, which is built around two cloisters, is the seat of the Venetian state archive. After the archives of the Vatican and Vienna, it is the third-largest archive in Europe with more than 15 million books and manuscripts.

Archivio di Stato

← *Titian's altarpiece »Assumption of Mary« (detail)*

✶ Santa Maria dei Miracoli

G/H 11

Location: Campo S. Maria Nova   **Quay:** Rialto

Opening hours:
Mon–Sat
10am–5pm,
Sun from 1pm

Photo p. 150 ►

Santa Maria dei Miracoli is an early Renaissance masterpiece, built between 1481 and 1489 from plans by Pietro and Tullio Lombardo to accommodate a miraculous painting of Mary (1408), which stands on the high altar today. On the exterior, the architects, instead of sculptural ornamentation, used marble which was worked into the façade in the form of rosettes, circles, octagons and crosses. The design of the exterior corresponds to that of the hall-like, barrel-vaulted interior, which further intensifies the effect of the golden dome over the grey-red marble walls. The coffered ceiling is covered by portraits of about 50 prophets (Pier Maria Pennacchi, 1528). The raised choir is separated by a wonderfully designed balustrade in the early Renaissance style with half-length figures.

✶ ✶ Santa Maria della Salute

F 13

Location: Fondamenta della Salute   **Quay:** Salute

Opening hours:
Daily 9am–12 noon,
3–6pm

The Baroque domed church at the mouth of the Grand Canal was built as a token of thanks for the deliverance of the city from the plague of 1630, which had claimed 40,000 lives, nearly one third of the population, in Venice. Baldassare Longhena was employed to build the church. In 1631, he began work over a foundation of about 100,000 wooden piles. The building was completed in 1687 – five years after the death of the builder. The church of Mary shows the Virgin as the »Ruler of the Seas« (Capitana del Mar): her statue on the 60m/197ft-high dome bears the staff of a Venetian high admiral. With its stairway, monumental portal and two mighty domes, the church has an astonishing width and enhances the whole appearance of the city. Viewed from the sea – the loveliest view of Venice – Santa Maria della Salute is the perfect complement to the ►Basilica di San Marco, the ►Palazzo Ducale and the Campanile.

Interior

The interior seems rather un-Baroque. Eight massive pillars support the tambour dome; there are six side chapels each on the right and left. The floor is also very beautiful. Of the numerous sculptures – there are said to be more than 120 figures on the entire building – the group by Giusto Le Court on the high altar is probably the most significant work: the Virgin fulfils the despairing plea of Venetia and drives away the pestilence. The Greek-Byzantine icon from the 13th century on the high altar was brought here from Crete in 1672 by Francesco Morosini. Every year on 21 November, Venice celebrates

The cityscape is unthinkable without them: the domes of Santa Maria della Salute

the **Salute Festival** by building a bridge across the Grand Canal to the church, and commemorates the end of the plague.

The sacristy (to the left of the high altar) houses **Tintoretto's** *The Marriage at Cana* on the long wall, and **Titian's** *St Mark* as well as the ceiling paintings *Cain and Abel*, *The Sacrifice of Abraham* and *David and Goliath* (1542–1544).

Santi Apostoli

Location: Campo dei Santi Apostoli   **Quay:** Ca' d'Oro

The church, which was consecrated in the 14th century and remodelled in the 18th century, is noteworthy for its magnificent tomb chapel of the Corner family in the right aisle, built on a square plan with a dome at the end of the 15th century by Mauro Coducci. This beautiful example of Venetian Renaissance architecture was originally intended to serve as the tomb of Catarina Corner, Queen of Cyprus (her tomb is in the church San Salvador, ►Mercerie). The richly decorated columns and the light dome create a surprising harmony. The altar painting by Giambattista Tiepolo, the *Communion of St Lucia* (1748), also fits in well.

✶ ✶ Santi Giovanni e Paolo • San Zanipolo

H 11

Location: Campo Santi Giovanni e Paolo   **Quays:** Fondamenta Nuove, Ospedale

»Museum of Venetian sculpture«
The imposing brick church, together with the adjacent Scuola Grande di San Marco, which is still used as a hospital, and the Colleoni equestrian statue in the courtyard, form an outstanding ensemble from the Gothic period and the Renaissance.

Towards the mid-13th century, Doge Jacopo Tiepolo granted the site to the Dominican order. Financing problems were probably the reason for the 200-year construction period: the nave was completed in 1369, the choir and the dome over the crossing only in 1450. In accordance with the Dominican ideal of poverty, the exterior of San Zanipolo, as the church is named in the Venetian dialect, is plain. The marble portal is a work by Bartolomeo Bon (1460), while the framing columns are from Torcello.

Interior
Its size is all the more impressive. With a length of 101.5m/333ft and a height of 35m/115ft, it is **Venice's largest church**. Its interior space, which is subdivided by tall columns, is proportioned with more vertical emphasis than the Frari church. Due to the absence of a choir screen, there is an unobstructed view all the way into the light-flooded apse. The church is also referred to as the pantheon of Venice, since 27 doges were entombed here. Its funerary monuments were created by renowned artists and reflect the development of sculpture from the late Gothic period via the High Renaissance to Baroque. The tombs of doges Pietro, Giovanni and Alvise Mocenigo lie at the west wall. The Renaissance funerary monument for Pietro Mocenigo (c. 1481, left) which extends down to the floor, with Hercules statues as pedestal reliefs, no longer shows the doge as a recumbent figure, but as a hero. The tomb completed around 1500 by Tullio Lombardo for Giovanni Mocenigo (right) is classically austere, the triumphal arch motif being replaced by an arrangement of columns. On the other hand, the colossal tomb of Alvise Mocenigo, who passed away in 1577, was built between 1580 and 1646 with inclusion of the church portal and bears the marks of early Baroque decorative design.

Magnificent Renaissance façade of the Scuola Grande di San Marco

The marble statue of the kneeling St Jerome on the first aisle altar was designed by Alessandro Vittoria (1525–1608). The tomb for Doge Nicolò Marcello with its base, columns, pilasters and entablature, which was created in 1481 by Pietro Lombardo, is next to the second round pillar. Beside it is the tomb monument for Doge Tommaso Mocenigo in the transitional style from late Gothic to Renaissance, using a fabric canopy for the first time, with shell niches and the portrait-like recumbent figure of the deceased. Not far away is the wall tomb of Doge Pasquale Malipiero in the early Renaissance style by Pietro Lombardo, decorated with a pietà relief, griffins and a fabric canopy.

Left aisle

The adjacent sacristy (16th century) has beautiful wall carvings of walnut wood and a ceiling painting by Marco Vecellio with *St Dominic and St Francis Praying to the Virgin* as well as an altar painting with a *Crucifixion* by Palma the Younger. In the left transept, on the facing wall near the entrance to the Cappella del Rosario, are three tombs for the doges of the Venier family: Antonio (doge 1382–1400), Francesco (1554–1556) and Sebastiano (1577–1578). Set into the left wall of the Cappella Cavalli is one of the oldest tombs in the church, for Giovanni Dolfin (1356–1361), a simple sarcophagus with reliefs of the doge and his wife before the enthroned Christ, the adoration of the magi and the death of the Virgin.

Sacristy

Santi Giovanni e Paolo • San Zanipolo *Plan*

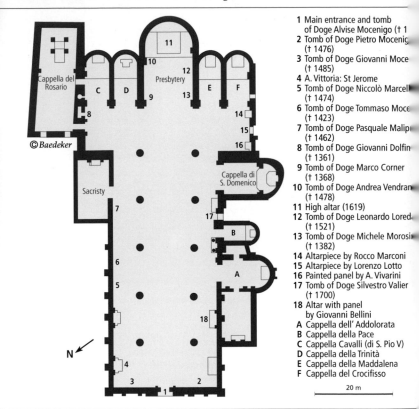

1 Main entrance and tomb
   of Doge Alvise Mocenigo († 1
2 Tomb of Doge Pietro Mocenig
   († 1476)
3 Tomb of Doge Giovanni Moce
   († 1485)
4 A. Vittoria: St Jerome
5 Tomb of Doge Niccolò Marcell
   († 1474)
6 Tomb of Doge Tommaso Moce
   († 1423)
7 Tomb of Doge Pasquale Malip
   († 1462)
8 Tomb of Doge Giovanni Dolfin
   († 1361)
9 Tomb of Doge Marco Corner
   († 1368)
10 Tomb of Doge Andrea Vendran
   († 1478)
11 High altar (1619)
12 Tomb of Doge Leonardo Lored
   († 1521)
13 Tomb of Doge Michele Morosi
   († 1382)
14 Altarpiece by Rocco Marconi
15 Altarpiece by Lorenzo Lotto
16 Painted panel by A. Vivarini
17 Tomb of Doge Silvestro Valier
   († 1700)
18 Altar with panel
   by Giovanni Bellini
A Cappella dell' Addolorata
B Cappella della Pace
C Cappella Cavalli (di S. Pio V)
D Cappella della Trinità
E Cappella della Maddalena
F Cappella del Crocifisso

20 m

Cappella del Rosario   The Cappella del Rosario, the votive chapel built in 1582 to commemorate the sea victory at Lepanto (1571), had ceiling paintings by Paolo Veronese (1528–1588) added to its new carved ceiling after the fire of 1867, among them *Adoration of the Magi*, *Assumption of the Virgin* and *Annunciation and Adoration of the Shepherds*. The rear wall of the chapel is ornamented by the *Nativity*.

Presbytery   In the presbytery, the impressive high altar in the form of a triumphal arch (around 1619) from designs by Baldassare Longhena has figures of St John and St Paul, the patron saints of the church (about 1660). On the left side wall, the eye first meets a Gothic tomb with the recumbent figure of Doge Marco Corner who died in 1368. The five-section retable above it with a Madonna figure was created by the Tuscan sculptor Nino Pisano. The adjacent Renaissance tomb (around 1492) for Doge Andrea Vendramin (doge 1476–1478), one of the main works of Tullio Lombardo, elevates the Roman triumphal arch motif out of the wall surface into a monumental sculpture. The recumbent figure, which is guarded by servants, rests on a sarcophagus surrounded by personifications of the virtues, above them in an arch relief the enthroned Virgin, while young warriors in poses from antiquity stand in the side niches. The opposite wall is graced by the funerary monument (1572), framed by colossal columns, of Leonardo Loredan (doge 1501–1521) who appears as a state official and peacemaker between the personifications of Venezia (left) and the League of Cambrai (right). The adjacent Gothic tomb for Doge Michele Morosini, who died in 1382 – the year of his election – shows the combination of architecture, painting and sculpture which was typical for monumental tombs of the 14th century. The end wall of the right transept is adorned by *Christ Bearing the Cross* (15th century) by Alvise Vivarini, the *Coronation of the Virgin* (16th century) by Giovanni da Udine and the altar painting (1542) by Lorenzo Lotto – showing the influence of Titian in its structure and coloration – *Alms-Giving of St Anthony Pierozzi* (an archbishop of Florence who died in 1459 and was canonized in 1523) as well as a large, glowing glass window (after 1470) from the workshops of Murano with saints George, John, Paul and Theodore in the lancet segments.

Right aisle

The Cappella di San Domenico from the early 18th century contains a fascinating major work of the Rococo period, a ceiling fresco full of movement and immersed in surreal light by Giovanni Battista Piazzetta (1682–1754), the *Apotheosis of St Dominic* (1727).

The right aisle in the direction of the exit leads to the tomb of Silvestro Valier, the doge who died in 1700 and was the last to be entombed in Zanipolo. The design is theatrical Baroque. The adjacent Cappella della Pace contains a Byzantine icon given to the Dominicans in 1349. The adjacent chapel of the *Suffering Mother of God* is basically a late Gothic room with paintings from the 17th century and an altar painting showing the cross being taken from Christ (19th century). A few steps farther is a triptych ascribed to Giovanni Bellini, in the early Renaissance style (around 1475–1480) with a beautiful original frame. The central panel shows St Vincenzo Ferrer, a Spanish Dominican, while St Sebastian and St Christopher are shown on the side panels and the predella depicts scenes from the life of St Vincent (1346–1419).

★
Monumento di Colleoni

The Colleoni monument in the courtyard, the second epoch-making equestrian monument of modern times after Donatello's Gattamelata statue in Padua, was modelled between 1481 and 1488 by the Florentine sculptor Andrea del Verrocchio and cast in 1496 by Alessandro Leopardi (photo p.41). The innovation is that the horse and rider are shown in movement. The figure itself has little in common with the army commander Bartolomeo Colleoni (1400–1475). Rather, it represents the ideal of a proud and power-conscious condottiere.

Colleoni fought for Venice on the terra ferma (mainland) from 1448, accumulating a huge fortune in the process. On his deathbed, he bequeathed his possessions to the state on the condition that he would receive a monument »in front of San Marco". The state did not want to fulfil the condition that was linked to the payment, but it did not want to lose the money either. Finally, it had the monument erected in front of the house of the brotherhood of San Marco – after all, the dying man had not explicitly stated that it had to be the church of San Marco!

Scuola Grande di San Marco

The scuola immediately left of San Zanipolo church was the house of the rich brotherhood of the goldsmiths and silk traders. Today, it houses the city hospital. Its beautiful Renaissance façade was begun around 1490 by Pietro Lombardo (lower section); his son Tullio created the reliefs and the two lions. Mauro Coducci finally completed the upper section around 1500. The illusionistic wall design of the ground floor, the sculpted arches and the figure decoration of the gable are highly effective. There is also a remarkable relief over the entrance gate, *St Mark Giving a Blessing* by Bartolomeo Bon, one of the masters of the Porta della Carta at the ▶Palazzo Ducale.

Santo Stefano

F 12

Location: Campo Santo Stefano   **Quay:** Accademia

Opening hours:
Mon–Sat
10am–5pm,
Sun from 1pm

At the upper end of the long **Campo S. Stefano**, which is lined by bars, restaurants and cafes, stands the 15th-century Augustine brick church with its hazardously crooked bell tower. It has a beautiful coffered wooden ceiling in the form of an inverted ship's hull. Two important Venetians are entombed in the richly decorated interior: in the nave is the tomb of Doge Francesco Morosoni (doge 1688–1694), who re-conquered the Peloponnese for Venice, destroying the Parthenon on the Acropolis at the same time – since the Turkish powder magazine was housed there. Before the first altar to the left lies **Giovanni Gabrieli** (1557–1612). The composer was active at the Basilica di San Marco from 1586 and is regarded as a pioneer of early Baroque music. Three paintings in the sacristy are by **Tintoretto:** *Last Supper*, *Washing of Feet* and *Christ on the Mount of Olives*. Furthermore, there is **Bartolomeo Vivarini's** *St Nicholas of Bari* (c. 1475).

Campo San Vidal

To the south, Campo S. Stefano merges into Campo San Vidal. In the east, it is bounded by the long **Palazzo Loredan** (16th century); in front of the palazzo there is a monument to the author Niccolò Tommaseo (1802–1874). On the opposite side stands the **Palazzo Morosini Gatterburg**, built for Doge Francesco Morosini who held

Santo Stefano with its beautiful wood ceiling

office from 1688 to 1694, and whose victories over the Turks are re-told on the portal ornamentation at the main and side entrances. A few steps farther south stands the magnificent Baroque palace of the Pisani family, begun by Bartolomeo Monopola around 1614. Today it is the seat of the Benedetto-Marcello music conservatory.
The long-secularized church San Vidal is the seat of the Interpreti Veneziani; regular concerts take place here (tel. 04 12 77 05 61; www.interpretiveneziani.com).

North of Campo Santo Stefano lies the picturesque **Campo Sant'Angelo**, which owes its name to a church dedicated to the archangel Michael which was torn down in the 19th century. All that remains is the small **Oratorio Annunziata** which was donated by the Morosini family. The composer **Domenico Cimarosa** (1749–1801) spent the last years of his life in Palazzo Duodo (no. 3584).

✱ Scuola Grande dei Carmini

D 12

Location: Campo S. Margherita   **Quay:** Ca' Rezzonico

🕐
Opening hours:
Daily 9am–6pm
Sun to 4pm
Nov–Mar
only to 4pm
Sun until 1pm

The Carmelite order, which was founded in the 13th century, owned a monastery, a church and a lay brotherhood in Venice. The Scuola dei Carmini was one of the six major scuole in Venice (► p.39). Its brotherhood building was constructed in 1663 to plans by Baldassare Longhena. The decoration of the large meeting hall on the upper floor is by **Giambattista Tiepolo**. Between 1739 and 1744, he carried out nine ceiling paintings, among them his most mature work: *Mary Hands the Scapular of the Carmelites to St Simon* (the scapular is a part of the vestments of this order). The fields in the corners contain personifications of the virtues and scenes from the life of the blessed Simon Stock. Also noteworthy: Piazzetta's painting *Judith and Holofernes* (c. 1743) in the passage from the hostel hall to the archive, and the beautiful marble floor there.

Santa Maria del Carmine (I Carmini)

Opposite, the Gothic church of the Carmelites from the 13th and 14th centuries was enlarged in the 17th century and given its high campanile. In the interior, some paintings show scenes from the history of the order. The most valuable works of art include Cima da Conegliano's *Adoration of the Shepherds* (c. 1504; second altar in the right aisle) and Lorenzo Lotto's *St Nicholas with John the Baptist and St Lucia* (c. 1523, in the left aisle) and in the right aisle, a Tintoretto: *Presentation in the Temple*. The former monastery next door houses the academy of art.

🕐
Opening hours:
Mon–Sat
2.30–5.30pm

! *Baedeker* TIP

Nightlife alla veneziana

Venetian nightlife is concentrated here on the campo. The few bars that are open late (by Venetian standards) are located here, including Il Caffè (No. 2963), Bar Salus (3112), Margaret Duchamp (3019) and Caffè-Gelateria Causin (2996).

The irregularly formed, large **Campo S. Margherita**, one of the few squares in Venice with trees, is one of the most lively places in the city with its many pubs, market stands and stores. The cube-shaped building at the centre was the Scuola dei Varoteri, the brotherhood of furriers. On the façade, an old inscription states the statutory minimum measurements for the sale of fish: eels must be longer than 25cm/10in, and sardines not shorter than 7cm/2.75in. The former church S. Margherita is lecture hall of the university today.

Palazzo Zenobio   Slightly farther south-west, at Fondamenta Soccorso 2596, is the Baroque Palazzo Zenobio, built between 1680 and 1685 by Antonio Gaspari. In its simple structure, the Baroque façade already shows classical style elements. Today, the palace is the seat of the Moorat-Raphael college for Armenian priests. The banquet hall painted by **Tiepolo** can be viewed by appointment (tel. 04 15 22 87 70).

On the other side of Rio di Ca' Foscari, it is worth taking a look inside the church San Pantalon (1686). For more than 20 years, from 1680 to 1704, Giovanni A. Fumiani worked on »the largest ceiling painting in the world«, a Baroque composition with figures from the life and death of the name-giving saint. The chapels of the church also contain a late work by Paolo Veronese (*The Miracle of St Pantaleon*, 1587) as well as a painting by Antonio Vivarini and Giovanni d'Alemagna (*The Coronation of the Virgin*, 1444).

San Pantalon

Pasticceria Tonolo, on the corner of Calle San Pantalon and Calle Crosera, sells truly delicious cakes and sweets.

✳ Scuola Grande di San Rocco

E 11

Location: Campo San Rocco   **Quay:** San Tomà

The brotherhood, which was founded in 1478 in the name of St Roch, patron of the victims of plague, was one of the richest scuole in Venice (►p.39). Its meeting house was begun under Bartolomeo Bon (1517); after his death, Antonio Scarpagnino brought the work to completion in 1549. Opposite the great façade of the church S. Rocco, in which the relics of the saint are kept, the Renaissance structure of the scuola seems almost modest. In 1564, Tintoretto, himself a member of the scuola, won the competition to decorate the building – instead of a sketch, he had submitted the finished painting. In the years to 1588, he created one of the most extensive biblical cycles in Italian painting, including some of his greatest works.

🕐
Opening hours:
Daily 9am–5.30pm

In the large columned hall on the ground floor, where the poor were once fed and the sick cared for, Tintoretto's cycle of paintings about the life of the Virgin begins on the left wall with the *Annunciation*. The Counter-Reformation is the historical background to Tintoretto's style of painting, which emphasizes the mystical with his exciting effects of light and shade, emotional coloration and dramatic gestural language. For example, the archangel steps into the Virgin's chambers, which are rendered as ruins, in blinding light and shrouded in cloud. The *Adoration of the Magi* is a complicated diagonal composition, in which the Virgin and Christ sit on a kind of bridge arch, surrounded by light, and accept the tribute. *Rest during the Flight* is dimly lit, but nonetheless the scene with the most naturalistic composition of landscape and figures. The *Massacre of the Innocents*, whose details remain somewhat in the dark, is – again – a dramatic representation. The paintings of Mary Magdalene and Mary the

Ground floor

✳ ✳
◄ Cycle: life of
the Virgin

Scuola Grande di San Rocco *Ceiling and Wall Paintings*

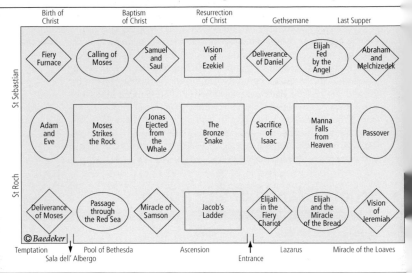

| | Birth of Christ | Baptism of Christ | Resurrection of Christ | Gethsemane | Last Supper |

St Sebastian — St Roch (left margin)

Top row:
Fiery Furnace · Calling of Moses · Samuel and Saul · Vision of Ezekiel · Deliverance of Daniel · Elijah Fed by the Angel · Abraham and Melchizedek

Middle row:
Adam and Eve · Moses Strikes the Rock · Jonas Ejected from the Whale · The Bronze Snake · Sacrifice of Isaac · Manna Falls from Heaven · Passover

Bottom row:
Deliverance of Moses · Passage through the Red Sea · Miracle of Samson · Jacob's Ladder · Elijah in the Fiery Chariot · Elijah and the Miracle of the Bread · Vision of Jeremiah

© Baedeker

Bottom labels: Temptation · Pool of Bethesda · Ascension · Lazarus · Miracle of the Loaves
Sala dell' Albergo · Entrance

Egyptian reflect a melancholy, serious mood, emphasized by the landscape of wilderness around the two figures, who seem not to be of this world. The cycle ends with depictions of the *Circumcision of Jesus* and the *Assumption of the Virgin*.

★★ Great Hall

A stairway with paintings of the plague raging in Venice leads to the meeting hall. The wall paintings show scenes from the New Testament, beginning with the birth of Christ on the long wall, then the baptism of Christ, the resurrection, the Mount of Olives and the Last Supper scene. On the other side, the cycle on Christ's life continues with the miracle of the loaves. These are followed by the resurrection of Lazarus, the ascension of Christ, the healing of the sick at the pool of Bethesda and the temptations of Christ.

The end wall of the hall is occupied by the San Rocco altar, framed by statues of St Sebastian and John the Baptist by Girolamo Campagna. A graceful annunciation scene (c. 1526) by Titian and the *Meeting of Mary and Elizabeth* (1588), a late work by Tintoretto are displayed on easels. Two paintings by Tiepolo from 1732, *Hagar in the Desert Comforted by an Angel*, as well as *Abraham and the Angels*, came to the scuola in 1789.

The wooden figures below the paintings were carved by Francesco Pianta in the 17th century. The male figure with the palette and brush (at the altar) is intended to represent Tintoretto.

Ceiling paintings ▶

The 21 ceiling paintings, which all give an underside view, show scenes from the Old Testament (there are hand mirrors for more convenient viewing). They refer partly to the wall paintings, and partly to the charitable tasks of the brotherhood – such as feeding the poor and caring for the sick. The central field of the ceiling describes the miracle of the bronze snake with Moses as saviour. In the scene in which Moses strikes water from the rock, he appears related to the figure of Christ and points out the spring of life as a source of salvation. *Jacob's Ladder*, which Tintoretto painted in an extremely tall format as a stairway to heaven with light swirling around it, has a fascinating perspective.

In the small meeting room for the leadership of the brotherhood, what is probably Tintoretto's most moving work, the *Crucifixion*, catches the eye. Christ, illuminated in glory, announces his victory over death and the salvation of humanity. On the entrance wall, there are scenes from the passion of Christ: Christ before Pilate, the

✴
Sala dell'Albergo

The Scuola S. Rocco is the only one with a fully preserved interior

misericordia domini and the bearing of the cross. The ceiling paintings are part of Tintoretto's first commissioned work; at that time, he won the competition with *St Roch in Glory*. The easel painting of Christ bearing the cross is ascribed to Titian or Giorgione.

San Rocco The choir of the church on the opposite side houses two noteworthy paintings by Tintoretto; both were painted around 1550.

★ Scuola di San Giorgio degli Schiavoni

J 12

Location: Calle dei Furlani/Ponte dei Greci

Quay: San Zaccaria

🕐 Opening hours: Tue–Sat 9.30am–12.30pm, 3–6.30pm, Sun 9.30am–12.30pm

The brotherhood building of the Schiavoni, the Dalmatian (or Slavic) merchants, which lies slightly hidden at Rio di S. Agostin, is a very plain 16th-century building which **Vittore Carpaccio** decorated with a wonderful cycle of paintings in 1502 and 1508. The scenes from the lives of saints George, Triphon and Jerome are the most significant work by this exceptionally gifted Renaissance painter, who achieved a perfect combination of realistic detail with a sense for decoration. The scenes on the left wall show the *Battle of St George and the Dragon* and *St George Brings the Dragon into the City*. To the left and right of the altar are *St George Baptizes a Heathen King and Queen* and *St Triphon Drives Out a Demon from the Emperor's Daughter*, on the right wall: *Christ's Prayer in the Garden of Gethsemane*, *The Calling of St Matthew*; *St Jerome Leads the Tame Lion into the Monastery*; *The Burial of St Jerome* and *The Vision of St Augustine*.

The so-called **Greek quarter** with popular trattorias and bars, beneath the crooked bell tower of the orthodox church S. Giorgio dei Greci, which was built in 1539, is evidence of the once important Greek community in Venice. In the Scuola di S. Nicolò in Palazzo Flangini (17th century, Longhena) immediately next to the church, a collection of valuable Byzantine icons can be seen (open: Mon–Sat 9am–noon, 2–4.30pm, Sun 10am–5pm).

Museo Dipinti Sacri Bizantini ►

❗ *Baedeker* TIP

Pearls

Outstanding craft products, guaranteed to be made locally, as well as real Venetian pearls, are available in the little store Il Coccio di Marina, Salizzada dei Greci, Castello 3446 (Mon–Sat 10am–12.30pm and 3.30–7.30pm).

★ **Riva degli Schiavoni**

Riva degli Schiavoni, the quay of the Dalmatians, extends from the Ponte della Paglia (► Palazzo Ducale) almost to the ► Arsenale.

Riva degli Schiavoni – there continues to be busy ship traffic on the »Bank of the Dalmatians«.

Where the large passenger ships still come in today and hawkers try to sell their wares to the tourists, the ships of the Dalmatian merchants once docked.

La Pietà The late Baroque church is also called Santa Maria della Visitazione or simply **Vivaldi's church**. The composer Antonio Vivaldi (1677–1741) was a teacher in the adjacent orphanage for many years. Regular concerts take place here even today. The church is presently being restored. In the meantime, the concerts take place in Palazzo Ca' Papafava, five minutes' walk from ► Ca' d'Oro (15th century; Calle Recheta 3764, information in the tourist offices or tel. 0 41 91 72 57 and www.vivaldi.it).

Teatro La Fenice

Location: Campo San Fantin   **Quay:** Santa Maria del Giglio

Risen from the ashes »The fabulous Teatro La Fenice is returned to Italy and the world«, said Venice's mayor Paolo Costa when, on 13 December 2003 after eight years of rebuilding, the curtain was first raised again in Venice's famous opera house, which had burned down completely in 1996.

Teatro La Fenice during the grand reopening on 20 July 1837

The project by the architect **Aldo Rossi** cost €55 million or more. It should have been completed in 1999, but spent years stuck in a »morass of objections«. Now, however, La Fenice has been restored to its former glory: 174 theatre boxes have been re-created in their original form, including gold leaf. Even the new chandeliers are exactly the same as the old ones. And the Graces dance on the turquoise ceiling as before. The opera now holds an audience of about 1,000 – approximately 150 more than before.

Venice's **opera house**, which faces water on two sides at a place where three canals meet, is among the most famous opera houses in the world, together with Milan's Scala and San Carlo in Naples. The luxurious house was built between 1790 and 1792 as a replacement for a predecessor which had burned down in 1773, the popular opera house San Benedetto. At that time, it received the symbolic name La Fenice, »the phoenix arisen from the ashes«. On 16 May 1792, the theatre was opened with Giovanni Paisello's *I Giochi di Agrigento*. In 1836, a major fire destroyed this opera house as well, but one year later, it had already been rebuilt, a faithful copy of the original in the neo-classical style. The theatre can be viewed (information and appointments: tel. 0 41 24 24).

Viewing ▶

The magnificent theatre probably owed its burgeoning reputation as the »queen of the opera world« in the 19th century to its well-considered statutes and the rich Venetian musical tradition. At its foundation the showing of two new operas annually was specified. Rossini, Bellini, Donizetti and Verdi composed major works especially for this opera house. In 1873, visitors to La Fenice saw Wagner's *Rienzi*, in 1881 *Lohengrin*, and shortly after the death of the celebrated composer, the Ring cycle was shown at La Fenice for the first time in Italy. In the 20th century, Igor Stravinsky conducted the first performance of his opera parody *The Rake's Progress* at La Fenice (1951). Later, Benjamin Britten's *The Turn of the Screw*, Sergei Prokofiev's *Fiery Angel* and Bruno Maderna's *Hyperion* premiered here. In 1960, Luigi Nono's *Intolleranza* triggered a staged scandal, and in 1985, Pina Bausch enjoyed an ecstatic reception at La Fenice for her idiosyncratic choreographies. The special atmosphere of the theatre is probably the reason why singers from Caruso to Pavarotti, conductors such as Leonard Bernstein and directors from Giorgio Strehler to Luca Ronconi were delighted to work here.

◄ Programme info:
www.teatro
lafenice.it
Fax 04 12 41 80 28

✴ Torcello

Population: 30

Location: North lagoon (get there via Burano; change boats to go to Torcello)

Torcello, the island of the little tower, was the first and for some centuries also the most important settlement in the lagoon, with its own bishop, churches and palaces, a large port and shipyards, its own laws and more than 20,000 residents. The unstoppable rise of Venice and the hazard of malaria in the increasingly swampy surrounding land were probably the reasons why the population gradu-

! *Baedeker* TIP

Al Ponte del Diavolo

The osteria on the way to the basilica, which is named after its location near the »devil's bridge«, is a good (and inexpensive) alternative to its better known neighbour Cipriani, not just because of its shady terrace (Al Ponte del Diavolo, daily except Wed, tel. 0 41 73 04 01).

ally moved away from the early 16th century. Today, reminders of a great past can be found in the Basilica S. Maria Assunta, the oldest building in the lagoon, and a handful of houses scattered across the island.

According to an inscription to the left of the high altar, the basilica was built in 639 in the Venetian-Byzantine style. In the 9th century, it received a crypt, a narthex and the two side apses. In the early 11th century, the naves were raised and the bell tower (accessible) completed. In front of the church, the foundation walls of the 17th-century baptistery are still identifiable. The floor tiles of the basilica date from the 11th century, while the mosaic of the sub-floor is even from the 9th century.

✴
Santa Maria Assunta

The oldest mosaics are found in the cross-vault of the right apse. **★** The angels bearing a medallion with the lamb of God (apse vault) **Mosaics** are very similar to Byzantine examples and reminiscent of the famous mosaics in Ravenna. The latter are from the 6th century, and it is thought that mosaic artists from Ravenna participated in the work on Torcello. The main apse with a stepped seat for priests is graced by 12th-century mosaic decorations: the Virgin with the apostles. The enthroned Christ with archangels in the right apse dates from the 12th and 13th centuries. The opposite wall is occupied by a large Last Judgment mosaic from the 12th/13th centuries. The six scenes on the wall should be read from the top to the bottom.

Next to the basilica stands the small church Santa Fosca, a significant **Santa Fosca** 11th-century building with a central plan, surrounded by a 12th-century arcade. The square interior space – analogous to tombs from antiquity – with its rectangular choir serves as a place of remembrance for St Fosca, a martyr from Ravenna, and has an unusually harmonious spatial effect.
The marble block in the form of a seat in the courtyard is said to be the 5th-century throne of Attila the Hun.

Exhibits in the adjacent museum document the long history of the **Museo di** island: capitals, fragments of mosaics, ceramics, icons and paintings **Torcello** from former churches are presented here, as well as writings, seals and everyday objects (open: Tue–Sun 10am–12.30pm, 2–5.30pm).

← *Santa Maria Assunta; as was the custom in Greek Orthodox liturgy, an iconostasis divides the altar room.*

INDEX

a

Accademia **193**
accident, ambulance **80**
administration **17**
airport **18**
Ala Napoleonica **239**
Alberoni **79, 216**
Alitalia **78**
Ando, Tadao **182**
Antico Granaio **175**
antiques **121**
Apostles **166**
Appartamento Ducale **235**
Archaeological Museum **243**
Archivio di Stato **261**
Arco Foscari **228**
Arsenale **158**
art academy gallery **193**
art galleries **122**
art history **45**
artists' supplies **122**
ATMs **118**
Aulenti, Gae **182**
autostrada toll **135**

b

bars **81**
Basilica di San Marco **160**
beaches **78**
Bellini, Gentile **50, 61**
Bellini, Giovanni **61**
Bellini, Jacopo **51, 61**
Benedizione del Fuoco **85**
Biblioteca Marciana **242**
Biennale **58, 206**
Bocca di Leone **230**
books **122**
Bosch, Hieronymus **235**
Botta, Mario **192**
breakdown service **135**
breakfast **92**
Bridge of Sighs **226**
bronze horses of St Mark **171**
brotherhoods **39**
Burano **171**

c

Ca' d'Oro **185**
Ca' da Mosto **177**
Ca' Farsetti **180**
Ca' Foscari **181**
Ca' Pesaro **186**
Ca' Rezzonico **188**
caffè **85**
Café Florian **241**
Café Lavena **241**
Café Quadri **241**
cafés **92, 103**
Calle dei Fabbri **146**
Calle Larga XXII Marzo **219**
Calle Vallaresso **219**
Campanile **241**
Campanile (S. Giorgio
  Maggiore) **247**
Campiello dei Morti **245**
Campo dei Mori **218**
Campo S. Bartolomeo **218**
Campo San Giacomo
  dell'Orio **245**
Campo San Polo **251**
Campo San Vidal **268**
Campo Santa Margherita **270**
Campo Santa Maria
  Formosa **257**
Campo Santo Stefano **268**
Canal Grande **173**
Canaletto **54, 61**
Canova, Antonio **183**
Capitaneria del Porto **184**
car parks **75**
carnival **85**
Carpaccio, Vittore **51, 274**
Carriera, Rosalba **189**
Casa del Tintoretto **218**
Casa Goldoni **251**
Casanova, Giacomo **62, 228**
Case Tron **151**
cash machines **118**
Casina delle Rose **183**
casino **81, 175**
Cavallino **216**
Centro Studi di Storia del
  Tessuto e del Costume **187**
Chiesa degli Scalzi **173**
children **79**
Chioggia **188**
Cimitero Israelitico **215**
Cini foundation **247**
city administration **180**
city dialling codes **119**
city tour **132**
clock tower **240**
Coducci, Mauro **49**

Collegium Ducale **130**
Colleoni monument **149, 267**
Collezione Peggy
  Guggenheim **190**
Colonne di Marco e
  Teodoro **241**
Concerto dell'Assunta **90**
concerts **130**
consulates **106**
Contarini church **160**
Corner, Caterina **176, 219**
Corte Cavallo **149**
costume museum **187**
country codes **119**
credit cards **118**
customs regulations **77**

d

Dante Alighieri **159**
dialect **108**
diplomatic representation **106**
directory inquiries **119**
disabled travellers **136**
discounts **120**
Dogana da Mar **184**
Doge's Palace **224**
Doge's private chambers **235**

e

economy **18**
electricity **80**
emergency call numbers **80**
entertainment **81**
environmental protection **28**
etiquette **82**
Ex San Vidal **269**
Ex-Macelli **247**

f

Fabbriche Nuove **177**
Fabbriche Vecchie **177**
fabrics **123**
Father Paolo Sarpi **149**
Fenice theatre **275**
Ferrovia S. Lucia **173**
Festa dei Morti **91**
Festa del Redentore **99, 210**
Festa della Madonna della
  Salute **101**
Festa di San Marco **85**
Festa di San Martino **91**

festival of the Saviour **90, 210**
festivals **85**
film festival **90, 215**
fish market **177, 243**
flagstaffs **161**
flood water **28**
Fondaco dei Tedeschi **190**
Fondaco dei Turchi **192**
Fondamenta Nuove **151**
Fondazione Cini **247**
Fondazione Querini-
  Stampalia **192**
food and drink **91**
football stadium **206**
forcole (gondola rowlocks) **126**
foreign exchange
  regulations **118**
Fortuny, Mariano **237**
Franchetti, Giorgio **186**
Frari church **257**
Fusina **75**

Galleria Franchetti **186**
Galleria Nazionale d'Arte
  Moderna **186**
Galleria Querini-
  Stampalia **192**
Gallerie dell'Accademia **193**
Galuppi, Baldassare **171**
Gesuati **253**
getting there **75**
ghetto **200**
Giardini Pubblici **206**
Giardini Reali **184**
Giorgione **50**
Giudecca **208**
Giunta, Lucantonio **59**
glass museum (Murano) **221**
glass workshops **125**
Golden Book **36**
Golden Lion **215**
Goldoni, Carlo **189, 251**
gondola ferries **133**
gondola regatta **90**
gondola rowlocks **126**
gondola shipyard **252**
Grand Canal **173**
grocery stores **125**
Guardi, Francesco **54**
Guggenheim collection **190**
Guggenheim, Peggy **62, 190**
guided tours **132**

Harry's Bar **79, 184**
Harry's Dolci **209**
health **105**
health insurance **77**
Hello Venezia **106**
hire cars **136**
history **31**
holidays **84**
horses of St Mark **171**
hospital **105**

I Carmini **270**
I Gesuiti **199**
I Redentore **209**
ice cream parlours **103**
internet addresses **107**
Interpreti Veneziani **128, 269**
island round trip **133**
islands in the lagoon **211**
Isola del Tronchetto **75**
Isola della Giudecca **208**
Isola di San Pietro **159**
Italian cuisine **91**
Italian National Tourist Office
  ENIT **105**
Itinerari Segreti **228**

Jesolo **217**
Jesuit church **199**
Jewish cemetery **205, 215**
Jewish museum **205**

La Fenice **275**
La Giudecca **208**
La Grazia **213**
La Pietà (church) **275**
lace **127**
lace museum **171**
lagoon **21**
Lagoon islands **211**
language **108**
lay brotherhoods **39**
Lazzaretto Nuovo **213**
Lazzaretto Vecchio **214**
Le Vignole **212**
Le Zitelle **210**

learning Italian **116**
left luggage **76**
Libreria Sansoviniana **242**
Libreria Vecchia **242**
Lido **214**
Lido di Jesolo **79, 216**
lion's mouth **230, 253**
literature **116**
Littorale del Cavallino **79, 216**
Lombardo, Pietro **49**
Longhena, Baldassare **54**
Longhi, Pietro **54, 188**
Lord Byron **181**
lost property offices **106**

Madonna dell'Orto **217**
mail **119**
main post office **191**
Malamocco **216**
Manin, Daniele **42**
Manutius, Aldus **58**
marathon **91**
Marco Polo Airport **76**
Marghera **28**
maritime museum **159**
markets **128**
mask and costume shops **128**
Massari, Giorgio **55**
Mazzorbo **153, 171**
medical aid **105**
menu **93**
Mercerie **218**
Mestre **75**
metal goods **129**
mint **243**
Monteverdi, Claudio **63**
Monumento di Colleoni **267**
Moorat-Raphaël priests'
  college **271**
MOSE **28**
Mulino Stucky **210**
Municipio **180**
Murano **220**
murazzi **216**
Museo Archeologico **243**
Museo Correr **240**
Museo d'Arte Orientale **187**
Museo del Settecento
  Veneziano **188**
Museo del Vetro **221**
Museo di Storia
  Naturale **192**

Museo di Torcello **279**
Museo Dipinti Sacri
Bizantini **274**
Museo Ebraico **205**
Museo Fortuny **237**
Museo Marciano **170**
Museo Storico Navale **159**
museum pass **120**

n

New prisons **226, 236**
newspapers **118**
nightclubs **81**
Nono, Luigi **209**

o

open-air cinema **251**
opening hours **119**
Oratorio Annunziata **269**
Oratorio dei Crociferi **150, 200**
osteria **92**

p

Pala d'Oro **168**
Pala di San Giobbe **194**
palace architecture **53**
Palazzo Balbi **181**
Palazzo Barbaro **182**
Palazzo Belloni Battagia **176**
Palazzo Ca' Papafava **275**
Palazzo Cavalli Franchetti **182**
Palazzo Cini **183**
Palazzo Contarini del
Bovolo **224**
Palazzo Contarini Fasan **184**
Palazzo Corner **183**
Palazzo Corner Ca' Grande **183**
Palazzo Corner della
Regina **176**
Palazzo Corner Mocenigo **251**
Palazzo Correr Contarini **149,
174**
Palazzo Dario **183**
Palazzo dei Camerlenghi **177**
Palazzo del Cinema **215**
Palazzo Dolfin Manin **180**
Palazzo Ducale **224**
Palazzo Flangini **174, 274**
Palazzo Giovanelli **150, 174**
Palazzo Giustiniani **181**
Palazzo Grassi **181**

Palazzo Grimani **180**
Palazzo Gritti **184**
Palazzo Lezze **149**
Palazzo Loredan **180, 268**
Palazzo Mangili Valmarana **177**
Palazzo Michiel **148**
Palazzo Michiel delle
Colonne **177**
Palazzo Mocenigo **181, 187**
Palazzo Morosini
Gatterburg **269**
Palazzo Pesaro **176**
Palazzo Pesaro degli Orfei **237**
Palazzo Pisani **269**
Palazzo Pisani Moretta **181**
Palazzo Sagredo **176**
Palazzo Soranzo **251**
Palazzo Vendramin Calergi **175**
Palazzo Venier dei Leoni **190**
Palazzo Zen **150**
Palazzo Zenobio **270**
Palladio, Andrea **49, 63, 209,
247**
Papadopuli park **250**
Paradise **234**
parking **75**
Pellestrina **216**
Pescheria **177**
pharmacies **105**
Piazza San Marco **237**
Piazzale Roma **75**
Piazzetta **241**
Piazzetta dei Leoncini **161**
Pilastri Acritani **163**
Pinacoteca Manfrediniana **184**
Pinacoteca Querini-
Stampalia **192**
Pinault, François **182**
pizzeria **92**
Podrecca, Boris **186**
Polo, Marco **64, 249**
Ponte dei Sospiri **226**
Ponte dell'Accademia **199**
Ponte della Libertà **148**
Ponte delle Guglie **148**
Ponte di Rialto **243**
population **17**
port office **184**
Porta del Frumento **227**
Porta della Carta **226**
Porto Marghera **28**
post **119**
power **80**
Prefecture **183**

prices and discounts **120**
Prigioni Nuove **226, 236**
printing **58**
probably **245**
Procuratie Nuove **239**
Procuratie Vecchie **239**
public transport **132**
Punta Sabbioni **75, 216**

q

Querini-Stampalia
foundation **194**

r

railway terminal Santa Lu-
cia **76, 173**
receipts **118**
Redentore church **209**
Regata Storica **100**
Regate delle Befane **85**
rental cars **136**
restaurants **97**
Rialto bridge **243**
Rialto market **243**
Ricci **54**
Rio Terrà Lista di Spagna **148**
Risorgimento Museum **240**
Riva degli Schiavoni **274**
Rizzo, Antonio **50**
road traffic **135**
Rossi **276**
Ruga degli Orefici **244**

s

Sagra del Mosto di
Sant'Erasmo **101**
Sagra del Pesce di Burano **90**
Sagra di San Pietro di
Castello **99**
Sala del Maggior Consiglio **234**
San Angelo Raffaele **151**
San Felice **150**
San Francesco del Deserto **154,
212**
San Francesco della Vigna **245**
San Giacomo in Paludo
(island) **153**
San Giobbe **246**
San Giorgio dei Greci **274**
San Giorgio Maggiore **247**
San Giovanni Crisostomo **249**

San Giovanni Elemosinario **244**
San Giuliano **75**
San Lazzaro degli Armeni **213**
San Marcuola **174**
San Michele (island) **211**
San Moisè **220**
San Nicolò (Lido) **215**
San Nicolò da Tolentino **249**
San Nicolò dei Mendicoli **151**
San Pantalon **271**
San Pietro di Castello **250**
San Pietro di Castello
 (island) **250**
San Polo **250**
San Rocco **274**
San Salvador **218**
San Sebastiano **252**
San Servolo (island) **213**
San Silvestro **244**
San Simeone Piccolo **173**
San Staè **176**
San Trovaso **252**
San Vidal (Ex San Vidal) **269**
San Zaccaria **253**
San Zanipolo **264**
Sansovino, Jacopo **48, 63, 169**
Sant' Elena **206**
Sant'Alvise **218**
Sant'Andrea (Lido) **215**
Sant'Angelo Raffaele **252**
Sant'Erasmo **212**
Sant'Eufemia **210**
Santa Fosca (Torcello) **279**
Santa Geremia **148**
Santa Lucia railway station **148**
Santa Maria Assunta
 (Torcello) **277**
Santa Maria dei Miracoli **149,
 262**
Santa Maria del Carmine **270**
Santa Maria del Giglio **220**
Santa Maria del Rosario **253**
Santa Maria del Rosario ai
 Gesuati **253**
Santa Maria dell'Orto **217**
Santa Maria della
 Presentazione **210**
Santa Maria della Salute **262**
Santa Maria della
 Visitazione **253, 275**
Santa Maria di Nazareth **173**
Santa Maria Formosa **257**
Santa Maria Gloriosa dei
 Frari **257**

Santi Apostoli **263**
Santi Gervasio e Protasio **252**
Santi Giovanni e Paolo **264**
Santi Maria e Donato
 (Murano) **221**
Santo Stefano **268**
Scala dei Giganti **227**
Scala d'Oro **230**
Scarpa **192**
Scarpa, Carlo **58**
Scuola dei Varoteri **270**
Scuola di Merletti **171**
Scuola di S. Nicolò **274**
Scuola di San Giorgio degli
 Schiavoni **274**
Scuola Ganton **201**
Scuola Grande dei Carmini **270**
Scuola Grande di San
 Marco **268**
Scuola Grande di San
 Rocco **271**
Scuola Italiana **201**
Scuola Levantina **201**
Scuola Spagnola **201**
Scuola Tedesca **205**
scuole **39**
secret pathways **228**
sestiere **17**
Sestiere Cannaregio **148**
Sestiere Dorsoduro **151**
Sestiere San Marco **143**
Sestiere San Polo **146**
Sestiere Santa Croce **146**
shopping **121**
shopping streets **121**
Silver Book **36**
Sottomarina **79, 189**
Sottoportego del Ghetto **148**
speed limits **135**
Spira, Johannes de **58**
Sposalizio col mare **89, 215**
Squero di San Trovaso **252**
St Mark's Basilica **160**
St Mark's Library **242**
St Mark's Square **237**
state archive **261**
Stazione S. Lucia **76, 173**
Strada Nova **149**
Stucky, Giovanni **58**
swimming **78**

Teatro La Fenice **275**

Teatro Malibran **249**
Teatro Verde **248**
telephone charges **119**
telephoning **120**
tetrarchs **163**
theatre **130**
Tiepolo, Giambattista **54, 65**
Tiepolo, Giovanni Domenico **65**
time **131**
Tintoretto, Jacopo **52, 65, 217**
tips **93**
Tirali, Andrea **55**
Titian **52, 66**
Torcello **277**
Torre dell'Orologio **240**
tourist guides **132**
tours **142**
traffic regulations **135**
transport **18, 132**
transport timetables **133**
travel documents **76**
Treporti **75**
trips **142**
Tronchetto **75**

vehicle papers **76**
Venice European Restoration
 Centre **213**
Venice International
 University **213**
Veronese, Paolo **52, 66**
Via Garibaldi **159**
Vivaldi, Antonio **67**

Wagner, Richard **175**
walks **142**
water taxis **134**
well heads **249**
when to go **137**
wood art **129**

y

youth hostel **208**

z

Zattere **253**
Zecca **243**
Zitelle church **210**

LIST OF MAPS AND ILLUSTRATIONS

Centro Storico Sestieri **18**
Venice in Italy **19**
Lagoon of Venice **22**
Mose Flood Protection Programme **29**
How Venice was built (3 D) **32**
Hotels and Restaurants **98 / 99**
Climate **137**
Tours through Venicei **140 / 141**
Tour 1 **144 / 145**
Tour 2 **147**
Tour 3 **149**
Tour 4 **152**

Basilica di San Marco **162**
St Mark's Basilica (3 D) **164**
Galleria dell'Accademia **196**
Il Redentore **210**
Palazzo Ducale **229**
Doge's Palace (3 D) **232**
Santa Maria Gloriosa dei Frari **258**
San Giovanni e Paolo **266**
Scuola Grande di San Rocco:
 Ceiling and Wall Paintings **272**

PHOTO CREDITS

PUBLISHER'S INFORMATION

Illustrations etc: 182 illustrations, 23 maps and diagrams, one large city plan

Text: Dr. Eva-Maria Blattner, Rupert Koppold, Michael Machatschek, Peter Peter, Dr. Madeleine Reincke, Anja Schliebitz, Reinhard Strüber, Wolfgang Veit

Editing: Baedeker editorial team (Anja Schliebitz, John Sykes)

Translation: all-lingua, John Sykes

Cartography: Christoph Gallus, Hohberg; Franz Huber, Munich; MAIRDUMONT/Falk Verlag, Ostfildern (city plan)

3D illustrations: jangled nerves, Stuttgart

Design: independent Medien-Design, Munich; Kathrin Schemel

Editor-in-chief: Rainer Eisenschmid, Baedeker Ostfildern

1st edition 2008

Copyright: Karl Baedeker Verlag, Ostfildern
Publication rights: MAIRDUMONT GmbH & Co; Ostfildern

Printed in China

DEAR READER,

We would like to thank you for choosing this Baedeker travel guide. It will be a reliable companion on your travels and will not disappoint you.
This book describes the major sights, of course, but it also recommends the most charming wine bars, as well as hotels in the luxury and budget categories, and includes tips about where to eat or go shopping and much more, helping to make your trip an enjoyable experience. Our authors and editors ensure the quality of this information by making regular journeys to Venice and putting all their know-how into this book.

Nevertheless, experience shows us that it is impossible to rule out errors and changes made after the book goes to press, for which Baedeker accepts no liability. Please send us your criticisms, corrections and suggestions for improvement: we appreciate your contribution. Contact us by post or e-mail, or phone us:

▶ **Verlag Karl Baedeker GmbH**
Editorial department
Postfach 3162
73751 Ostfildern
Germany
Tel. 49-711-4502-262, fax -343
www.baedeker.com
E-Mail: baedeker@mairdumont.com

Baedeker Travel Guides in English at a glance:

▶ Andalusia

▶ Dubai · Emirates

▶ Egypt

▶ Ireland

▶ London

▶ Mexico

▶ New York

▶ Portugal

▶ Rome

▶ Thailand

▶ Tuscany

▶ Venice